TERENCE CONRAN'S
Kitchen Book

TERENCE CONRAN'S

Kitchen Book

A COMPREHENSIVE SOURCE BOOK AND GUIDE
TO PLANNING, FITTING AND EQUIPPING YOUR KITCHEN

Contributing Editors

Elizabeth Wilhide and Deborah Smith-Morant

Consultant Editor

Rick Mather

THE OVERLOOK PRESS
WOODSTOCK • NEW YORK

To Caroline

With fond memories of the many happy hours spent in our kitchens together

First published in the USA in 1993 by
The Overlook Press
Lewis Hollow Road
Woodstock, New York 12498

Originally published in the UK
by Conran Octopus Limited

Contributing Editors   Elizabeth Wilhide
                        (parts 1–3 & 5)
                        Deborah Smith-Morant
                        (parts 4 & 5)
Consultant Editor   Rick Mather (part 4)

Library of Congress Cataloging-in-Publication Data

Conran, Terence.
  [Kitchen book]
  Terence Conran's kitchen book / Terence Conran with Deborah Smith, Elizabeth Wilhide.
    p. cm.
  Includes bibliographical references and index.
  1. Kitchens. 2. Interior decoration.
I. Smith, Deborah. II. Wilhide, Elizabeth.
III. Title. IV. Title: Kitchen book.

NK2117.K5C66 1993
643′.3—dc20

ISBN: 0-87951-513-9

                              92-23164
                              CIP

Art Editor   Helen Lewis
Project Editor   Simon Willis
Americanizer   Emily Van Ness
Editor   Charyn Jones
Picture Researcher   Jessica Walton
Production Manager   Sonya Sibbons
Editorial Assistant   Charlotte Coleman-Smith
Visualizer   Jean Morley
Illustrators   Sarah John (colour)
                Joy FitzSimmons (line)

PUBLISHER'S ACKNOWLEDGMENTS
The publisher would like to thank the following for their assistance with this book: The James Beard Foundation, Gerd Bulthaup, Michelle Clark, Annette DePaepe at the National Kitchen and Bath Association, Paul King and Walter Jaffe, Fay Maschler, Narash Ramchandani and David Buonguidi, Mr and Mrs N. Spencer, Chan Starke at the Hydronics Institute, Deborah Weintraub.

Typeset by Servis Filmsetting Limited, Manchester
Printed and bound in Italy

Contents

FOREWORD	**7**
INTRODUCTION	**8**
THE PROFESSIONAL KITCHEN	**24**
The Restaurant Kitchen	26
Le Pont de la Tour	32
Bulthaup: Planning the Cook's Kitchen	36
THE HUB OF THE HOME	**40**
Kitchen Life	42
Defining Areas	44
Decorative Potential	52
Kitchen Character	56
The Built-in Kitchen	58
The Unfitted Kitchen	62
The Contemporary Kitchen	64
The Country Kitchen	70
The Family Kitchen	76
The Small Kitchen	78
The Idiosyncratic Kitchen	86
The Vernacular Kitchen	88
Display and Concealment	92
Eating in the Kitchen	98
The Conservatory Kitchen	102
The Outdoor Kitchen	104
KITCHEN DESIGN	**108**
The Well-designed Kitchen	110
Planning	115
Planning from Scratch	116
Getting Your Priorities Right	118
Design Challenges	120
Ergonomics	122
Plan 1: A Family Kitchen	126
Plan 2: Opening Up the Workspace	128
Plan 3: A Farmhouse Conversion	132
Plan 4: New Space for Old	134
Plan 5: A Cook's Kitchen	136
Universal Design	140
Essential Services	142
Kitchen Lighting	144
Ventilation	148
Waste Disposal	150
Fitting	153
Flooring	154
Walls	158
Countertops	162
Cabinets and Units	168
Storage	174
Screening and Dividing	180
Kitchen Furniture	184
Equipping	189
Ranges, Ovens and Cooktops	190
Refrigerators	196
Sinks and Faucets	198
Dishwashers and Washing Machines	200
THE WELL-STOCKED KITCHEN	**202**
The Essential Pantry	204
Basic Kitchen Accoutrements	210
Useful Addresses	214
Index	219
Acknowledgments	223

Foreword

A kitchen provides physical and spiritual nourishment, and for many homes is now the heart and soul of family life. A constant source of pleasure if it has been intelligently planned and designed, your kitchen may become a source of frustration if it has not.

There is a vast amount of information you need to consider before you can even start to think about the appearance of your kitchen. If it does not work well you will never enjoy it to its full potential, however beautiful it may look. Beware of unnecessary gadgets and glossy leaflets for built-in kitchens: it is too easy to be seduced by their surface appeal and to make rash decisions you may regret later on. Time invested discussing your ideas and carefully examining all the options open to you is always time well spent.

The purpose of this book is to provide both practical information and inspirational ideas to create a kitchen environment that suits your way of life and responds to your specific needs. Elizabeth David's enduring advice about the preparation of food – to keep it simple – may also be applied to the design of your kitchen. Use good quality materials in a simple way and your kitchen life will be a pleasure.

Terence Conran.

The kitchen is defined by the activities it accommodates. Devising a working arrangement that matches your style of cooking is the secret behind successful kitchen design (LEFT).

The custom-built kitchen gives scope to originality and flair. Deep purple walls forge a strong partnership with machine finishes (ABOVE).

A wood-burning inset stove, split logs stacked neatly underneath for drying, forms a glowing focus for the heart of the home and an echo of the kitchen hearth (LEFT).

Kitchen esthetics celebrate good food and fresh ingredients. A senstive mix of materials here contributes character without diffusing practicality (BELOW).

Introduction

A strict segregation of the kitchen from the dining room was standard throughout the nineteenth century. In this print, published around 1850 in Würtemberg, a waiter communicates with a below-stairs restaurant kitchen via a speaking tube (ABOVE).

"Kitchen Interior" (1815) by Martin von Drölling (1752–1817). Many aspects of this early nineteenth-century kitchen remain appealing today – pans neatly ranged above the working area, high shelves for large utensils, practical tiled floor and, above all, generous natural light. (RIGHT).

*O*ur ideas about kitchens derive from many different sources. When kitchen appliances began to be introduced in the 1930s, revolutionizing domestic work, a new machine aesthetic was born. The post-war American kitchen, sleek, hygienic and fitted with a myriad of labor-saving devices, was a powerful modern image. To this we have added the influence of the professional cook's kitchen, with its emphasis on practicality and its efficient work centers.

At the same time, more traditional notions of kitchen design have persisted, expressing a very different ideal. The country kitchen in all its manifestations – from the kitchens of great houses full of arcane equipment and pantries stacked with rows of preserves to the farmhouse kitchen with its cozy Aga, racks of drying herbs and quarry-tiled floor – exerts a no less powerful pull on our sensibilities. It is unlikely that, in pursuit of the simple life, cooks of the future will ever exchange their stoves for cauldrons and chimney cranes or abandon their built-in ovens for outdoor hearths. But, just as it has done for centuries past, the kitchen will continue to reflect the way we want to live.

KITCHENS OF THE PAST

Kitchens may have been at the heart of existence for thousands of years, but they are one of the least written about rooms. Few representations of early kitchens survive; when our ancestors showed any interest in depicting their surroundings, it was usually the finest rooms, with the best decoration and furnishings, on which their attention was focused. The kitchen, by and large, was inconceivable as a subject worthy of recording, rather in the way we might find few reasons for photographing the boiler room or the tool shed.

Most of the pictorial evidence for early rooms comes from the royal palaces and the homes of the wealthy. They are relatively well documented; not merely because their inhabitants had the money to do so, but also as part of the process of preserving a heritage for succeeding generations. Further down the social scale, little remains to give a picture of ordinary life, in homes where cooking, living and even sleeping all went on in the same room.

The kitchen has been described as "the Cinderella of rooms." A large part of its obscurity came from the fact that in great houses, from Tudor times well into this century, it was largely the domain of servants and increasingly segregated from the rest of the household. This state of affairs reached its climax in Victorian England, just as technology was emerging that would enable the radical changes of the twentieth century to take place.

For exceptions, you have to look back to the communal kitchens of the Middle Ages, or to early colonial settlements where labor was scarce and mistress and kitchen help worked more closely together.

The rapid changes in technology which have occurred during the course of this century have affected the kitchen more than any other room. Up to modern times, however, the kitchen changed very slowly. When changes happened, they were usually the result of a change in the type of fuel used, or in the availability of labor.

THE EARLIEST KITCHENS

Most historians believe that a series of happy accidents account for the early history of cooking. Peking Man, who lived half a million years ago, is thought to have been the first to have used fire. But he was unable to make the connection between its warming flames and the raw food he was eating. Much later, some time between this point and the emergence of the Neanderthals, 75,000 years ago, cooking was discovered. A chunk of meat that dropped off a bone was grazed by fire and proved tastier and more tender after roasting must have prompted the experiments humans have performed on food ever since.

Utensils and reusable containers were a long way off. Wrapping food in leaves or covering it in clay before baking in a pit lined with hot embers, spit-roasting, and stewing food in a reptile's skin, animal's stomach or hide pouch are all natural solutions which may have occurred to early humans. Later still came the first cooking pot: a large stone with a hollow in the middle was left in the center of the fire and the hollow filled with water; food was boiled by adding hot stones.

The cultivation of grain and domestication of animals mark the next turning point. As early civilizations established themselves in the fertile lands in the Near East, Central America and Southeast Asia, life changed from a nomadic hunting and gathering existence to a more settled state, where farming could develop and animals could be husbanded for their resources of wool and milk as well as meat. Unleavened bread was a staple food of these early grain producers, baked on a flat stone beside the hearth, and this led eventually to the first primitive ovens. Soon the development of pottery containers greatly increased the possibilities for experimentation.

Linked with bread making was the discovery of fermentation. Ale was important to the Sumerians, but it is thought to have been the Egyptians who, in turn, dis-covered how to make leavened bread as a result of their brewing activities. The Egyptians also used salt as a preservative. At the height of their civilization, cooking had progressed a long way from the subsistence level. Sweet pastries, pickled fish, cheese and fresh figs were some of the delicacies enjoyed by the pharaohs.

The Greeks evolved an early specialization in wine and olive oil, both of which they exported in great quantities. Their simple cooking methods reflected the fact that life was largely lived outdoors.

Roman cuisine was more varied and sophisticated; their kitchens, well equipped with utensils and ingredients, are the true forerunners of the kitchen as we know it today. Early Roman kitchens were located in the atrium, where smoke from the fire could escape without risk. Later, when the atrium became the living area, the kitchen was assigned to a separate back room. The poor lived in crowded tenements where the risk of fire was great, and relied on food cooked in communal cook shops. At the height of the Empire an estimated one in three of the population depended on the ration of free grain.

The preferred fuel of the Romans was charcoal. The Mediterranean climate made quick methods of cooking infinitely preferable to burning large fires that threw off an uncomfortable heat; in any case, timber stocks were increasingly depleted and could not have supported such an extravagant use of fuel. Grilling and spit-roasting were favored and there were tripods to support cooking pots over the fire.

Basic cooking implements found in a Roman kitchen changed little over succeeding centuries; the pestle and mortar had ancient origins and so, surprisingly, did the apple corer, the first examples of which were made from sheep's bones. The principle of the double boiler was discovered by the Romans and there was also a type of *bain marie*, an open vessel in which separate jars of different foods could simmer

Roman cooking arrangements from the kitchen at the House of Vettii, Pompeii. Liquamen, a salty fermented fish sauce similar to the present-day fish sauces of Southeast Asia, was a popular flavoring in Roman cooking, and helped to disguise the taste of meat that had begun to go off. Regulating supplies of fresh produce without any means of refrigeration was a constant problem (ABOVE).

away without mingling the tastes. The pottery amphora was the standard Mediterranean storage jar, its spiked base allowing it to be stuck in earthen floors.

The expansion of the Empire brought exotic ingredients to a society eager for variety and refinement. Spices from the East, particularly pepper, were highly valued. Spice enlivened a starchy diet, and also disguised the rancid taste of meat.

THE DARK AGES

The barbarian hordes that swept over the Roman Empire in the fifth century brought the cultural refinement of the Classical world to an abrupt end. Life in the Dark Ages is generally assumed to have returned to a basic, brutal level, where the rigors of survival replaced the cultivation of taste.

Famine, plague and marauding Vikings brought periodic havoc that made progress extremely slow. Whether or not they were unremittingly harsh, the Dark Ages are truly dark to us: few records survive to illuminate this corner of history.

In Northern Europe, cooking was carried out over a central fire fueled by logs, fallen branches or peat. Smoke escaped as best it could through the roof. Naturally, since most buildings were made of timber, there was a great risk of fire.

The blazing heat of a wood fire limited cooking methods. In great hall houses whole animals might be spit-roasted, especially on special occasions, filling the air with smoke and smells. The spit had to be turned laboriously by hand, often for hours, to ensure even cooking.

By the end of the Roman Empire, cooking had grown in sophistication. Feasting was a popular pastime for the rich, who could afford both the slaves to prepare these elaborate banquets and the expensive imported ingredients of exotic dishes. Some banquets went on for days; tradition decreed that the ideal number at dinner was nine. This fourth-century mosaic shows a roast piglet on a dish (ABOVE).

Cooking and eating in the early Middle Ages lacked all the refinement and finesse evident in the cuisine of the Classical world. Although the nobility used bowls and dishes, most people made do with "trenchers," slabs of bread that served as edible plates (RIGHT).

Most people, however, survived on bread and whatever could be boiled up in a cauldron kept simmering on the hearth. Different foods, each tied up in a linen bag, might be boiled together, but most cauldrons contained a basic brew concocted from whatever was available. Since the fire was rarely allowed to go out, such broths could be kept simmering for weeks. A slab of bread or "trencher" served as a plate.

Central hearths meant that baking had to be done alongside the fire, usually under an upturned metal cover. The peasant baked on a griddle covered with a pot and piled hot embers over the top.

Early religious communities fared little better, especially since abstinence from certain foods, particularly meat, as well as fasting for prolonged periods was a requirement of the Church. Gradually, however, rules relaxed, the number of monasteries increased and monks became skilled at all kinds of cultivation, from growing medicinal herbs to tending vineyards and keeping bees. Monastery bees supplied the monks with precious wax candles; until the Reformation, their honey was also an important sweetener for the populace at large.

THE MEDIEVAL KITCHEN

Despite improvements in agriculture, daily life for European peasants changed slowly in the centuries between the Norman Conquest and the beginnings of the Renaissance. Central hearths were still common and the basic diet remained grain, beans or cabbage, supplemented by occasional fresh meat or fish. Few households could feed domestic animals over the winter, and salted, smoked or dried pork and fish (particularly herring) were the main source of protein for half the year.

As the population grew and concentrated in towns, market trading, cook shops for meat, and bakeries where homemade dough could be baked into bread addressed the convenience of the town dweller. But towns also fostered the spread of disease. Food poisoning from decaying produce and epidemics brought on by contaminated water were ever-present hazards.

When stone began to replace timber as a building material, the hall house was transformed. Gradually, in castles, abbeys and fortresses, fireplaces were set into the wall with ovens frequently built in alongside, sharing the same flue. The kitchen was now adjacent to the great hall, or else in a separate building altogether to minimize the fire risk and exclude the smoke and odours of roasting meat. This stage marked the beginning of the segregation of the kitchen from the main living area.

Cooking in these great medieval kitchens was a communal affair. The men lifted heavy cauldrons and stoked fires with logs, as well as doing the cooking and serving. Huge hams, salt fish and dried herbs hung from massive rafters, while bread was suspended well away from mice. Surrounding the kitchen were numerous specialized chambers for baking, brewing and storing spices, wine and grain. Herb gardens, ponds stocked with fresh fish, dairies, hives, vineyards and orchards kept communities of several hundred people self-sufficient from one season to the next.

Spices had been rediscovered by the Crusaders and once again played a vital role in making unreliable or monotonous food palatable. For the rich, cooking began to regain the sophistication of classical times, with the number of dishes on the table and the variety of spices they contained being an indication of wealth and status. Meals were served on trestle tables and people ate largely with their fingers, dipping into bowls shared between two or four at a time. Stale bread trenchers were being replaced by wooden platters, but there were no forks in common use for centuries to come.

NEW HORIZONS

It is hard to imagine the importance of spice to the North European in the fifteenth century. But some idea can be gained by the fact that the desire for spice (as well as gold) led to the first attempts to reach India by a direct sea route, which accidentally resulted in the discovery of America and the establishing of new trading frontiers. The expansion of trade brought increased prosperity to the merchant classes, but contact with the New World also brought new types of food.

The restored kitchen of a medieval abbey at Lavau Franche, France shows the huge hearth used for spit-roasting with a baking oven built in to the side of the recess. The table and chairs date from the nineteenth century, while earthenware and pewter is of eighteenth-century origin (LEFT).

By the fifteenth century, cooking had regained a degree of sophistication, largely due to the availability of spices. This fifteenth-century illustration from the *Roman de Renaud de Montauben* shows aristocrats at dinner, served from a serving table (the ancestor of the sideboard) and entertained by a gallery of musicians (ABOVE).

The central fire remained a feature of country life for centuries after the wall fireplace appeared in palaces and castles. "Visit to the Farmhouse" (*Besuch auf dem Bauernhof*) by Pieter Brueghel (1564–1638) provides a vivid evocation of one-room living around the central hearth. Mother and children warm themselves beside a cauldron suspended over burning logs; in the background there is a table set for a hearty meal, a couple churning vigorously and a woman setting off to fetch water in a bustling display of self-sufficiency (LEFT).

The centuries that followed saw an increase in comfort on the domestic front. The fortified castle gave way to the manor house, just as self-sufficient, but less communally organized. Women servants were not common until the seventeenth century, but the mistress of the household played an increasingly prominent role in supervising the home production of ale, candles, cheese, butter, cream and bread, as well as remedies and preserves.

Most changes in kitchen technology from the twelfth to the seventeenth century addressed the problem of how to regulate the heat of an open fire and cook more easily. Since the fire could not be "turned down," various devices were developed to vary the distance of the pot from the flames for quicker or slower heating.

In medieval times, cauldrons had been generally suspended by chains from an iron bar. This unsatisfactory arrangement was followed by a ratchet and crane system, which enabled pots and kettles to be swung over the fire at different levels. "Idlebacks"

allowed kettles to be tilted for pouring without burning the fingers, while flat-bottomed pans were set on trivets. Spits rested on andirons, with dripping pans beneath to catch the fat and screens in front to protect the unfortunate turnspit. The tops of some andirons were shaped to hold cups for warming drinks and cast-iron fire-backs reflected the heat, making the most of the fuel. By the end of the period the kitchen fireplace positively bristled with complex ironmongery.

Another seventeenth-century innovation was the sideboard, which evolved from a flat board fixed to the wall where tasters checked food for poison before it was offered to the master. The original purpose is revealed by the Italian for sideboard, *credenza*, which derives from the verb "to believe." From the flat board with shelves above, the sideboard developed into a single item of furniture with a solid back, extending to the full height of the room. Enclosed cupboards at the base were used to store linen with plates above.

A sixteenth-century kitchen, portrayed in an engraving by Justus Sadeler (1555–1630), after Antonio Tempesta. Fowl is spit-roasted over an open fire, while low pans on tripod legs are set down to warm over a bed of charcoal. The cook, with an impressive collection of knives tucked in his belt, lays out dishes for collection by serving boys, and dirty plates are brought back from the dining hall for washing up (ABOVE LEFT).

This seventeenth-century woodcut depicts a cook in his kitchen rolling out dough on a large table in preparation for baking bread in the oven behind him (ABOVE).

The Great Kitchen at the Royal Pavilion, Brighton, England was built by Nash in 1816 for the Prince Regent (later George IV). The Prince was a connoisseur of good food and many famous chefs, including Carême, worked here. The kitchen featured an innovative system of steam heating and had many other facilities, including a smoke jack in the chimney, powered by using hot air, which turned the spits. The Prince was so proud of the kitchen that he often showed visitors around it. The oval table in the center is a steam table for keeping dishes warm (RIGHT).

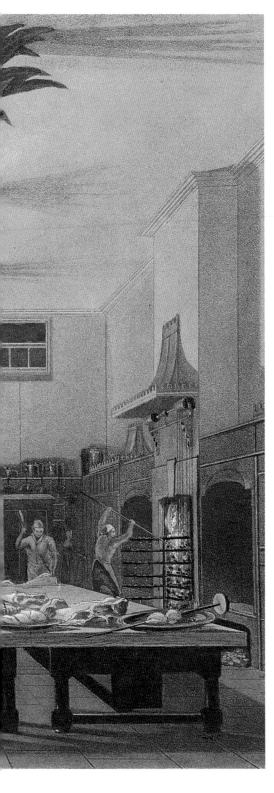

This Swedish kitchen at Hazelins House, Stockholm, typical of the late eighteenth century, shows a traditional kitchen fireplace with a deep hood to take smoke away. Round-bottomed copper pots on three legs stand on the raised hearth ready to be set down over the fire; a stack of split logs dry out underneath; the copper container to the right of the fireplace held fresh water for cooking and drinking (LEFT).

A CHANGE OF FUEL

By the beginning of the eighteenth century, timber stocks in Northern Europe had been seriously depleted. In England, laws were passed which only permitted certain types of wood to be burned. The rural poor were allowed to collect "dead" wood for their open hearths. Elsewhere, coal began to take over.

The new fuel meant a new type of hearth since coal needed a draft coming from underneath to burn freely. By the mid-century, the oven grate was in common use, which enclosed the fire in a raised firebox flanked with iron plates. Many such hearths included a hole in the wall fitted with an iron door for baking. But coal was expensive and in cities many ordinary households relied on ready-prepared dishes, roasts and baking from cook shops.

In the country houses of the wealthy, great kitchens, served by a range of ancillary offices, catered to a gentry increasingly keen on entertaining. Some kitchens had long stone sinks with a piped cold-water supply and large estates might have their own ice houses for cold storage, brick-lined cellars cut into a hillside and filled with ice from a frozen river or pond.

Spit-roasting was still carried out over huge open fires, the spit sometimes powered by a smoke jack which harnessed the smoke rising in the flue. A new development was the hastener or roasting screen, a cylindrical polished metal screen whose open front was placed in front of the fire. The roast was suspended inside and the polished metal reflected the heat of the fire and hastened the cooking.

The dining room became established as a room in its own right at this period, while the craze for tea drinking which swept through society had an important civilizing effect on domestic life. But some of the changes in manners originated in the new spirit of comfort and informality which

A typical kitchen in a large house of the late nineteenth century, with an accompanying plate showing a range of utensils and equipment. An important development was the close range or stove, fueled in this case by coal and incorporating hot plates and baking ovens. The array of pots and pans, the kitchen sideboard and scrubbed floorboards display an emphasis on practicality and efficiency (LEFT).

grew up in the salons surrounding the French court of Louis XV. Intimate suppers replaced formal banqueting and the acknowledged French supremacy in matters of taste – particularly in cuisine – became established during this time. Cooking was a way of displaying refinement and cultivation, not merely a matter of domestic management and basic sustenance.

UPSTAIRS, DOWNSTAIRS

The Industrial Revolution speeded up the pace of kitchen development. The central innovation was the close range or kitchener, an enclosed iron stove which allowed better regulation of heat and a more economical use of fuel. The range incorporated an oven for baking or roasting meat and top plates for heating water or cooking; many also heated boilers for a ready supply of hot water. It warmed the kitchen, supplied hot water for washing and blazed away in summer and winter.

But the new stove had its disadvantages. It was hideously difficult to clean. At the crack of dawn, before a fire could be lit and the first kettle boiled, the range had to be raked out, swept, blackleaded and polished, a punishing daily routine which generally fell to the poor kitchenmaid. "Slaving over a hot stove" meant exactly that to the Victorian cook, condemned to spend hours tending the family's dinner in overheated, poorly ventilated conditions.

Burnt meat and badly timed meals were still by no means uncommon. Without any reliable means of gauging temperature, cooks relied on trial and error. One cookbook advised that the oven was ready for baking cakes when you could hold your arm inside and count to 40. A less painful method was to throw a handful of flour into the oven to see how quickly it burned.

As it had always done, the kitchen still played an essential role in maintaining daily life, but it was no longer an integrated part of the household. Except in the cottages or simple homes of the poor, where everything largely happened in one room, the kitchen was now the domain of the army of domestic servants the Victorians employed to cook, clean and run their homes. Victorian women seldom ventured into their own kitchens, except to consult the cook on the day's menu or intervene in a domestic drama. Far from exercising those self-sufficient skills of previous generations, many were entirely ignorant of the most basic procedures and could not even have made themselves a cup of tea.

Upstairs, downstairs depicted in an illustration from a German cookbook, 1875. Many kitchens at this time were located in the basement or well away from living areas, in a rigorous form of social segregation (FAR LEFT).

The Victorian kitchen, at any level of society, was dominated by the close range. These massive iron stoves required constant maintenance, were extremely difficult to clean and could become uncomfortably hot. In these views of a small kitchen in a Glasgow tenement, freshly laundered dish towels air in front of the stove, pans hang from a shelf on hooks and a small wooden table in the middle of the floor serves as a working area (LEFT and BELOW).

In larger houses, particularly outside the cities, kitchens could be well-run, practically planned and attractive places, with high ceilings, good ventilation and an abundance of natural light. They were accompanied by the usual service rooms, which grew increasingly specialized, although the "room where the butler ironed the daily newspaper" may well be an exaggeration. There were certainly rooms where the chief activity was knife-sharpening (which until the invention of stainless steel was an arduous task), pantries where the plates were kept, rooms where the housekeeper did her bookkeeping, sculleries for washing up and larders with external, north-facing walls to benefit from natural refrigeration. In the country, there might be a separate dairy, built on a shady site, with tiled walls and stone floors to keep it cool.

In the middle-class terraced house, the kitchen was a less hospitable place. It was usually located in the basement, which could be poorly lit and badly ventilated. Walls were often painted brown, so as not to reveal the discoloration caused by coal fires and gas lighting. Floors were made of flagstone or quarry tile to withstand daily scrubbing. A scullery for washing was a nineteenth-century addition to the basic kitchen, reflecting the increased appreciation of the role of hygiene in health.

The abundance of cheap labor did not guarantee good results. Course upon course of French-style dishes represented the height of fashion but severely taxed the skills of most kitchen staff. To fill the gap in culinary knowledge, many new books were published, the most famous by a young housewife, Isabella Beeton.

The utility and spare beauty of the Shaker kitchen has given it a timeless appeal. The distinctive interior style adopted by this small religious sect is appreciated today for its functionalism, purity and attention to detail. Wall-mounted pegboards were used to hang everything off the floor, keeping rooms rigorously ordered and scrupulously clean (LEFT).

The main kitchen of a hotel in the latter part of the nineteenth century. The layout of the professional kitchen, with an island of ranges and pans hung neatly overhead, is already evident (RIGHT).

France was the center of gastronomic excellence in the nineteenth century. This allegorical illustration is a title page from a book called "Les Aliments" (OPPOSITE).

NEW WORLD INFLUENCES

Life for the early colonists of North America was harsh, and even as new frontiers were opened up by pioneer families, much depended on the ability to husband meagre resources. Everything that was used or consumed had to be made at home, although at particularly busy times of the year, people in neighbouring districts often pooled their efforts.

There was no shortage of timber, and wood was the major source of fuel. But it was also the principal building material and it was not unusual for early colonial kitchens to be located in a separate building to reduce the risk of fire. In the South a further incentive was to remove the heat of cooking from the main living quarters. In basic one-room cabins and farmhouses, cooking was done over an open fire. A brick-lined root cellar dug under the earthen floor preserved vegetables throughout the winter months. Cauldrons (known as kettles) were indispensable pieces of equipment.

As the new colonies established themselves, gained independence and flourished, there were new opportunities to recreate Old World comforts. It was natural for those with close ties to England to try to imitate the English way of life as closely as possible. But with the great waves of immigrants from Central and Northern Europe that poured into the country during the nineteenth century, new customs and types of food were introduced and American cooking began to acquire its variety.

The labor-shortage was the major difference between European and American ways of life that affected how kitchens developed in the New World. From the outset, the wife tended to work alongside her servants; in many cases everyone sat down to eat together. There were always those who tried to maintain the distinctions of the Old World, and the slave economy of the South before emancipation proved an exception to the rule, but the general lack of cheap labor meant that Americans were pioneers in the drive to make kitchens more efficient and pleasant places.

As early as 1869, Catherine Beecher (sister of Harriet Beecher Stowe) analysed what we would call the "work sequence" in a kitchen and went on to put her findings into practice. Anticipating a time when there would be no domestic help, her aim was to transform the kitchen so that it could be easily managed by one person.

By the end of the nineteenth century, the North American kitchen, particularly in towns and cities, was much less segregated from living areas than its European counterpart. Wood-burning stoves had replaced open hearths and the kitchen, conveniently located near the dining room to make serving easier, provided a warm focus to the ordinary home.

KITCHEN TECHNOLOGY

Many of the labor-saving devices that have transformed the kitchen in modern times were first envisaged in the late nineteenth century. The principle of artificial refrigeration was discovered in the 1870s. The gas stove made its first appearance in the 1850s but it was another 50 years before the public overcame their suspicions and began to adopt it. There was even an American design for a dishwasher dating from the 1850s. Canned food, the pressure cooker and the carpet sweeper also first appeared during this period.

Early domestic gadgets such as mincers, mixers and grinders were cumbersome and hard to operate, and only when the small electric motor was developed in the 1920s did these ideas become practical for daily use in the average kitchen. Electrification and the rise in gas consumption were other agents of change: most homes in England were without either before 1914.

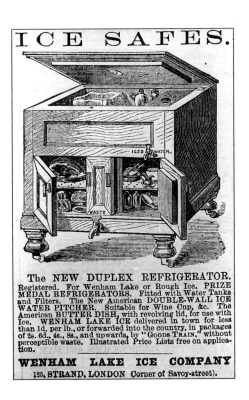

ICE SAFES.

The NEW DUPLEX REFRIGERATOR.
Registered. For Wenham Lake or Rough Ice. PRIZE MEDAL REFRIGERATORS. Fitted with Water Tanks and Filters. The New American DOUBLE-WALL ICE WATER PITCHER. Suitable for Wine Cup, &c. The American BUTTER DISH, with revolving lid, for use with Ice. WENHAM LAKE ICE delivered in town for less than 1d. per lb., or forwarded into the country, in packages of 2s. 6d., 4s., 8s., and upwards, by "GOODS TRAIN," without perceptible waste. Illustrated Price Lists free on application.

WENHAM LAKE ICE COMPANY
125, STRAND, LONDON Corner of Savoy-street).

The 1920s saw the birth of the modern kitchen as we know it. In the United States, the closed kitchen cabinet had been in use for some time; standard prefabricated kitchen units were now designed embodying the results of the latest time-and-motion studies. By the 1930s the development of plastic laminates produced hygienic, easy-care work surfaces. The arrival of stainless steel in the 1920s took the drudgery out of keeping utensils clean and sharp.

Appliances were redesigned, too, in the new streamlined aesthetic borrowed from aeronautical engineering. Sleek, and with gleaming white enameled finishes, the new refrigerators, electric and gas stoves brought the machine age into the home. The labor-saving kitchen, bright, convenient and powered by the clean new fuel, electricity, was the selling point of the suburban housing that sprang up between the wars. It often incorporated an eating area or "breakfast nook" where the family could have informal meals.

In Britain, change happened more slowly. Although it was obvious by the 1920s that the servant army upon which the Victorians had relied was retreating from view, it had not yet quite disappeared. Old kitchens were gradually updated to provide a better environment that might keep staff happy and persuade them to stay. Linoleum proved a popular substitute for hard stone floors, and walls were painted light colors. Closed kitchen cupboards replaced open sideboards, keeping their contents free from dust. Gas rings and eventually electric stoves supplanted the kitchen range, but refrigerators remained rare.

The turning point came with the social upheavals brought on by the Second World War. For the first time, the middle-class housewife had no option but to manage single handedly. And working in a cramped, dingy kitchen with outmoded equipment was not a prospect that many relished. The built-in kitchen – the product of the latest ergonomical knowhow – was

initially seen as a status symbol as much as a necessity for the working women of the 1950s. But thermostatically controlled ovens, electric toasters, high-level grills, washing machines, refrigerators and tumble dryers were no longer unimaginable luxuries for many people. Convenience foods and supermarket shopping addressed the same need: to save time and trouble on the domestic front.

With mass tourism came a new awareness of the culinary traditions of other countries, particularly those bordering the Mediterranean. New ingredients began to appear in the supermarkets which enabled dishes sampled abroad to be recreated at home. The new wave of cookbooks published after the war, designed to give the housewife confidence and expertise, was matched by a steady stream of advice on kitchen design and decorative possibilities. From the 1960s, eating and even entertaining in the kitchen lost its stigma, a powerful indication of its significant shift in status. After its long eclipse, the kitchen was back at the heart of the home.

Ovens that clean themselves, multipurpose food processors, waste-disposal units, freezers and microwaves represent a continuing refinement of the technological advances that have changed kitchen life for good. Manufactured kitchens are now available in every conceivable color, and in a vast range of finishes and materials all designed for easy care, cleanliness and efficiency. Appliance manufacturers are keen to persuade us of the merits of their latest innovations. Yet, alongside the demand for technology, there remains a persistent attachment to traditional ways, best encapsulated in the "country kitchen style" with its emphasis on natural rather than synthetic finishes. Even if the experience of working in real country kitchens would have daunted most of today's home cooks, what they represent remains a powerful inspiration for those who now find that the kitchen is the center of family life.

Technological advances have transformed the kitchen in the twentieth century. Before artificial refrigeration, this "ice safe" of 1874 was cooled by a block of ice that was delivered to the door by the iceman (OPPOSITE).

North America led the world in labor-saving kitchen appliances and fixtures. But in the early twentieth century there was still little attempt to make the kitchen an attractive room in its own right, as is apparent from this Canadian kitchen (ABOVE).

Ahead of its time, this kitchen designed by Mrs Darcy Braddell was displayed at the Academy Exhibition of British Art in Industry in 1935. The stove and sink are arranged in a tightly planned layout, positioned to benefit from artificial or natural light. There is a ventilating grill over the cooker (ABOVE).

The classic post-war built-in American kitchen, with bright shiny surfaces and a full range of storage units integrated with the latest appliances (LEFT).

The Professional Kitchen

In the Dordogne, Helen Hamlyn's hotel kitchen at Château Bagnol maintains traditional cooking methods such as spit-roasting over an open fire (ABOVE).

The professional kitchen with its heavy-duty appliances, gleaming stainless steel surfaces and rigorous organization may appear a world away from the home kitchen, but there are many useful lessons each side can learn from the other. The kitchen at Le Pont de la Tour in London combines sophisticated technology with a humane working environment (RIGHT).

Kitchen professionals of all descriptions, from food writers and editors to restaurateurs, exert a considerable influence on the home kitchen. Today, the experience of eating out is widely enjoyed, not merely by the privileged few, but by a much broader cross section of the population than ever before. This regular point of contact with professional cooks and their kitchens has had a crucial impact on culinary ambitions and expectations at home.

Innovative chefs introduce new styles of cooking which more adventurous restaurant-goers attempt to recreate in their own kitchens. Most food-lovers are equally serious about kitchen design and equipment, and the professional cook's standards in these areas provide important points of reference.

But it is not merely a one-way process. The trend for restaurant kitchens to be more open and accessible, so that customers catch a glimpse of all the activity behind the scenes, is a direct reflection of the new informality of entertaining at home. Despite the obvious differences of scale and expertise, there are many useful lessons that each side can learn from the other.

THE RESTAURANT KITCHEN

Considering how central to our lives is the enjoyment of good food and company, restaurants have a surprisingly short history. According to the celebrated French gastronome Brillat-Savarin, the first restaurants opened in Paris in the second half of the eighteenth century.

Cook shops, where precooked food was sold or slabs of meat could be taken to be roasted or bread to be baked, have ancient origins. Taverns and inns also provided hungry travelers with set meals. But the concept of a restaurant, with a choice of different dishes, including specialties of the house, was entirely new.

The term "restaurant" originated as a typically canny marketing ploy. A Parisian soup-seller, Boulanger, promoted his products as "restaurants" or "restoratives" and won a famous legal battle which enabled him to broaden his repertoire to include a dish he had devised (sheep's feet in white wine sauce, according to *Larousse gastronomique*). From this unlikely beginning in the middle years of the eighteenth century, restaurants rapidly grew in popularity. After the French Revolution, they became established as places where ordinary citizens could savor a refinement of cooking formerly enjoyed only by the rich.

The chefs Beauvilliers, Baleine and Vefour were among the founders of early restaurants, some of which became associated with a particular specialty. Many of these eighteenth-century establishments survived well into the nineteenth century, providing a forum for intellectual life as well as helping to consolidate France's reputation for gastronomic excellence.

It is generally acknowledged, however, that the true founder of classic French cuisine was the great chef Antoine Carême (1784–1833), who worked for the French diplomat Prince Talleyrand, the Prince Regent (later George IV of England), and many other grand households. His various books and treatises resulted from a lifetime's dedication to the culinary arts.

The restaurant kitchen of innovative chef Michel Guérard features the traditional arrangement of central ranges where chefs exercise their culinary skills. With the introduction of color on vitreous enameled surfaces, neat checkered tiled border and plenty of natural light, such a setting dispels any notion that the professional kitchen is a soulless place (LEFT).

Guérard's personal kitchen, no less formidably equipped, displays the appeal of professional fittings in the home (ABOVE).

Recently restored, Villa Turque in the Swiss Jura was designed by the pioneer of modernism, Le Corbusier, in 1916. The sympathetic renovation was carried out by Ecart, Andrée Putman's interior-design firm: harmonious geometries and the introduction of machine finishes into the home make for a powerful expression of the modern aesthetic. The kitchen is a serenely functional place, fitted with stainless steel, tile and glass bricks (RIGHT and FAR RIGHT).

The modern restaurant kitchen has come a long way from its eighteenth-century origins. With the intense commercial pressures of modern restaurant cooking, a restaurant kitchen represents one of the greatest design challenges of all. Out of what is often a restricted and awkward space, the professional designer must create a working environment where a team of people can produce a great quantity and variety of different dishes to a reliable, even excellent, standard day after day. It may seem that today's restaurant kitchens share little more than a basic French vocabulary with their predecessors. But the basic problems of managing intense heat, providing an efficient sequence of work and integrating the needs of different disciplines have probably changed very little, even if we are now technologically very well equipped to deal with them.

In any commercial kitchen, time, space and efficiency must be maximized or the restaurant simply won't make money. The need for tight, focused planning is further complicated by health and safety regulations which seem to increase in scope and complexity every year. For most of us, preparing a dinner party for 20 people is a major task, and would stretch our cooking and organizational skills to the limit. Naturally, in this situation, few people would complicate matters further by offering guests very much choice in what they ate. In a large restaurant on a busy evening, there may be 100 people or more, each one choosing a variety of different dishes and all expecting to be served quickly and with precisely what they ordered. The fact that good restaurants routinely manage this minor miracle to their customers' satisfaction is a tribute not only to highly skilled and dedicated staff, but also to thoughtful and rigorous planning on the part of the kitchen designer or architect.

Space is a fundamental consideration. Most restaurant owners naturally want to maximize the floor area available for seating. Traditionally, the chef has had to make do with what is left over, often a space that is not only too small, but may be awkwardly shaped and with little natural light. Increasingly, however, a new attitude is emerging which puts the kitchen at the center of the process of restaurant design. As typified by the kitchen at Le Pont de la Tour (pages 32–35), this approach starts with the needs of the chef and the type of

The kitchen at Hoexter's Market, Boca Raton, Florida is treated as a shop front, in full view of passers-by. The bustle of food preparation pulls crowds of onlookers, who, appetites whetted, are drawn into the restaurant to sample the fare. Such a level of exposure has the added advantage of allowing customers to appreciate the immaculate cleanliness of the working kitchen (RIGHT).

The immediacy of food cooked and prepared in full view and brought straight to the table has long been part of the experience of eating out in the Far East. In London's Wagamama, a Japanese noodle bar designed by John Pawson, the "cook and serve" philosophy is accentuated by the long lines of the counter and refectory dining (ABOVE).

Japanese food, with its emphasis on freshness and quick cooking, demands precision. Pots and pans are subjected to repeated, frequent use. Everything must be in the right place, readily to hand (LEFT).

food he or she will be producing and allows the kitchen to be better integrated with the restaurant as a whole.

Nevertheless, in kitchens where up to 30 people will be working at one time, if the kitchen designer were to allocate space on a strictly ergonomic basis, the result would be a vast area that was unprofitable and probably unworkable. With experience, designers learn how to confine certain activities in a more compact fashion, relying on the ability of an experienced kitchen team to work in close quarters with an almost instinctive sense of what each member of the group is doing.

The precise work sequence will depend on how the chef operates and the type of food which the restaurant intends to offer. There may be distinctly zoned areas for making sauces and rolling pastry, broiling and so on, each organized so that the right equipment, surfaces, servicing and utensils are at hand. Professional kitchens are organized either with stoves or ranges in a central island or lined up against a wall. The range provides the hot surface on which the food is cooked and may also incorporate ovens and high-level salamanders or browning ovens. A stockpot on a low burner may be nearby. All professional equipment is designed to withstand incredible punishment. Tradition has it that oven doors on ranges must be strong enough to bear the full weight of the heftiest chef, since standing on the door is often the best way to reach the range hood for cleaning it at the end of the day.

Preparation areas, dishwashers, cold stores, collection points, freezers and broilers may also line the walls. It saves time and cuts down on unnecessary traffic if waiters can collect dishes from a point near the range. Again, it is helpful if storage for cold desserts is also nearby. Juggling a host of such individual requirements adds up to a planning process of considerable complexity. It may take four or five complete redesigns to get it right.

The head chef – or chef de cuisine, to use the traditional term – hardly cooks. The chef's role is to create a dish, teach it to the staff and then control the quality of the output on a daily basis. The kitchen layout therefore has to take into account how the chef performs this supervisory role and must allow plenty of room for overseeing and observing everything that is happening in different areas of the kitchen. Chefs may also have a say in the choice of equipment, especially if they have a favorite gadget they feel they cannot do without. However, designers try to restrict the amount of incidental machinery: expensive to run and subject to failure, many ancillary pieces of equipment may not be any faster or more efficient than a skilled pair of hands.

New health regulations, which vary from state to state, municipality to municipality, place further burdens on space and layout. The Department of Health in each municipality is charged with inspecting and licensing restaurants. In general, there must be sufficient refrigeration and work space to ensure that no cross contamination of foods occurs during storage and handling. Equipment must be washed and sanitized immediately after use. Some health departments require that food preparation be segregated with color-coded chopping boards for meat, fish and vegetables.

Basic surfaces and finishes should be robust and easily maintained; flooring as non-slip as possible. In commercial kitchens, stainless steel counters and sealed, non-absorbent walls and floors are now standard. Surfaces must be as seamless as possible to facilitate cleaning, joints and gaps sealed tight to prevent a build-up of grime. Thorough cleaning is part of the daily routine and may be carried out with a steam cleaner. Drains built into the floor help to eliminate surface water.

Lighting is another vital element. A busy staff working under pressure with razor-sharp knives, gallons of boiling water and hot ovens need to see precisely what they're doing, otherwise there is a real risk of serious injury. Chefs need bright light to illuminate their working areas; low-energy fluorescent is the most practical and economical source. The brashness of such lighting can be mitigated, however, by restricting ceiling lights to the areas of intense activity and using supplementary halogen lights where possible.

Good ventilation is also critically important. Ovens, broilers and hot plates generate a blast of heat which can quickly turn a kitchen into an inferno. To counteract the effect, a supply of cool air is essential, setting up a massive cycle of convection that literally stirs up the atmosphere.

Anyone who has ever installed a new kitchen and appliances will be aware of the risk of incorrect measuring or specification. Even with careful planning, there is always a chance that what has been ordered will turn out not to fit the space precisely. Designers of home kitchens can allow for this by incorporating a margin for error; or, if an appliance proves to be too big for the area left for it, it can be exchanged for a model that will fit. Designers of commercial kitchens have to be infinitely more precise. With every millimeter of space accounted for, the process of specification is fraught with anxiety. Custom-built ranges, equipment ordered from manufacturers all over the world, and custom steel construction mean that tolerances are practically zero. Everything must fit absolutely and work as it should. When the gigantic range at Quaglino's in London was fired for the first time it expanded in length by 2in (5cm) and knocked over a wall. Designers also have to know which way doors and lids hinge, and ensure that machinery can be serviced if something breaks down.

As the restaurant kitchen becomes more accessible, customers gain a unique insight into the creative skills of those who cook for a living. A thoughtfully planned kitchen is the first stage in the process that culminates in the perfect meal at your table.

LE PONT DE LA TOUR

TERENCE CONRAN'S THAMES-SIDE RESTAURANT, LONDON

My introduction to restaurant life came when I worked as a young dishwasher and vegetable boy in a Paris brasserie. But the lowest rung can provide a good vantage point and the experience taught me a great deal about kitchens and inspired a fascination with the whole way of life that has stayed with me ever since.

Le Pont de la Tour is my tenth restaurant. Ever since I opened the Orrery back in the 1950s, I have come to appreciate the unique challenge restaurants offer the designer. There is the technical expertise required to plan and lay out a professional kitchen, the interrelated practicalities of making food and serving it and the interior-design skills that come into play in creating a welcoming and exciting place to eat. Then there are the more intangible factors. No successful restaurant is without its own special atmosphere. When you get it right, there is nothing to equal the buzz of a roomful of people enjoying themselves.

On the other hand, if you get it wrong, the price is high. There are few second chances in the restaurant business. Customers are highly critical, especially when they're spending their own money, and staff are equally quick to complain if they can't do their jobs properly.

A riverside restaurant where people could appreciate one of London's most neglected natural assets has always been a personal ambition. With spectacular views of Tower Bridge and the constant hum of Thames traffic, the character of Le Pont de la Tour owes a great deal to its setting. The warehouses at Butler's Wharf offered me the chance to realize another dream – to create a "gastrodrome" of restaurants, shops, bars and cafés to cater to every food lover. Le Pont de la Tour is the hub of a complex that includes a bar, grill, smoked-fish shop, wine merchant, food store and – most recently – a Mediterranean café-cum-restaurant called Cantina.

The design of a restaurant should suit the food it serves. At Le Pont de la Tour, we had the opportunity to take this basic principle to its logical conclusion and begin the whole design process with the kitchen. At the same time, we wanted to break down some of the traditional barriers between kitchen and restaurant. When people have the chance to see chefs at work preparing the food they are eventually going to eat, the experience of eating out becomes more natural and less contrived. The showmanship of Japanese cooks who prepare food right in front of you, or the accessibility of the Mediterranean restaurant, where customers are invited into the kitchen to approve the freshness of the ingredients and appreciate the skills of the cook, demonstrate the powerful attractions of this level of participation.

Co-designed with Keith Hobbs – who has worked with me on other restaurants, notably Bibendum, also in London – and chef David Burke, the kitchen at Le Pont de la Tour places cooking at the heart of the restaurant, just as the kitchen is the heart of the home. It achieves this largely through making the kitchen visible from the main restaurant and from the bar/grill – and, unconventionally, from the street.

From the restaurant, two large portholes cut in the kitchen double doors defuse the mystique inherent in traditional restaurant layout, whereby guests often have no clue as to where the food has come from. In the bar/grill, a large window reveals the grill chef working at a black slate counter. At the back of the restaurant, large windows and glazed doors allow passersby to view kitchen activity in full swing. The pastry chef has pride of place in front of one of the largest back windows.

This accessibility works both ways. For the guests, the display of craftsmanship and fresh ingredients whets the appetite and makes an enjoyable backdrop for eating. For the kitchen staff, there are other positive repercussions. A kitchen on view must be able to withstand scrutiny, which means that in addition to designing for practicality and efficiency, other factors more to do with style have to come into play. The average commercial kitchen is not a thing of beauty. Because the kitchen at Le Pont de la Tour is visible, it has to be easy on the eye and this has, in turn, created a more sympathetic environment for the staff.

Lighting has been a key element in this process. Chefs and kitchen staff were pleasantly surprised to find that they could work just as effectively with a lower overall level of lighting. Bright overhead light is reserved for those areas where it is essential, such as over chefs' preparation areas and the ranges. Elsewhere, lighting is softer. Halogen lights over the pass tables at collection points give a more attractive, sparkling effect as well as keeping food hot. Light-colored surfaces and the ceramic-tiled floor brighten the room, while daylight from windows on the street side lifts the spirits and provides a more natural atmosphere in which to work.

Working in an "open" kitchen enhances the performance aspect of cooking. Being on view keeps staff on their toes, aware of their audience. The effect extends down to the level of detail. Using decent bowls and storage jars instead of the ubiquitous plastic tubs reinforces the basic message of quality and craftsmanship.

The kitchen at Le Pont de la Tour is at the center, not only of the restaurant, but of the entire "gastrodrome." The separate, dynamic areas of interest provide character and vitality, but the physical organization would have been unworkable without a nervous system of computer technology. Terminals at each waiter station allow orders to be placed at the touch of a button anywhere within the complex and facilitate central control of supplies. However vital the technology, this is one aspect that remains firmly behind the scenes. At the table, the waiter takes the order down on paper: some things never change.

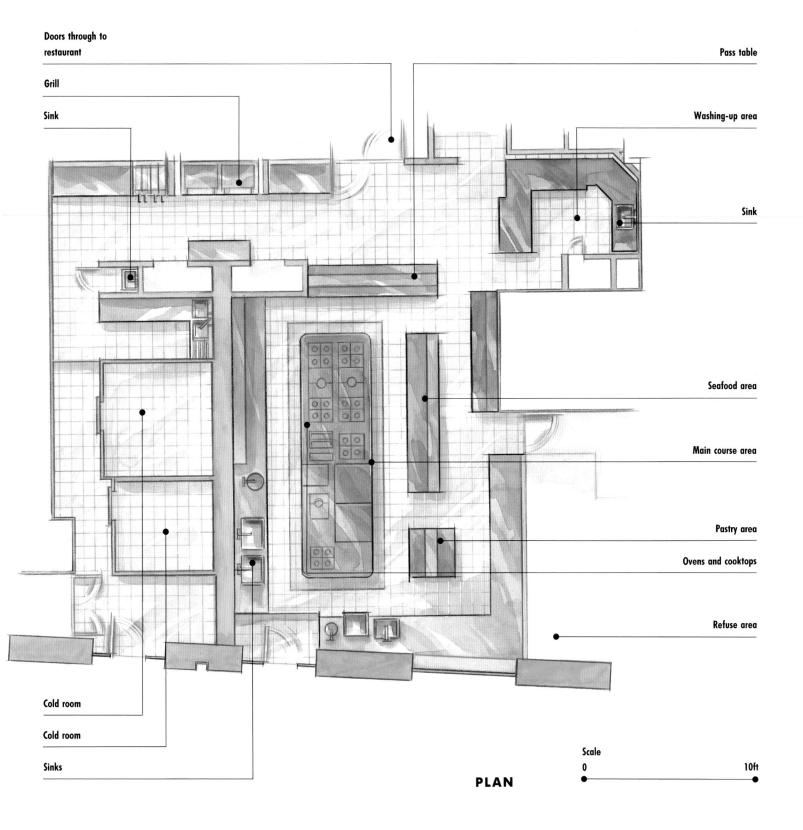

Doors through to
restaurant

Grill

Sink

Pass table

Washing-up area

Sink

Seafood area

Main course area

Pastry area

Ovens and cooktops

Refuse area

Cold room

Cold room

Sinks

Scale
0   10ft

PLAN

The kitchen in full swing for lunchtime trade: all of the food preparation areas lead to the pass table, where the food waits to be taken out to the restaurant. Bill slips hanging at eye level remind waiters which plates are for which table (ABOVE).

Illuminated countertops provide excellent task lighting: here, a cook whisks the sauce to accompany the fish course. Chill cabinets beneath the counter keep ingredients in peak condition (RIGHT).

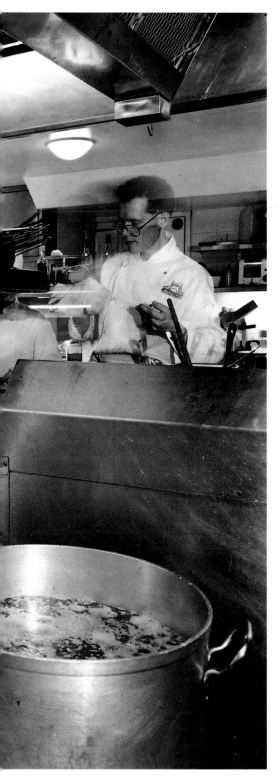

A huge pot of vegetable stock constantly simmers. Beyond, cooks cluster around the giant ranges preparing the main courses (LEFT).

Eye-level broilers are positioned directly above the burners, with bowls to the side and industrial-grade exhausts close by (RIGHT).

The pastry chef adds the finishing touches to a *tarte aux pommes*. Positioned at the back of the kitchen close to a street-level window, his expertise at the pastry counter provides a fitting show to passersby of the culinary delights on offer in the restaurant (RIGHT).

BULTHAUP: PLANNING THE COOK'S ROOM

Accessible from all sides, the Bulthaup kitchen workbench bridges the gap between built-in and unfitted kitchens and brings a new professionalism to the home environment. In combination with the ventilation hood, large double refrigerator and high-tech oven, it provides a professional-standard kitchen in a home environment (RIGHT).

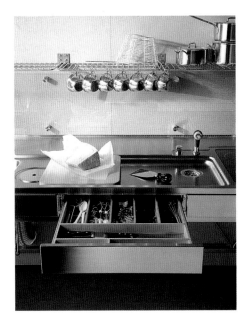

The cooktop area of the workbench can be equipped with a variety of heat sources: gas burners and electric rings or, as here, gas burners and an electric grill (ABOVE LEFT).

Drawers are fitted with integral compartments to make storage better organized and easily accessible (LEFT).

The professional cook's choice on the home front, Bulthaup kitchens have acquired an international reputation for quality, efficiency and thoughtful design. This German-based company, with retail outlets all over the world, produces a range of kitchens and kitchen accessories that enshrine Bauhaus principles of functionalism and form, a direction influenced by the company's design mentor, the late Otl Aicher. Years of research and conceptualization lie behind each new line. The result is a refinement of detail and precision of finish that draws on the lessons of the professional kitchen but remains fully in tune with the wishes of the home cook.

Reflecting the relationship between professional and home kitchens, Bulthaup's innovative kitchen workbench draws on the

Versatility is a cornerstone of Bulthaup planning philosophy. Designed as a free standing unit, the workbench can equally be placed against a wall and equipped with appliances such as an oven and dishwasher, and with a combination of drawers and cupboards. Storage above the workbench is just as adaptable: hanging rails at arm height and behind the light fitting hold a range of utensils; blinds hide cooking pans and ingredients stored on shelves (RIGHT).

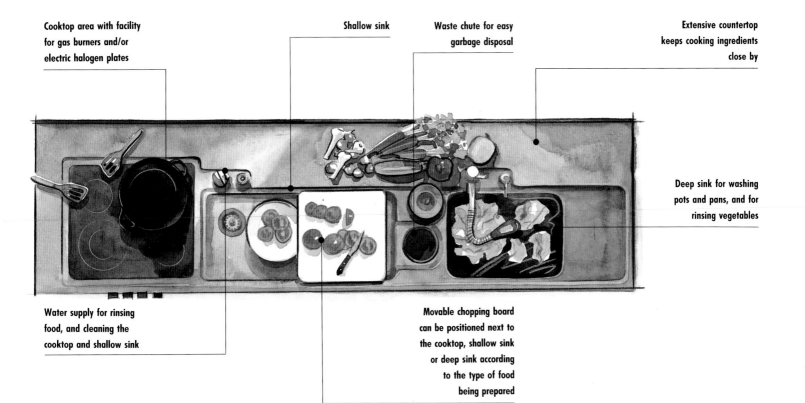

Cooktop area with facility for gas burners and/or electric halogen plates

Shallow sink

Waste chute for easy garbage disposal

Extensive countertop keeps cooking ingredients close by

Deep sink for washing pots and pans, and for rinsing vegetables

Water supply for rinsing food, and cleaning the cooktop and shallow sink

Movable chopping board can be positioned next to the cooktop, shallow sink or deep sink according to the type of food being prepared

principles of restaurant design, but adapts them for the home. Power and water connections apart, the bench is a totally independent unit, providing all the main cooking functions in one. Like a table, it is accessible from all sides, so two or more people can comfortably work at it without getting in each other's way. Before they start a family, most people lead less fixed and settled lives; they may move frequently or change jobs. Bulthaup's workbench, which can be readily moved from place to place, is a response to the habits of this group. The next stage, when family life becomes established, demands a larger, more versatile kitchen to accommodate growing needs. Then, finally, when the family has grown, the kitchen can be made simpler and more compact.

Kitchen manufacturers tend to respond to the demands of industry or the needs of retailers before they consider their customers. They may design units around standard components that are easily processed or shipped, or attempt to create stylistic niches to sell their products on image alone. Bulthaup, however, holds fast to the sound principle that good design unites material, function and form in an ideal solution that has little to do with cosmetics or passing trends. The classic Bulthaup kitchens prove that the best design is the design you can't see.

The years of development that go into each product concentrate on investigating exactly what people want. Inspiration comes from being aware of the way people live and use their kitchens and from the experience of eating out. Gerd Bulthaup and his team of designers try to reflect the central role kitchens play in ordinary life: the openness of the modern kitchen, integrated with the rest of the household, is an important factor; environmental concerns and the new role of the home as a focus for entertaining are other considerations. The inspiration for the new line, System 25, came from a dinner in a Swiss farmhouse, not from a drawing board prototype.

Kitchens are expected to last about 15 years on average. The challenge to designers is to create durable and well-made products that will withstand daily use over a period of many years, and also to anticipate changing habits so that the basic organization remains relevant. Ergonomics changes constantly: people are getting taller – the average height has increased by 6in (15cm) since 1920 – which means proportions, head room and counter heights all need to be adjusted accordingly. Kitchen practices also change – the way we cook, what we eat and how we shop.

Most people expect to invest in a new car at least half a dozen times during their driving life and tailor their choice to suit their requirements at a particular time.

Bulthaup believes that kitchens, too, have a natural life span and are worth that same level of investment, both in relation to usage and in terms of quality. A kitchen that functions poorly or is not relevant to the type of life you lead is a daily source of frustration and inconvenience.

As well as extensive research into the needs and habits of different households, Bulthaup designers spend a great deal of time analysing basic kitchen functions. The mundane tasks performed in the average kitchen – sorting trash, preparing vegetables, storing packaged goods, unpacking groceries – vary little from week to week. In a well-designed kitchen, the routine is pleasant and easy to perform, in a badly planned space, mistakes will happen. The care taken to match the materials to the task, and in attention to the fine details of operation and organizational flexibility, shows up time and again in everyday use.

This type of thinking has resulted in details such as drawers that pull out to their full depth, deeper eye-level cabinets to take new types of produce, and as a host of ingenious storage facilities that enables units to be adapted precisely to suit what is being stored – a far cry from the bland basic boxes of many built-in kitchens which rarely offer any specific storage.

With a range of kitchen systems that encompasses over 600,000 distinct parts, delivering the goods to the customer is equally important as designing them. Bulthaup's solution has been to build up a "distribution culture" by establishing its own centers where the traditional ordering bottleneck can be bypassed. Specially trained personnel, typically with architectural or interior-design backgrounds, advise on installation and ordering, so that clients can make an informed selection that will suit their individual needs. In Bulthaup terms, the kitchen is an arena for communication. Applying the same thinking to the design process as to customer relationships is basic company philosophy.

Bulthaup's System 25 was conceived to combine the instinctive comfort of a farmhouse kitchen with the highest degree of utility. Seven years in development, each detail of the entire system was intensively planned in terms of function and use of material (LEFT).

A fitted knife drawer and sliding countertop chopping board are two of the elements of System 25 designed to increase convenience and pleasure in daily kitchen use (ABOVE).

The Hub of the Home

The appealing rusticity of this Tuscan kitchen connects indoors and outdoors, a fit environment in which to savor the taste of freshly picked vegetables and herbs (ABOVE).

The Conran kitchen at Barton Court, England is a huge family room where the pleasures of cooking and eating happily coexist. The island unit allows a basic separation of activities, reinforced by a change in flooring from oak boards in the eating area to pale ceramic tiles in the kitchen. An aluminum hood provides efficient ventilation and space for utensils (RIGHT).

The demands of kitchen technology mean that the kitchen is likely to be one of the most intensely planned areas in the home. Yet, as manufacturers are well aware, the "dream" kitchens of popular imagination are not merely about efficiency and spatial logic. Most people have some idea of the kind of kitchen they would like, even if only in very general terms, and these issues of "style" are just as important as ergonomics. In the end, the kitchen will only work for you if you positively enjoy being there.

Style is not something that can be superimposed on any room, but really ought to come out of the way the room is lived in and used. In the kitchen, this means specifically the kind of cooking that you do. But, since kitchens are increasingly the arena of much of daily life, it means taking into account broader issues that affect the rest of the household as well.

At the same time, it is important not to forget that beneath all the appliances, fittings and fixtures, the kitchen is still a room. All the elements of color, character, decoration and furnishing we use to express personal taste in other rooms are just as critical here.

KITCHEN LIFE

The social changes of the past decades have transformed the kitchen from a neglected service room to the hub of the home. But there can never be one solution to all kitchen needs. Thinking about these basic patterns of use can save a great deal of time, money and frustration. If you live alone, eat out frequently and entertain rarely, it is pointless to devote too much precious living space to a function that plays a relatively minor role in your life: a galley, tailored to your requirements and level of skill, or an efficient kitchen area integrated into a main room, would reflect your pattern of kitchen use.

For a busy family with young children, life is likely to be more home based and daily routine more centered on mealtimes. Here a larger kitchen which allows you to oversee children's play while you cook and gives you enough space to gather the family round the kitchen table for dinner provides the right degree of versatility. To create that much elbow room it might be worthwhile knocking down a dividing wall and integrating kitchen and dining room or kitchen and living area.

The self-sufficient working counter and the generously proportioned kitchen/great room represent two extremes. In between,

Efficient ventilation is perhaps the single most important element that makes multipurpose kitchen and living areas possible. Tucked around a corner but far from hidden away, this neatly planned kitchen adjoins the main living area in a clever allocation of space (ABOVE).

there are many other permutations, and space may not necessarily be the critical factor. Time is just as precious a commodity as space for some people and any appliance or gadget that promises to minimize the time spent on kitchen chores has instant appeal. But while kitchen machines have undoubtedly liberated households from

For those who delight in cooking, the kitchen should be a place where the enjoyment of food comes through. This can be expressed by some open display of utensils, dishes and food itself – there is nothing more hospitable or appetizing than piles of fresh produce ready to be transformed into mouthwatering dishes. And, unless you are

The merest suggestion of separation is provided by the supporting framework of old beams in this warehouse-style conversion. The simplicity of layout and cheerful kitchen clutter create an hospitable, unpretentious room in which to cook, eat, or relax (ABOVE).

drudgery, saving time is not necessarily a matter of investing in a push-button kitchen. Simplicity is often the greatest kitchen short cut of all. Restricting yourself to a minimum of basic equipment, intelligently arranged, can save time as well as space, while those tempting pieces of gadgetry can often involve you in spending more time on maintenance and cleaning than you had bargained for. Think about how often you will use different gadgets, and whether the tasks you'll put them to are truly labor-saving: it's quicker and easier to chop a few nuts with a sharp knife than to throw them into a food processor.

reluctant to place your cooking skills on view, kitchens that connect with living or eating areas allow friends and family to participate in the pleasures of cooking so that you integrate eating with entertaining.

The best kitchens have a sense of vitality which fundamentally arises from suitability to purpose. For this reason, the latest state-of-the-art kitchen where no cooking is done can be just as dispiriting as a cramped, awkwardly planned kitchen that frustrates everyone who uses it. Style and decoration are not irrelevant, but they are only part of the process of creating a kitchen that is appropriate for the way you live.

A separate, self-contained kitchen is not simply a room for cooking. The kitchen table provides additional countertop space as well as a gathering point for snacks and informal meals (ABOVE).

DEFINING AREAS

Color is a powerful way to create unity in a room devoted to different activities. This cozy country kitchen and eating room with its mellow walls and fresh blue trim marries comfort and practicality. There's an appealing directness in such simple surroundings where a single step brings warm food from Aga to table (ABOVE).

Cooking is not a single activity, but a series of related tasks, each with its own specific demands in terms of space, equipment and fittings. Marshaling these separate functions into a smoothly coordinated whole is the job of the kitchen planner who works to integrate technical infrastructure with a given layout of space.

But there are other aspects to space planning which have a more personal dimension. Whether the kitchen is open to view or has a greater sense of enclosure, and to what degree it is integrated with the rest of the house, are basic questions of emphasis that particularly arise now that the kitchen occupies a more central role in day-to-day living for so many people.

With adequate servicing and an efficient ventilation system, a kitchen can be located almost anywhere. But integrating kitchen areas with living areas requires a lot more finesse than merely knocking down a partition wall. Unless you are prepared to live with uncomfortable contrasts of mood and decor, you will have to consider the space as a whole, defining distinct areas of activity while unifying the room on a more fundamental level.

Color can equally be used as a defining element, marking the transition from one area to the other. Armchairs comfortably upholstered in bright patterned fabric add dash and flair to a dining area, while the more sober, utilitarian kitchen remains discreetly in the background – proof that two divergent styles can live happily together (LEFT).

A wonderfully architectural solution to defining areas, a wedge-shaped partition that conceals a staircase provides an interesting slant on kitchen accessibility. The soft, matt colors and the play of geometries add character to simple unobtrusive built-in units and an expanse of plain countertop (ABOVE).

United by a shared aesthetic, the living, cooking, eating (and swimming!) areas in this architect-designed space have a cool, linear quality: open-plan living subtly defined and organized (LEFT).

Wrap-around counters and projecting ceiling framework turn the kitchen into an open box, where much remains on view but there is equally the opportunity to screen unwanted clutter and provide the cook with a sense of enclosure. In the kitchen area, the dark floor, countertops and rear wall give further contrast with the light, airy open spaces which surround it (RIGHT).

An island plan is a good way of controlling the design of a kitchen/eating area, preventing a blurring of boundaries while retaining a sense of openness. Here a large-scale painting adds life and color to the dining side of the arrangement, while soft neutral shades are used in the kitchen. The arched ceiling of brick and metal straps offers dramatic potential for the lighting: tungsten strips are fitted on top of the wall units and are controlled by dimmer switches (BELOW).

The opposite approach to decoration places the emphasis on the central kitchen core, dramatically fitted in black. The half-height space divider holds racks for storing wine on the facing side and provides an informal eating area with angular bar stools arranged around the counter (BELOW RIGHT).

A huge butcher block on wheels gives great flexibility – it can be easily moved around within the kitchen area and used in a variety of different ways. Such a large preparation surface also encourages several people to work together – a positive pleasure in this galleried kitchen with its dramatic sense of space. The kitchen forms a part of the general living space, the division of tasks indicated by a change of flooring levels and materials (LEFT).

Screening a certain amount of kitchen activity with counters, sliding panels, half-height partitions or island units is often a good solution for an integrated room. Even the most professional cooks appreciate a degree of separation or enclosure and feel more comfortable when their every move is not on full view.

In addition to concealing some of the clutter of kitchen paraphernalia and providing a convenient place for informal meals, such partitions form natural boundaries that can make a change of flooring, for example, look more considered.

Small, enclosed spaces pose the opposite problem. No one likes to cook in a space that is shut off from any outside contact, but there may be situations where it is not feasible to take down all or some of the walls. In these circumstances, puncturing walls with internal windows or portholes, or widening doorways can help to restore a vital sense of connection.

Areas can also be defined in a less architectural fashion. In an open-plan kitchen/dining room, the part of the room where eating takes place can be simply designated by making it more decorative and comfortable, with free standing furniture and softer lighting. If there is an opportunity to put some of the noisier or bulkier appliances into an adjoining service room, in a modern version of the scullery, the kitchen will be more relaxing and consequently more pleasant to spend time in.

Extending floor and wall finishes throughout a multipurpose area helps to keep it all together, providing a visual link between, say, the cooking and sitting areas. If the basic surfaces are made of the same material, a change of color can highlight a change of use or mood. The same strategy works the other way round – keeping to the same color scheme while varying the materials provides just enough visual consistency to unify the room.

Tucked into an alcove of the living room and with a tiled floor for easy maintenance, this kitchen neatly incorporates the basic essentials. An intelligent idea for a small kitchen, the peninsular table serves as worksurface and dining table all in one. The kitchen, two steps down from the general living area, positions the table at a convenient height for food preparation, while the dining end is just the right level to sit at in comfort (BELOW).

For those that like their materials natural, wood finishes have a strong appeal. Here, wood is used throughout an open-plan scheme to provide a strong sense of unity. The warmth and graininess of the surfaces, combined with the rugged rusticity of the stone-faced closed-fire, create a sleek, luxurious version of the log-cabin look in a timber-framed house (ABOVE).

An idiosyncratic U-shaped layout pulls the kitchen counters round to mark the distinction between cooking and eating areas. With adequate storage below the worksurfaces and no wall units, the above-counter shelves can be used to display purely decorative objects, bringing the two parts of the room closer together visually. The warm tones of the wood-faced units are echoed by the film poster in the eating area, while the diagonal pattern of the flooring draws the eye through the space (LEFT).

There's no sense of a battle of styles in the integration of a modern kitchen in a beamed room. The emphasis on natural tones and materials mean that whitewashed roughly plastered walls, granite countertop and new wooden staircase harmonize in a sensitive yet practical conversion of an old building (LEFT).

With a view through double doors into a book-lined living room, the design and decoration of this kitchen show a considered response to its period setting. Panels on the unit fronts pick up on existing architectural detail, while the L-shaped layout has been carefully aligned with the large opening between the rooms (LEFT).

Even with a large amount of space at your disposal, a big kitchen is not necessarily the best use of floor area. Small kitchens can function every bit as effectively as those of more generous proportions and may suit your needs better. Unobtrusively fitted into an alcove, this kitchen allows an indulgent enjoyment of space elsewhere (LEFT).

DECORATIVE POTENTIAL

A far cry from the dingy basement of Victorian days, the kitchen is no longer "the Cinderella of rooms." This modern kitchen, bathed in natural light, enjoys a stunning panorama, a view guaranteed to cheer the busy cook however mundane the task. Even if the view from the average kitchen sink is not as spectacular as here, natural light is an obvious asset when decorating any room (ABOVE).

Dynamic color articulates the plain surfaces of this seamless kitchen, standing in for architectural detail and breaking up the monotony of smooth surfaces. Using strong color successfully is often a matter of balance; here, strong yellow walls are offset by the glossy red-brown of the floor and the blue-green ceiling. Although each color is intense, the overall effect is harmonious (RIGHT).

Ever since we began to live in kitchens, rather than merely cook in them, the decorative potential of the kitchen has increased in scope. With its integration into the home, the kitchen has grown progressively lighter, brighter and more colorful.

Color, pattern and texture are the main elements in any decorative scheme, and kitchens are no exception. But the creative freedoms offered by modern varieties of paints, wall surfaces, flooring, countertops and cabinet finishes must be tempered by questions of utility and practicality.

Natural light is an important issue when it comes to choosing kitchen colors. Daylight has always been the cook's ally and, even with the sophistication of modern artificial lighting, there is no substitute for its clarity. Sight is one of the cook's most important senses (along with smell and taste), and neutral backgrounds that make the most of natural light promote greater accuracy in judging the color and condition of all kinds of food, cooked or raw. Restful and uncompetitive, white and other light-enhancing tones also tend to increase the sense of space. And white and cream have powerful connotations of cleanliness, freshness and efficiency which reinforce their prevailing use in kitchen decor.

In modern kitchen design, gray is one of the most popular neutrals. Unrelieved expanses of gray may be dreary but, used as a background, gray is sophisticated and subtle with none of the faintheartedness of many pastels. The ability of gray to enhance any bright color that is set against it makes displays of fresh fruit and vegetables, for example, look electrifying.

Blue is another color which has strong kitchen associations. The age-old belief that blue naturally repels flies once made it a common feature of kitchen decor. On its own, especially in rooms with little direct sunlight, blue can be chilly, but in partnership with white, it has the appealing domesticity of Delft tiles, willow-patterned dishes and striped linen.

Yellow, on the other hand, was once thought to attract insects, which made it an unpopular kitchen color. But sunny yellow kitchens can be uniquely cheerful provided the shade is well judged, and the range of colors from pale yellow to buffs and creams all make excellent partners for natural finishes. In the same spirit, the darker earth colors such as terra cotta create warm, rich backgrounds that are not too insistent on the eye.

Brilliant color has a place in many kitchens. Slabs of Mondrian-like primaries or hot secondaries can create vitalizing accents on unit fronts or be used to articulate partitions. But bear in mind that you may grow tired of a strong color scheme faster than you can afford to buy new kitchen units. And dramatic decoration also tends to shift the emphasis away from where it belongs – on the food.

Texture is a powerful element in kitchen decoration and can provide depth and variety if the range of colors is necessarily limited. Cooking is as much about touch and feel as it is about taste, and a kitchen composed of uniformly smooth and artificial surfaces negates this vital element: there is something deadening about the all-laminate, all-plastic kitchen which goes

Planes of bright color enliven a modern kitchen, linking the eating and cooking areas together and generating a great sense of vitality and movement (LEFT).

Reminiscent of a 1950s' diner or trailer home, the streamlined curves of this built-in kitchen are emphasized by the steel strips that protect the laminated edges from chipping. A small circular table swings out from beneath the countertop in a neat detail (BELOW).

beyond the fact that plastic and food are not happy companions. Natural finishes, by contrast, offer in-built textural variety and actually improve with use. Wood, slate, stone, ceramic tile, marble, zinc and steel: each suits different kitchen applications and contributes its own visual qualities.

Pattern enriches and gives rhythm to our surroundings. Used indiscriminately it can also become superficial and overwhelming. In the kitchen, patterns that run riot over walls and unit fronts in an ill-conceived attempt to disguise the true nature of the room are ultimately unsatisfactory. But patterns that add definition and detail or arise naturally out of the arrangement of things are full of vitality. A defining band of contrasting tiles, a sculptural array of cook's utensils, and open shelves of glassware and pottery all make kitchen patterns that enhance the enjoyment of cooking.

Kitchens resist grand decorative statements. But color to brighten and clarify, texture for depth, and pattern to excite the eye all have a role to play in creating the kitchen that speaks for itself.

Sweeping curves compete with strong planes of color to define this highly architectural kitchen area. A breakfast table encircles one end of the peninsular counter (TOP).

A sure touch with color gives this kitchen a decorative edge, carried through in the display of pottery on shallow curved shelves. Robust and confident, the color scheme suggests a positive enjoyment of fresh food and good cooking. The pots and utensils hanging over the sink are no less attractive (ABOVE).

Color is literally built in to these eye-catching units. The strategy adopted here is to keep floor, ceiling and walls white so the rest of the room does not compete for attention (ABOVE LEFT).

The traditional country kitchen, with blue-and-white tiled walls and shiny copper pans, can be equally colorful. The combination of blue and white always suggests freshness and domesticity (ABOVE).

The use of color as a unifying detail is well judged in this simple, fresh-looking kitchen. Basic utensils, used every day, are stored on plain shelves supported by metal brackets – nothing over-elaborate or contrived, just good common sense (LEFT).

KITCHEN CHARACTER

The best built-in kitchens develop a room's character. This beautifully detailed scheme provides a bank of drawers in different widths and depths along one wall, while the other side incorporates open shelves with cabinets, wall units and drawers. The refrigerator is similarly built in and the built-in concept extends around the corner to provide a kitchen/office area (ABOVE).

A new built-in kitchen, discreet and clean-lined, in a London warehouse conversion (RIGHT).

The kitchen used to be a room that had no definable style of its own; it was simply a utilitarian place which was organized as practically as possible with little account taken of decorative niceties. In its most basic incarnation, this could only be described as the utility or – in the style-language of today – "grunge" kitchen. However, there is something to be said for this no-nonsense approach, and it is ironic that it is this type of kitchen which forms the basis for one of the most popular styles of today – the country kitchen.

There is no escaping the fact that kitchens have entered the realm of style and there is an inexhaustible choice of colors, finishes and designs to enable almost any type of mood to be created, from traditional to modern, country to city, minimal to cluttered. These categories, however, are not blueprints to be adopted wholesale, but merely approaches that provide a starting point for you to develop your own ideas.

In recent years a basic division has developed between the built-in and the unfitted kitchen. After several decades in which the kitchen-buying public has remained enamored of the sleek, built-in efficiencies of fitted units, it is not surprising that fashions have now swung back to a renewed appreciation of traditional kitchen furniture.

What such issues highlight is the need to be aware of the architectural qualities of the kitchen. A built-in kitchen is in some ways a room within a room, an inner skin that essentially forms part of the basic construction. The unfitted or furnished kitchen, on the other hand, places sideboards, hutch cabinets tables and other free standing pieces of furniture at strategic points around the kitchen, accommodating them within the general framework of the room.

In reality, most kitchens necessarily contain both built-in and unfitted elements. Reconciling the two will always be a feature of kitchen design, just as there is always a need to balance display with storage, or screened areas with those in full view.

Strong on character, the unfitted kitchen makes use of free standing furniture rather than built-in units and surfaces. Old kitchen equipment, restored to use, can be very handsome, as well as practical – this oven range incorporates a plate-warming compartment. A desk has been called into service as an additional preparation counter (ABOVE).

The base of a Welsh dresser, with drawers to take kitchen clutter and a stout wooden top for displaying fresh fruit and vegetables, furnishes a country kitchen. Decorative pottery is arranged along a deep plate rail above the tongue-and-groove paneling, while the farmhouse table doubles as a robust worksurface between mealtimes (FAR LEFT).

Neat paned wall units and mesh-fronted base units combine in a modern interpretation of the Shaker ethos (LEFT).

THE BUILT-IN KITCHEN

The rich mellow tones of pine-clad walls, built-in cabinets and drawers transform a kitchen into a snug den. Wood wears and ages attractively (ABOVE).

White unit fronts, glazed doors and open shelves keep the kitchen light and airy in a nicely judged balance of concealment and display. A pine kitchen cabinet blends happily with the modern built-in elements (RIGHT).

A highly crafted custom-built built-in kitchen, with idiosyncratic detailing, incorporates traditional features such as the deep Belfast sink and pull-out storage baskets. Small metal lights fitted to the top of the wall units illuminate the worksurface; the grooved draining board is angled to allow water to run freely into the sink (ABOVE).

Reflective, incredibly tough and long lasting, stainless steel brings a professional esthetic to the home kitchen. The wall-mounted knife rack and metal hanging rail for copper pans and cooking utensils make an impressive, practical working display (RIGHT).

The quintessential built-in kitchen – sparkling clean, and with clutter neatly stowed behind closed doors. With seamless stainless steel countertop and backsplash there are no awkward grooves or corners in which grime can build up. The black-and-white tiled floor completes the picture (BELOW).

Within an archetypal built-in kitchen, all of the elements are integrated either above or below a countertop that spans one or more of the walls. Refrigerators, ovens, cooktops, dishwashers and other paraphernalia are built in between cabinets which are traditionally available in three basic units: base, wall and tall. Mass-production, which lies at the heart of the built-in kitchen, tends to encourage thoughts of uniformity. However, in addition to the choice of color and materials used, there are other elements of design that allow some expression of personality, such as shelf displays and hanging racks. Integration with existing structural features is important, to prevent awkwardness and incoherence. Built-in kitchens are often seen as good solutions for modern rooms where there is little architectural detail, or for rooms where such features can be easily suppressed or removed.

Gray-green painted units create a peaceful kitchen mood, the contemplative atmosphere enhanced by a pleasant view (ABOVE).

Ideas for built-in interiors can come from more traditional, vernacular sources – think of shipshape cabins, weekend cottages by the seaside or country retreats. Evocative of such places, this paneled wood interior has an appealing simplicity and trimness which suggests it would be an easy place to visit for a short stay and leave in good order. Vivid blue cabinet doors make a sharp accent for all the mellow wood; useful drawers fit into the base of a built-in window seat (RIGHT).

A forthright mix of styles pairs an almost minimally detailed modern kitchen with Arts and Crafts furniture. The long unbroken line of the wall units is echoed in the long refectory table placed in parallel, underscoring the affinity of design (ABOVE).

The reverse approach focuses attention on the unusual detailing of the open kitchen shelving and keeps to a basic pattern for table and chairs. With so much interest in the kitchen structure, color is kept to a soothing, neutral blue-gray, highlighted by lemon yellow (LEFT).

THE UNFITTED KITCHEN

The unfitted kitchen traditionally conjures expectations of the warm farmhouse. Certainly, most unfitted kitchens naturally work better in older rooms where there are strong points of structural interest that are harder to ignore. Sideboards and free standing cabinets may be more at home in the type of room which has an existing fireplace, with alcoves at either side of it, or where there is paneling on the wall or any other strongly articulated surface. However, with skill and careful planning, the principles, elements and furniture of an unfitted kitchen can be incorporated into even the most contemporary designs and layouts.

The unfitted kitchen is not necessarily traditional. Industrial and commercial sources have been plundered for this bold high-tech kitchen, with typists' chairs ranged around galvanized-steel corner tables, sleek catering units and wire-mesh storage shelves (LEFT).

It is not hard to imagine good cooking coming from this kitchen. The reassuring solidity of the white enameled range, the rows of serviceable copper pans ready for use, and the simple, unpretentious decoration convey a sense of charming domesticity (RIGHT).

Cozy and cluttered, this tiny kitchen leaves everything on view. Shelves over the pair of suspended sinks carry condiments and ingredients in daily use; wine is racked beneath. Pans hanging from a metal rail, cookbooks ranged on a shelf beside the stove, and vegetables in hanging mesh baskets keep it orderly but well within reach – a busy, well-stocked space for one-person operation (RIGHT).

A rudimentary cottage kitchen takes cooking back to basics. Weekends away in less-than-perfect surroundings with only minimal equipment available can serve as a useful reminder of just how little specialist equipment you actually need (LEFT).

A custom-made steel kitchen with wire-mesh door and drawer fronts marries a handcrafted approach to industrial materials. Mesh baskets inserted into a steel shelf keep air circulating around fresh fruit and vegetables, while moody purplish-blue walls counterpoint the hard shiny metalwork. Casters fitted to the base units allow them to be pulled out, moved to a different configuration and even packed up and moved to a new home with their owner (LEFT).

THE CONTEMPORARY KITCHEN

A light touch for a contemporary kitchen built in to an older building maintains respect for existing materials. The glass sides of the ventilation hood reduce its impact, while plain white wall tiles and shiny steel surfaces complement the painted timber ceiling and natural wood floor (ABOVE).

A blend of modern and traditional materials adds variety and character. Glass bricks, mosaic tilework and wire-mesh shelving are combined with basket drawers, wood-faced workbenches and wood flooring (ABOVE RIGHT).

The contemporary kitchen has evolved out of early twentieth-century advances in domestic-appliance technology and the way modern manufacturers have integrated all of this new machinery into a neat, ergonomically planned whole. The typical approach is essentially fitted, with units providing the bulk of the storage and appliances built in to the overall scheme wherever possible.

At the same time, the contemporary kitchen increasingly draws inspiration from the professional cook's kitchen (pages 26–31). The influence of professional cooking has resulted in an upgrading of kitchen apparatus, with the home cook enjoying almost the same standard of utensils and equipment as those who cook for a living. The notion of the island plan, a feature of many modern kitchens, is borrowed directly from the chef's range, the central cooking area in many restaurants.

All kitchens require careful planning. But the modern kitchen, with all its built-in facilities, makes especial demands in this respect. Manufacturers of built-in kitchen units attempt to accommodate a wide variety of options for different layouts and work sequences to enable their kitchens to be tailored to suit individual requirements. However, it may be worth investing in professional guidance to ensure that you are buying precisely what you need and what the space at your disposal can support: less can be more. Some "standard" units promise versatility but prove less flexible in practice. Adjustable shelves, interior racking or integral compartments can make a basic unit much more adaptable. Building in existing appliances can be another area of potential difficulty, particularly if you plan to replace them in a short time.

The modern kitchen has brought industrial finishes and materials into the home. Stainless steel and laminates are easy to maintain and promote the seamless quality which is all part of the modern aesthetic. Ceramic tiling on walls and floors and crisp paintwork make eminently compatible backgrounds. But there is room for natural surfaces, too. Wooden countertops and unit fronts, for example, do not detract from the basic approach and prevent the kitchen from becoming too bland and clinical.

The ultimate modern kitchen in the home of architect Richard Rogers and his wife Ruthie, proprietor of London's River Café. Incorporating cooktop, double sinks, a sunken knife block and dispensers for paper towels, the steel plinth recalls aeronautical engineering in its sophisticated streamlining and functionalism. Located beneath the mezzanine level in the double-height living area, this is accessibility taken to the limit, a perfection of design in a pure space (RIGHT).

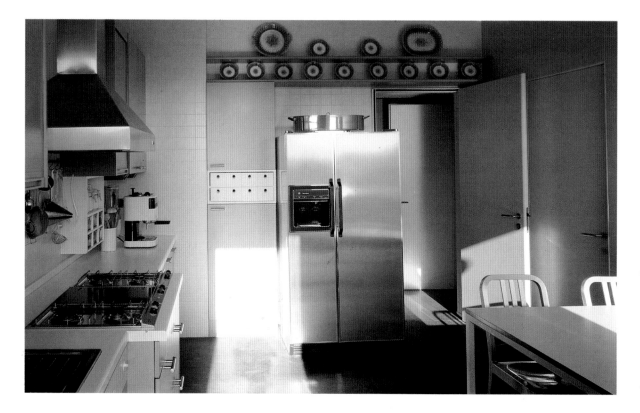

White laminate, tile and polished steel make a clean-lined kitchen with the emphasis on efficiency. The modern kitchen is a machine room, accommodating a range of different appliances in a tightly planned layout (LEFT).

The contemporary kitchen is all about convenience and efficiency. These principles are relevant in town or country, on a small or large scale. Few people would willingly forgo all of the labor-saving advantages the modern kitchen has to offer.

It's important, however, not to go overboard, equipping a kitchen with every conceivable gadget available, particularly – as is often the case – when space is limited. Cappuccino machines, coffee grinders, food processors and other electronic "wonder machines" quickly clutter the worksurface, leaving precious little useful counter space for preparing and cooking food. Although the emphasis is to some extent on technology, the contemporary kitchen looks and works best when ideas are contained and streamlined. Think minimal, and resist the temptation to cram the kitchen with a gleaming array of ingenious gadgets you will seldom actually use.

Like an oversized pendant light, a ventilation hood descends over an island cooktop through a slot in the ceiling. The rounded ends of the island unit are a sympathetic echo of the detailing of the full-height window and the arched doorway; careful alignment of features and a considered use of materials and finishes displays the elegance of contemporary design (RIGHT).

Glossy and glamorous, this sleek and sophisticated black and stainless steel kitchen is the natural habitat of the city slicker. Tiny ceiling lights catch the shiny walls and worksurfaces (BELOW).

The grace and style of a cruise liner is evident in this well-considered galley kitchen, with shallow tapering shelves and chrome bumper rails defining the built-in elements. White lacquered surfaces makes a narrow corridor seem spacious – a simple, yet elegant, solution for an awkward space (LEFT).

Open-plan multipurpose areas benefit from some sense of definition, otherwise the space will seem unfocused and amorphous. Such simple means as a change in the color of flooring helps to make different areas distinct without sacrificing the basic quality of openness. Here a curved pathway in a lighter tone links indoors and outdoors (LEFT).

An internal window rising through two levels provides a dynamic view of cooking activity from an open stairway – a spatial arrangement which places the kitchen at the center of everyday life (RIGHT ABOVE).

In this elegant modern conversion, the conventional segregation of activities into separate rooms does not apply. A stepped partition houses a double oven, while a long counter faced in reinforced glass demarcates the boundary of the kitchen area, matched by a glass-topped dining table (RIGHT).

A kitchen designed by Philippe Stark bears all the hallmarks of this original and influential designer. The unashamed indulgence in marble as a finish for wall, floor and island counter defines the space; matt gray finishes elsewhere concentrate the attention on quirky detail, such as the twisted metal table legs (ABOVE).

The crowded city skyline from this glassed-in terrace provides a vital backdrop to a breakfast counter. The breakfast bar forms part of a peninsular countertop that also incorporates a gas cooktop and electric grill – fresh coffee and toast are just an arm's length away (LEFT).

THE COUNTRY KITCHEN

Time has done little to dim the appeal of the country kitchen – it may be a modern fantasy, but it seems to satisfy many people's deepest yearnings. All the elements are here: drying herbs and gingham curtains; deep porcelain sink and earthenware pottery bristling with wooden spoons; and, best of all, a pie fresh from the oven (LEFT).

Town or country, traditional kitchen arrangements recall a gracious past. A well-worn wooden table serves equally as a preparation area and a place for family meals. Natural surfaces and finishes are forgiving of both age and wear (BELOW LEFT).

The country kitchen as we understand it never really existed. A blend of nostalgia and nature, the style harks back to those traditional farmhouse kitchens which teemed with resourceful activity, or the service rooms of great country houses with their ready supplies of fresh, dairy produce and estate-grown fruit and vegetables. But, rather than arcane equipment and practices, it is more what these kitchens seem to represent in terms of ambience that has made the country kitchen such a perennially popular approach to decoration.

Ever since people began to congregate in towns and suburbs, "country" has been synonymous with all that is wholesome, undoctored and natural. The association is never more powerful than in the case of the kitchen. By concentrating on the elemental associations of natural materials, country kitchens preserve the best of tradition, without sacrificing the benefits of modern convenience or becoming sidetracked into spurious reproduction detail.

Terra cotta, stone and scrubbed wood are the principal materials of the country aesthetic. All wear and weather well, and indeed often improve with age. Colors are subdued and natural, surfaces robust and not highly finished. The emphasis is on simplicity and rugged practicality.

The focal point of the traditional kitchen was the kitchen fireplace or range. Solid fuel stoves, such as the Aga, first introduced in the 1920s, provide the same cozy focus and have become something of a talisman for those enamored of the quintessentially country look. Scrubbed pine or oak tables which double as food preparation areas and the setting for family meals, hutches displaying a cheerful array of dishes, deep Belfast sinks, wooden plate racks and butcher block chopping tables are equally popular features, combining practicality with the lure of tradition.

Because the country kitchen is commonly associated with the hustle and bustle of activity and – more practically – often contains many separate elements, it works best on a fairly generous scale. Then there is room, too, for hanging displays of pans and cooking utensils, for baskets and bowls of fruit and vegetables and for the simple enjoyment of cooking and its results.

There is no real reason why you cannot create a country kitchen wherever you live, even in the heart of the city. Nevertheless this approach does work best where there is the opportunity to emphasize the connection with nature, providing a constant visual reminder that the kitchen, at its most basic, is a place for the preparation and cooking of food. A ground-level kitchen with larder that leads out to a well-stocked vegetable garden or herb plot represents the country style in its fullest sense.

A massive stone fireplace is a reminder of the days when the open fire sustained every aspect of daily life, providing heat, light and power for cooking and hot water. Now it is the focus of an hospitable room where modern facilities slot neatly in beside an old sideboard and farmhouse chairs (ABOVE).

This modern built-in kitchen is based on the proportions of the traditional Welsh dresser, with utensils ranged on open shelves above closed cabinets (LEFT).

There's nothing particularly planned about this arrangement – jugs find a home suspended from a low beam alongside a grater, pottery makes a cheerful display on old pine shelves and a slate records reminders of ingredients that have run out (LEFT ABOVE).

Blue and white are natural partners in country decor, a familiar partnership in striped linen, gingham and, as here, tiles and kitchenware (LEFT CENTER).

Battered trays and bread boards line up in a domestic still life (LEFT BELOW).

Traditional in mood, if not overtly countrified, this charming French kitchen, practical, comfortable and easy on the eye, accommodates a cozy clutter of cooking utensils, serving dishes and basic ingredients – all the unselfconscious accompaniments to daily life. In such surroundings, style is barely an issue and attention is focused on the simple enjoyment of good food and company (RIGHT).

Very little gets hidden away in this kitchen, with fresh ingredients close to hand, a galaxy of utensils suspended overhead and patterned plates waiting to be used. Varying the countertop height accommodates the ergonomic needs of different tasks (TOP).

Brightly polished pans testify to the age-old traditions of good housekeeping. The well-used *batterie de cuisine* suggests a cook who delights in good, honest food (ABOVE).

Inky blue distempered walls, patchy and uneven, make an enveloping background for a low-ceilinged country kitchen, complete with Aga, butcher block and built-in window seat (ABOVE).

A white, tiled recess frames a modern stove, one concession to twentieth-century technology in a blissfully unfitted farmhouse kitchen. Woodwork and walls are a surprising deep shade of indigo blue (RIGHT).

The Windsor chair in all its variations is a classic piece of traditional country furniture, made to the same basic pattern for several hundred years (ABOVE).

The sympathy of natural materials finds a perfect expression in the country kitchen, with unfinished brick walls, a stone floor and natural wood (RIGHT).

THE FAMILY KITCHEN

Articulated by brilliant blue detail on door fronts and moldings, this kitchen forms a connecting link between a living room and a dining area set up in front of large french windows. The sense of space and light is reinforced by the clean white walls and ceiling and the unifying wooden floor (BELOW).

Warm and welcoming, the family kitchen can draw a household together, happily accommodating a range of pursuits, not all of which have to do with cooking. It may be where the baby takes its first tottering steps, where children play or wrestle with their homework or music practice, where messages are exchanged and routines planned, not to mention the place where informal and impromptu meals occur throughout the day.

Discreetly laid out behind tongue-and-groove boarding, an extended counter screens the working area of the kitchen. The kitchen table is the focus of family life, while the relaxed harmony of brick flooring, paneled walls and distressed cabinets underscores the informal mood (RIGHT).

family life, while the other half forms the focus for cooking activity. A direct connection with the outdoors is another positive advantage when there are young children who need to let off steam.

Safety is a major consideration. Children at different ages and degrees of mobility find their own levels of danger in the kitchen and this must be taken into account before inviting them into what is potentially the most hazardous area in the home.

children are young, and it is advisable to keep powerful cleansers and detergents out of children's reach.

A family kitchen often functions as an unofficial nerve center, where messages are relayed and the day-to-day routine of the household is managed. You can keep lines of communication open by making space for a phone, notice board or even a desk where all those vital pieces of paper can be kept safely in one place.

Spacious, warm and unpretentious, this family kitchen accommodates a wide variety of activities, from busy family meals to relaxed evenings with friends. Flagstone floor and large open fireplaces contribute character and charm, while a thoroughly modern kitchen is built-in along the length of the window wall (LEFT).

In most cases, managing such overlapping spheres of interest means providing enough room for untroubled coexistence. Overcrowded, restricted space means short tempers and potential accidents as everyone treads on each other's toes. For a family kitchen to be successful, it must be generously proportioned, even if that means opening out into adjoining rooms. One half of the resulting space can then be fitted and furnished as an eating room and center of

You can't foresee every disaster but it is common sense to guard against sharp corners and edges, trailing appliance cords, pan handles within easy reach, floors that prove excessively slippery when wet and open shelves or racks packed with tantalizing packs of food, utensils and equipment. Conventional ovens are best at upper levels to prevent children burning themselves on hot doors. A guard rail fitted to a cooktop or stove may also be a good investment when

If children are going to spend time in the kitchen, there should be room to store toys and whatever they need for creative play. And it obviously saves time and trouble if surfaces and finishes are easily cleaned and practical in daily use.

Above all, a family kitchen needs built-in flexibility. It has to accommodate everyone's day-to-day needs, but must also be capable of responding to the changing interests and needs of a growing family.

THE SMALL KITCHEN

Small kitchens can be every bit as effective and enjoyable as kitchens on a larger scale, but they demand a fundamentally different approach. The biggest hurdle is to stop thinking of restricted space as an inherent problem and to turn such limitations to your advantage.

Succeeding with a small kitchen depends on making it feel like a large one – achieving a perception of space. The beauty in conquering small spaces is distilling the best and most efficient ideas into one compact, complete package. Strong design, use of color and clever planning ensure that the dynamics are right and that space is deftly used. Small kitchens are usually simple and streamlined. They turn cooking into choreography, making it possible to close a drawer with your hip, and letting you turn, spin around and put something down in one smooth, simple action.

The first step is to acknowledge that a small kitchen will never be able to support the breadth of activities you might expect to accommodate in a larger space. Inevitably, its prime function will be cooking, which means that you can ruthlessly exclude any element that does not serve this purpose. Since most small kitchens are best operated by one person, there is also the opportunity to plan and equip the space in a very specific way.

In a small space, whatever equipment you include should work hard for its living. There isn't the room for gadgets that are rarely used or utensils that serve only one minor function. Good knives, a few decent-sized pans and flame-proof casseroles are indispensable, but you may well find that it is easy to do without, say, a pasta maker. Consider the kind of cooking you do, then you can eliminate the optional extras which take up valuable storage space but have little role to play in the daily routine. If space is tight, it might be sensible to opt for small-scale appliances, as long as these will not become redundant if you then move to bigger surroundings.

As compact as a ship's galley, this steel-encased kitchen manages to accommodate a range of appliances in a very tight space by opting for small-scale models and employing exceptionally careful planning. A washing machine fits under a wall oven, next to the small cooktop in a concentrated use of space. Nothing superfluous finds house-room here (OPPOSITE).

A different esthetic, but the spatial problems are the same: here a simple L-shaped layout keeps clutter to a minimum and makes for ease of working. Pans are stowed on a metal shelf over the cooktop and oven, and trays are kept in the "dead" space beside the oven (ABOVE).

Kitchens don't come much smaller than this Scandinavian kitchen in a closet. Kitted out with a small sink, ventilation fan, downlighters, cooktop, mini refrigerator, and shelving inside the doors, it all goes to show that efficiency doesn't depend on huge amounts of space (ABOVE).

Detail matters in a small space — when there is limited room to maneuver, anything awkward about the arrangement will be a constant source of annoyance. This beautifully finished kitchen is thoughtfully fitted with discreet downlighters over countertops. The opening in the partition wall prevents the kitchen feeling enclosed and turquoise tiling provides cheerful color (LEFT).

Located in little more than an alcove leading off the main room of a studio flat, this kitchen has to stand up to constant scrutiny. Basic affordable units have been dressed up with good handles, accessories which lift standard merchandise out of the ordinary. A slimline dishwasher, oven and cooktop are neatly integrated (LEFT).

A basic U-shaped layout comprises three distinct areas of activity in a version of the classic work triangle. Sink, dishwasher and preparation area occupy one wall, cooktop and oven another, and refrigeration and food storage take up the remaining side. Small kitchens have many positive aspects, not least of which is the fact that, with only a few steps between each main function, effort is minimized and work sequences streamlined. The handsome symmetry of this plan accentuates a sense of order and efficiency (RIGHT).

A glass-fronted display cabinet divides the main living space from a compact kitchen area. Wrapping around the corner, the top of the cabinet provides additional high-level counter space. Stepped wall cabinets offer versatile storage in a tight corner (ABOVE).

Truly below stairs, there can be few sites more awkward than this. Small kitchens often bear the burden of unusual shape, tucked into leftover areas. The stepped stairs form a module for storage; the counter divides the working area from the rest of the room (RIGHT).

One of the things you will learn from time spent in a small kitchen is to clear and clean up as you go, an essential discipline for every good cook. A respect of space will educate you to put it to good use.

Ships' galleys and mobile homes provide good ideas for space-saving. Making full use of wall space for hanging racks, fitting pull-out counters or fold-down preparation areas and investing in multipurpose cookware that can move from oven to cooktop to table are all ways of maximizing room.

Through lateral thinking and focused planning, the small kitchen can be an efficient and productive place, not an unhappy compromise. Restricted space can be the spur to some of the cleverest and most efficient kitchens: with absolutely everything in easy reach and nothing superfluous to requirements, cooking on a small scale becomes a positive pleasure.

The unusual T-shaped layout of this kitchen creates two distinct working areas, one for preparation, the other for cooking. Placed in an alcove off the main living area, there's still room for a two-person breakfast bar (LEFT).

Faced with such a defining feature as this curving ceiling, there are two options: ignore it, or make the most of it. The second alternative has been chosen here, the sloping surface wittily decorated with a mural of a suspension bridge and the kitchen laid out in an L-shape into the remainder of the space. Glass display shelves mark an entrance to the kitchen area. The strategy acknowledges the limitations of an awkward space and plays up to them, with a great sense of fun and style (RIGHT).

Two views of a tiny kitchen show how clever design can triumph over spatial limitations. Occupying the corner of an attic studio, the kitchen has to cope with awkward angles as well as a shortage of square feet. Potential light is maximized by the recessed downlighters together with skylights cut into the slope of the roof. A high countertop screens the kitchen area from view. Pale gray detailing matches the abstract effect of the ventilation fan recessed into the wall. This controlled scheme makes a virtue of its drawbacks (ABOVE and ABOVE RIGHT).

Careful planning and an eye for detail create a kitchen tucked into the alcove of the living room that is compact without feeling cramped. A flap-down extension to the countertop gives an extra preparation area when it's needed (LEFT).

Strong color and open display shelves pack a small kitchen corner with interest. Full use is made of wall space, while a gleaming *batterie de cuisine* is suspended from a plain metal rail screwed to the window frame (OPPOSITE BELOW).

Older houses often have a great deal of redundant space in hallways and under stairs. Tucked under the main staircase, this tiny built-in kitchen adopts the traditional proportions of the country dresser as a unifying idea, with wide display shelves above closed base cabinets. The wholehearted approach is full of character (ABOVE).

Dead corner space is not wasted in this kitchen layout which places a sink in the angle between two walls. Cutaway counters allow easy access and full benefit is gained from the expanse of window on either side, a lively and ingenious solution which adds great interest and a sense of openness to a tight plan (ABOVE RIGHT).

THE IDIOSYNCRATIC KITCHEN

The kitchen as dream machine in a cool interpretation of the modernist esthetic. A working wall fitted in polished patterned stainless steel reflects the light pouring in through floor-to-ceiling windows. Circular wall-mounted radiators like giant hubcaps make a bold visual statement in a robust, hard-edged setting (LEFT).

Spatial limitations can inspire an individual approach to design. In this basement room the kitchen is contained within a shallow recess in a corridor leading to the main living area. A high-level steel shelf supports a mini oven, along with essential ingredients. The refrigerator, set under the counter, is also small scale. The attention to detail and quality of fittings belie the pressure on space and justify the open approach (BELOW).

For some people, the architecture of their home or their own, highly developed sense of space, color and design will take the kitchen in new and unexpected directions. Not for the fainthearted, idiosyncratic approaches to kitchen design capitalize on the bold and the breathtaking, but – in the best examples – without sacrificing the basic, essential practicalities of layout and function. Necessarily bespoke, such grand gestures command not only respect but a big budget as well. The results won't be to everyone's taste, but that's part of the point and half the fun.

The ultimate in open plan, this "garage" kitchen glories in its exposed location. Cane blinds roll down to diffuse the brilliant sunshine. Gleaming white surfaces match the pristine façade of this crisp modern house (RIGHT).

Rough-hewn granite isn't everyone's idea of a kitchen material, but in the hands of a French sculptor it's transmogrified into a countertop of undeniably imposing impact (BELOW RIGHT).

A customized steel construction pushes kitchen architecture to the limit. The attentuated countertop and dynamic sweep of steel arm – housing top lighting, plate rack and fruit bowl – challenge every notion of conventional kitchen arrangement (BELOW).

THE VERNACULAR KITCHEN

The Mediterranean country kitchen, with its delight in rustic materials and bright cheerful color, expresses enthusiasm for fresh flavors and ingredients and a delight in robust, unpretentious regional cooking. The electric partnership of sunny yellow and vivid blue in this raftered farmhouse kitchen is more than a match for strong southern light, but this decorative approach would work equally well in less hospitable climates (ABOVE).

When Elizabeth David's *Mediterranean Food* (1950) and *French Country Cooking* (1951) were first published, they ushered in a whole new approach to food. In America, just beginning to emerge from years of rationing and wartime shortages, many of the ingredients in Miss David's recipes were still not widely available; others were unheard of. But an entire generation found its culinary inspiration in the evocation of hearty regional cooking, with its emphasis on fresh ingredients and a blend of strong flavors.

What proved just as beguiling as garlic, *herbes de Provence* and olive oil was the vision of good cooking at the heart of family life. Along with all the other changes in post-war society, this attitude helped to bring the kitchen into the central role it enjoys today. The trend was reinforced as mass travel enabled many people to sample Mediterranean cooking for themselves. Ever since, the vernacular traditions of other cultures have had a powerful effect on the way we see the kitchen.

This new appreciation of simplicity and directness in the cooking and serving of food has transformed eating habits. The impact on the kitchen was considerable, as it became a place where people sought to reproduce the warmth and conviviality they had experienced abroad. Cooking had long been regarded as an art; now it was something for everyone to enjoy and share.

Today culinary influences come from far and wide, not solely from Europe. American supermarkets now sell lemongrass, fresh coriander and Jalapeño chili peppers, while 20 years ago it was difficult enough to track down fresh parsley or fresh garlic. Cajun, Indian, east Asian, Japanese, Chinese, Mexican and Eastern cookery are no longer regarded as exotic and esoteric but are the popular themes of television programs and cookery books.

All this comes at a time when many people are becoming convinced that technology does not provide all the answers in the kitchen. What is just as appealing as intense new flavors and intriguing ingredi-

With rough whitewashed walls, beamed ceiling and a shallow sink tucked in a corner, this cottage kitchen reflects the stirring simplicity of life with the bare essentials. The appeal of the vernacular transcends mere nostalgia and makes a powerful antidote to the sophistication of modern, technological life (ABOVE).

An elegant summary of Mexican decorative style: chalky white walls, a collection of vivid ceramics, quarry tiled floor and farmhouse furniture (RIGHT).

ents is the basic, time-honored cooking methods which accompany them. Low-tech rather than high-tech, stir frying in a wok, steaming in a bamboo basket and grilling on a charcoal brazier are infinitely more satisfying than popping a pre-cooked meal in the microwave. The performance of cooking itself, intrinsic to many of these traditions, conveys pleasure and enjoyment at the most basic level.

A passion for Chinese or Mexican food, say, need not dictate the look of the kitchen beyond your choice of ingredients and cooking equipment. The simplicity of Japanese kitchens requires a degree of discipline to reproduce that won't necessarily increase your cooking skills and may even hamper them, whilst the riot of color we associate with parts of the Mediterranean demands a skilled eye if it's not to make cooking a headache. As always, a scheme will only work if it's rooted in careful planning and attention to detail.

The discipline of this Japanese kitchen reflects a cuisine which relies on impeccable standards of freshness and exacting preparation (ABOVE).

A European kitchen with a Japanese flavor combines familiar Western features, such as the cooktop and tiled backsplash, with decorative details more suggestive of the Orient – the neat gridded window screen and timber slats applied to unit fronts (RIGHT).

Oriental cooking, with its specialist paraphernalia, is increasingly practised as well as appreciated in the West (FAR RIGHT).

The gaudy exhuberance of this Mexican kitchen, alive with bold patterned tiles and swathes of vibrant color, is a fitting accompaniment to the spiciness of a cuisine renowned for its use of hot peppers and chili (LEFT).

A kitchen which has evolved comfortably over time, this Mediterranean family room, cool and spacious with whitewashed walls and terra cotta tiling, places the enjoyment of good cooking at the center of life. An *ad hoc* display of pestles and mortars fills the gap between wall and pillar (RIGHT).

Chunky storage partitions echo the thickness of old farmhouse walls, extending the architectural mood of the room to encompass the fittings. Pale natural colors and textures harmonize effortlessly (BELOW).

DISPLAY AND CONCEALMENT

Whatever else it may be, the kitchen is undoubtedly a room which houses an inordinate amount of diverse things, from eggs to whisks, wooden spoons to garbage bags, detergent to fresh herbs. It also contains areas where some of the most regularly used supplies and utensils need to be within easy reach. Deciding what is to be concealed in closed storage and what can be displayed has important ramifications, not only for the appearance of the room but also for its practicality in use.

With the first closed kitchen cabinets, many people thankfully abandoned their sideboards and open shelves where dishes, utensils and storage jars had sat collecting soot, dust and kitchen grime. Hygiene, as well as efficiency, was part of the thinking behind the development of the built-in kitchen, which promised to reduce dramatically the time spent in cleaning and maintenance. Coal- or wood-burning stoves that charge the air with soot are a fixture of the past, and modern ventilation systems have minimized the effects of steam and grease. Even so, an awareness of basic cleanliness should inform your decisions about what to leave out on view.

Visually speaking, sleek high-tech kitchens, where everything is hidden behind unit doors, can have all the appeal of an operating room. But kitchens where clutter reigns supreme are ultimately just muddled and tiring to work in. Somewhere between these extremes lies the right balance between display and concealment to suit your tastes and cooking habits.

Any display, no matter what it comprises, is an invitation to appreciate and enjoy the visual qualities of what is on view. Kitchen displays are unique in that they celebrate the beauty of everyday things. A bowl of lemons, copper-bottomed pans hanging from a rack, a wire basket of eggs, and bunches of freshly dried herbs have just as much intrinsic appeal – if not more – than the most tastefully arranged collection of china on a mantelpiece.

There's nothing half-hearted about this wall of display shelving, solidly constructed to a variety of different depths to take all shapes and sizes of kitchen objects. It's easy to imagine the satisfaction of arranging each compartment and the daily pleasure of seeing everything on view (OPPOSITE)

Built-in to the fabric of the wall, a deep grid of storage recesses is used to house wicker baskets, dishes, pots and assorted kitchen treasures (ABOVE)

Glass-fronted wall units show off glassware and pottery that is too attractive to be hidden away. The lightness of this approach works well with the small paned windows which border the countertop and form a visual counterpart to the wall units (ABOVE).

Stoneware pots, arranged like art objects, make a dramatic display against a built-in wall of seamless white units. With a splendid landscape on view, little has been allowed to distract the eye indoors. Such reticence is well considered – think of the difference if the shelf had been packed with clutter. The elegant minimalism allows the room to breathe (LEFT).

There's little color in this muted display, but a tremendous harmony of materials, textures and shapes, pleasing to the eye and evocative of those "below stairs" rooms in country houses (LEFT).

Spongeware bowls, baskets and old china, stacked ready for use, are vividly set off by deep blue woodwork of the cabinet door (LEFT BELOW).

Fiestaware, in vibrant clashing shades, clamors for attention in a brazen display that celebrates an enjoyment of color for its own sake. The dark painted wood acts as a perfect foil for this stimulating collection, which would look just as good in almost any permutation of colors (RIGHT).

Backlit glass candlesticks on a glass shelf add an ethereal quality to kitchen display, the delicacy nicely echoed by the black-and-white mosaic tiled panel (OPPOSITE).

At the same time, it is this everyday aspect which gives such displays their practicality. Fresh food that will be eaten in a day or two, ordinary utensils that are pressed into service every day, favorite flavorings and condiments do not hang around collecting dust but are part of the day-to-day life of the kitchen. In the same spirit are the latest refrigerator designs with glass-fronted doors enabling you to see the contents.

The simple honesty of kitchen displays does not rule out keeping other things from view. Cleaning products, waste disposal and bulk foodstuffs are the type of necessary but unlovely items most people keep behind closed doors – and with good reason. Gadgets that are needed infrequently are often better stored away from the main preparation area, both to keep counter space free and to cut down on heavy-duty cleaning between each use.

Organizing a kitchen is largely a matter of common sense. The equipment and utensils which relate to each area of activity should be stored or displayed close by – pans near the cooking surface, knives near the preparation area and so on. These natural associations occur to most experienced cooks, but there are always personal idiosyncrasies which resist any formula, as anyone who has tried to cook in an unfamiliar kitchen is well aware. Good behind-the-scenes organization that works for you plays a vital role in making the kitchen a coherent and attractive place.

A deep shelf at picture-rail height carries a collection of decorative objects; kitchen pottery and glassware are neatly arrayed on invisibly supported shelves (ABOVE).

Glass shelving and metal countertop make a sympathetic pairing, reflective and hard edged against the muted walls (ABOVE RIGHT).

A positive enjoyment of material is obvious in this association of glass vase and containers on suspended glass shelf, and the metallic glint of kitchen knives against a tiled wall (ABOVE FAR RIGHT).

A matchboarded wall fitted with wooden shelves recalls the traditional arrangement of the Welsh dresser. Neat rows of preserves and platters combined with cuphooks for jugs and mugs suggest good housekeeping. There's room for the kitchen clock and a framed engraving (LEFT).

Free standing catering-style metal storage-shelving may suggest an industrial esthetic, but it works equally well with an assembly of traditional kitchen paraphernalia — baskets, earthenware crocks, jugs and trugs (RIGHT).

Decorative ceramic plates and vases complement stainless steel cookware on these wire-rack shelves. The combination of decorative and practical objects in a display can enhance the esthetic quality of pots, pans and other kitchen utensils if the juxtaposition is nicely judged (TOP).

More is definitely more for this enthusiast of cooking equipment, recreating the effect of a professional catering supplier in the confines of a private home (ABOVE).

EATING IN THE KITCHEN

In a predominantly woody kitchen, staining the table and chairs injects a note of color without having to resort to manufactured materials. This comfortable eating area in a large kitchen places the table in front of a wide stone fireplace to provide a cozy focus on a cold day, the relaxed setting for convivial family mealtimes (RIGHT).

Placing the dining area adjacent to but beyond the kitchen allows the cook to work unimpeded without being totally segregated from family or guests. Benefiting from abundant natural light during the day, this small dining table is lit at night-time by pendent lights or, on more intimate occasions, by a pair of elegant candlesticks (OPPOSITE).

Eating in the kitchen was unthinkable in polite society in the last century, and only a few decades ago it was still regarded as dangerously bohemian in some circles. Pre-war American kitchens were the first to include "breakfast nooks" and counters for informal family mealtimes; since then, in a slow but steady change in social mores, formal dining rooms are used mostly for formal occasions and the kitchen has become the most popular place for entertaining friends and feeding the family.

The advantages are obvious. In the modern household, food can be conveyed by the cook directly to the table without having to be ferried to a different part of the house. And with the kitchen open to guests as well as family, the cook doesn't have to feel excluded, toiling away in seclusion while everyone else has a convivial time in another room. Eating in the kitchen turns cooking into a participatory activity, rather than one person's chore.

But there are, equally, disadvantages, even if most arise out of lack of space or proper planning. Not every cook is a kitchen performer and some understandably prefer a little privacy or quiet when concentrating on a particularly tricky recipe. Then again, close proximity to a humming refrigerator, a sink full of dirty pots and pans or a countertop littered with clutter is not conducive to everyone's digestion. Eating and cooking are inherently related activities but nevertheless benefit from a degree of separation between the two.

One answer is to use whatever intrinsic spatial qualities your kitchen possesses to create a natural demarcation between activities. It's easy enough when you've increased the kitchen area by knocking down a partition between two rooms. In this case, one half of the new space becomes the cooking center and the other half is where you eat. It's even better if some structural remnant still exists – an archway or partition that makes the distinction clear. Alternatively you could bring

A dagger-shaped island counter with accompanying stools makes a stylish place for catching a quick bite to eat in the kitchen. The counter is sited away from the main working area between the oven, cooktop and sink (RIGHT).

An alcove raised up a step from the main floor area achieves a sense of separation between cooking and eating. The eating area, minimally furnished with bench seats cantilevered out from the wall, is painted white in contrast to the steel-finished kitchen. A large window bathes the area in natural light (RIGHT).

the kitchen counter round to create a barrier. In L-shaped kitchen plans (page 124), there is a similar natural break; alcoves and bay windows offer the opportunity to set up a table and chairs out of the main traffic flow.

The style of furnishing, lighting and, to some extent, decoration can also mark the transition from one activity to another. Too big a contrast with the cooking part of the kitchen will be uncomfortably jarring, but a subtle distinction helps each area retain its own identity. Wall and ceiling finishes are probably best kept uniform throughout the room, but a change in flooring material can be very successful, particularly if you keep to the same tone, such as the pleasing combination of light ceramic tiling in the working end of the room and pale hardwood flooring in the eating end.

Choice of table and chairs is critical. Above all else, eating in the kitchen should be a comfortable experience. In a severely modern setting, dining furniture in natural materials can supply warmth. There should be enough room for everyone to fit round the table; chairs should be sturdy and untippable, finishes robust and practical. You can always dress up a basic table with a cloth and candlesticks for a special dinner, but a highly polished dining table is utterly impractical for regular family meals. Farmhouse tables with deep drawers at either end, glass- or marble-topped tables on metal bases, trestles, or simple wooden or laminate tables offer just the right blend of simplicity and versatility. Bentwood, cane or upright wooden kitchen chairs are equally practical, and weather the everyday knocks and spills that inevitably occur.

An eating area can be simply a table and chairs or a counter and stools. In kitchens that are combined with the main living room, a counter that forms the divide between the two areas can be used as a simple breakfast bar. Where space is at less of a premium, you may prefer a more furnished look: shelving units or a hutch cabinet for storing dishes, linen and cutlery can be useful as well as appealing. Prints, pictures and collections on the theme of eating and food make suitable decorative touches, space permitting.

Light the table with a low pendant or downlighters, supplemented by side lighting or spotlights. Dimmer switches allow you to vary the light level and adjust the mood. Glaring overhead light, impractical and inefficient in the kitchen, is uncomfortable and depressing at mealtimes.

An old Welsh dresser packed with plates and platters dominates the eating end of a large family kitchen. A circular table and ladderback chairs are in keeping with the homespun mood. Dressing the table with paisley cloth and flowers turns an ordinary supper into an occasion (BELOW LEFT).

A counter that divides the working part of the kitchen from the rest of the room provides a long, uninterrupted countertop for food preparation that doubles as a breakfast bar big enough for the largest of families (BELOW).

THE CONSERVATORY KITCHEN

A room for light, rather than a room for plants, this glazed addition to a New York brownstone, with curved roof, is fitted with a gleaming steel kitchen, the pans lined up in orderly rows on metal hanging rails. The metal surfaces make the most of the generous daylight (LEFT).

Blurring the boundary between outdoors and in, a glassed-in kitchen faced in white tile appears enclosed in greenery. There is a marble-topped counter, for informal meals or preparation, and a solid wooden block on top of a brick plinth for chopping. Fine venetian blinds filter the strong light (LEFT).

The conservatory, one of the most popular home additions, is not necessarily for the horticulturally minded. In a variable climate, such sheltered spaces allow enjoyment of the garden without exposure to the elements. Perfect as eating areas, they are best furnished simply so as not to detract from the view. Elegant metal chairs, a beautiful tiled floor and a window-sill display of ceramics generate a sense of tranquillity (RIGHT).

The regular gridded effect of paned windows has been carried over in the design of this light-filled kitchen. A waist-level bank of glass-fronted cabinets occupies one wall, with deep storage bins on wheels slotted in underneath. The movable butcher block is versatile, the green paintwork fresh and cheerful (OPPOSITE).

Extending your kitchen into the back yard can bring enormous benefits: a view of the outdoors helps to generate a feeling of space and tranquility. Skylights, stool windows and sliding glass doors transform an add-on kitchen or eating area into a light-filled conservatory. With a backdrop of plants, it's the next best thing to eating outside, but with the added advantage that you are not at the whims of the seasons. In northern climates, a glazed conservatory kitchen will trap even the weakest of the sun's rays, while in hotter parts of the world use blinds and shades to provide an escape from the blazing heat.

In most homes, a kitchen conservatory will be a purpose-built conversion or add-on, allowing you the opportunity to plan your kitchen from scratch. If you intend to use the conservatory area as a working kitchen rather than as an extension to the kitchen in which to sit and eat, it's unlikely you'll want or be able to combine cooking with plant-rearing: the demands of the two activities are competing rather than complementary. But even in the heart of the city, a kitchen that leads to a roof garden, a patio or a balcony provides a harmonious link with outdoors.

THE OUTDOOR KITCHEN

A cool shaded terrace under a pantiled roof is equipped with a full-scale outdoor kitchen, complete with corner grill. Drying herbs hang from the beams, perfuming the air; wine to be served with the meal is kept cool in terra cotta cylinders. The stone counter and stone table blend happily with old walls. In hot climates, outdoor eating can be more of a permanent arrangement (RIGHT).

The simple pleasures of eating outdoors are evoked by this view of a rustic terrace set up for lunch, sheltered from the scorching midday heat (ABOVE).

Even the most sophisticated gourmet or technologically minded aficionado of kitchen gadgetry generally finds it hard to resist the simple delights of eating and cooking in the open air. For most of us, picnicking, barbecuing or any kind of eating *al fresco* provides a happy reminder of the elemental pleasures of food. Marauding ants, threatening thunderclouds or charcoal that stubbornly refuses to light fail to detract from the fact that almost everything tastes better out-of-doors.

Part of the enjoyment is the impromptu nature of such occasions. A blanket to spread over the ground, and a hamper packed with cold chicken, chilled wine and crusty bread can be sheer perfection. But if

you have a yard – of any size – or even a large balcony or roof terrace, it can be well worth setting up a more permanent arrangement that will entice you to cook and eat outside whenever the weather is fine. A well-stocked kitchen garden or herb plot to supply some of the ingredients and flavors multiplies the satisfaction.

In areas of the world where the climate is warm and sunny, outdoor eating is an established part of life. Vine-shaded Mediterranean terraces, sheltered beachside tavernas, town squares strung with twinkling lights and packed with café tables may be difficult scenarios to recreate in less hospitable climes but nevertheless provide excellent sources of inspiration.

Diffusing the strong heat of the sun overhead is one of the most important factors in creating a comfortable eating area outdoors. This vine-shaded terrace, dappled in sunshine and simply furnished with a scrubbed wooden table, benches and chair, makes a delightful eating area (RIGHT).

A Parisian balcony is just the place for breakfast in the sunshine, surrounded by pots of geraniums (FAR RIGHT).

An outdoor eating area needs careful positioning. Shelter from strong breezes and at least partial shade are basic requirements; eating with the full strength of the midday sun beating down on you is not particularly enjoyable. It is often most practical for the table and seating to be near the house, for easier access to the kitchen. But make sure that wherever you site an outdoor eating area, the view is worthwhile.

BARBECUES

Native Indians showed the first settlers to the New World a primitive but effective way of baking in the sand. The method, also known to South American Indians and thought to have originated among Pacific Islanders, consisted of digging a pit, lining it with stones which were heated to a fierce

temperature by fire, and then layering the pit with seaweed, seafood such as clams, and vegetables such as corn. A wet covering of animal skins or cloth, green leaves or more hot stones sealed with a layer of earth slowly cooked the contents of the pit.

Barbecuing, or grilling over an open charcoal brazier, is another basic method which has rather more modern appeal. And a barbecue is likely to be the basis for most

In areas where much of daily life can take place outside, outdoor cooking does not need to be a temporary affair. A countertop and a sink plumbed into the main water supply brings the cook out of seclusion (RIGHT).

A massive outdoor grill with its own flue and wood-storage area underneath redefines the meaning of barbecue. A large market umbrella provides shade from intense sun (BELOW).

A fresh fish stuffed with rosemary and skewered vegetables is all ready for the grill (OPPOSITE).

Carved into a terraced hillside, a sheltered eating area incorporates a small barbecue under cover (LEFT).

Split cane or "canisse" makes an attractive covering for an outdoor dining room. The flagstone floor is cool and durable; the vines frame a peaceful view of the courtyard beyond (ABOVE).

outdoor cooking. Varieties range from disposable trays to huge free-standing contraptions with mechanized spits. Cast-iron hibachis are versatile and robust; serious cooks may want their own permanent fixture, to one side of a paved area or adjoining a garden wall. Sited where smoke won't billow into the house, but close enough for appetizing aromas to whet the appetite, the barbecue provides what is probably our closest connection with the ancient origins of cooking, which may explain its universal and almost ritual attraction.

SETTING THE SCENE

There is a wide variety of simple patio furniture, from picnic tables to wicker chairs, slatted benches to stone-topped tables, folding metal park chairs to canvas director's chairs. Designs should be unfussy so as not to compete with the greenery and robust enough to take a certain amount of weathering even if you don't leave them outside all year round.

Provide shade with awnings, a trellis or any kind of framework for climbing plants. You don't have to cast the eating area into deep shade; the type of dappled light that filters through a covering of split cane or a trailing vine takes the power out of fierce sun without losing all of the brightness or warmth. This type of covering also allows you to brave an occasional summer shower. At night, small points of light overhead and diffused garden lighting to illuminate beds and trees add a magical quality.

Kitchen Design

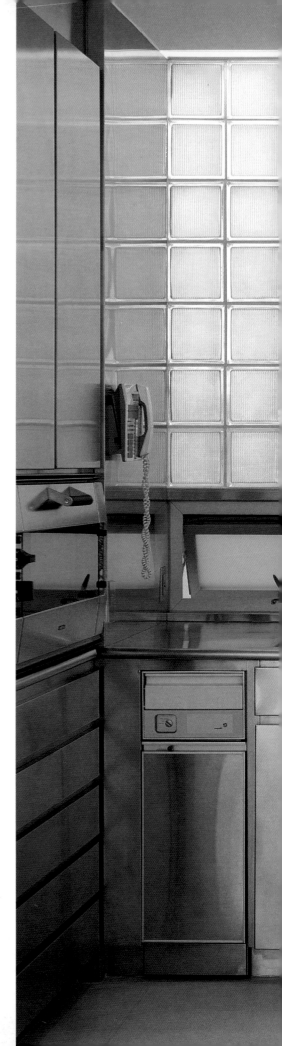

When square feet are at a premium, as in this Manhattan apartment, design is critical in getting the most out of available space. A table slots between dishwasher and countertop; a serving hatch connects to the dining room (ABOVE).

No matter how attractive the kitchen looks, good planning must underpin the design. Correct positioning of the basic elements – sink, stove and refrigerator – is vital for efficient use. Handsomely fitted with a panel of glass bricks and stainless steel finishes, this kitchen provides a well-considered layout of basic utilities (RIGHT).

*T*houghtful, careful design is the linchpin of a good kitchen. It will enable you to move smoothly from task to task in a logical sequence of activities, to work comfortably, safely and efficiently, to integrate the complex technical requirements of a variety of diverse appliances within the confines of four walls. It has nothing to do with superficial gloss and glamor, everything to do with making informed choices that meet your requirements on every level.

The basic approach is the same, whether you are starting from scratch in a new home, or upgrading facilities and implementing key improvements to reflect changing needs and circumstances. The process can be broken down into three distinct stages: planning the allocation of space and its servicing; outfitting with appropriate finishes and fixtures; and, finally, equipping with the appliances that function best for you.

Good design saves money by helping you to allocate your budget effectively. It saves time and trouble by creating an efficient environment attuned to your way of working. And the benefits are long-lasting, resulting in a kitchen you use with pleasure, day after day.

THE WELL-DESIGNED KITCHEN

A new or revitalized kitchen can significantly add to the value of a home. The trick is to reconcile the cost of improvements with the resale value it adds to the house. If you want to recoup the cost of your kitchen renovation when you eventually sell, it is wise to ensure that the changes you make reflect mainstream taste. Plan the kitchen so that it's not so idiosyncratic that it can't be used by someone else. Even in a disposable world, people expect kitchens to be made to last.

Kitchen upgrades generally add more to the market value of a home than they cost to accomplish. Depending on how long you intend to stay, plan carefully, avoid unusual color schemes – off-white and neutral colors are inoffensive – and beware of deluxe super-model appliances. But making a kitchen nondescript is also inadvisable. If yours is an older home, try to retain the character and period details. An odd-shaped room, glass cupboard doors, unusual moldings and wood countertops are financial as well as aesthetic assets.

Smart financing can save you lots of money in the long run. You might consider getting a home-equity loan to cover the cost of kitchen improvements, a sensible alternative to remodeling a kitchen on credit. It would be a great error, however, to install a kitchen that didn't reflect your needs or taste simply because you believed it may add value to your property.

ELEMENTS OF THE DESIGN

The function of a kitchen in the home has come full circle. Kitchens are the family room; and as the focal point of the home, a kitchen must be as serviceable as it is alluring. Begin your planning by prioritizing and making a list of what's right and wrong with your present kitchen. Once you outline what you would like amended, you might start the design process with an image or a material. For instance, if you harbor rural fantasies, wood might be a focal point. If yours is an industrial back-

Architectural features can provide a good starting point for kitchen design. Although the kitchen is a practical place, which must function efficiently and may contain many built-in elements, there is no need to obliterate all existing detail. With plenty of natural light pouring through a wall of windows, and a high raftered ceiling, this kitchen retains a strong sense of space and individual character (RIGHT).

In contemporary rooms, with little or no distinguishing features, the design of the kitchen may be called upon to supply additional definition. The treatment of the exhaust hood and high-level units, breaking up the expanse of the wall in a smooth unbroken line, adds punchiness and character in a modern space (FAR RIGHT).

ground, you might patronize streetwise aluminum or steel. One item you're crazy about could set up the kitchen's vocabulary. For example, requesting a specific range, like an Aga or Viking, means the kitchen wouldn't include wall ovens or require a big vertical block, or you might yearn for a style of kitchen, such as vernacular (pages 88–91) which will require a specific approach.

As well as a visual design, there should be planning about spatial design too. Ergonomics is essentially the study of how, in your working environment, machines and general conditions can best suit you so that you and they work to maximum efficiency. This theory of spatial organization has resulted in standard heights for countertops, kitchens that are adjacent to dining areas, major appliances placed to save needless steps, and the organization of storage. When you can cut vegetables at a counter without stooping, take dinner plates out of the dishwasher and put them in a convenient cabinet, or not bump your head on the range hood, it's the careful thought and work of ergonomists you're taking for granted.

The sweeping curve of a glass-filled wall provides a panoramic bay view for a kitchen/eating area. Here the kitchen has been conceived as part of the architecture itself and the result is a dynamic space with optimum conditions of natural light. A tall free standing bank of cupboards punctuates the space, dividing the kitchen from the dining area and offering a degree of enclosure in an otherwise wide-open room-plan (LEFT).

With a suggestion of Art Nouveau in the details of its construction, an island unit segregates an internal kitchen from the main route to a bathroom and from adjacent living space. A panel of opaque glass allows light to spill through from the bathroom window, maintaining a sense of connection and openness (BELOW).

The essential ingredients in every kitchen are adequate work surfaces, cooking equipment, a sink, a draining board, a refrigerator and ample storage space. The best kitchens are flexible and multifunctional. Nothing should be single use.

BREAKING THE RULES

Although the accepted wisdom is that good kitchen design is synonymous with the work triangle, kitchens now are for living in. These days they are frank and more open spaces that integrate a "good neighbour" policy with ergonomics – places where friends, kids and cooks toss conversation and salads with equal enthusiasm and aplomb. Though technically all we consume in kitchens are food and fuel, we gravitate to them for psychic and aesthetic sustenance as well. And so hardline functionalism, and the work triangle, may be forgotten or compromised as the kitchen is laid out to accommodate the soul.

There is a lot to think about, many hard questions to answer and budgets to balance. The following pages will help you to do this and plan your dream kitchen.

The period character of this house demands a respectful solution. The Aga is built into a fireplace recess, the mantelshelf used for a display of chrome teapots, coffee pots and pans. A checkered floor, laid diagonally, unifies the entire ground floor, leading the eye through to connecting rooms (RIGHT).

The well-planned kitchen of food writer Fay Maschler, designed by architect Rick Mather, makes a graceful accommodation of a range of different functions. It may all look easy, but such effortless organization depends on a rigorous investigation of all the possibilities (LEFT).

A redundant chimney houses a microwave oven in a tidy conversion (TOP).

A sliver of space between units in a small kitchen is pressed into service as a rack for wine storage (ABOVE).

Planning

Planning is the key element in good design. Essential before undertaking any major alteration, planning is even more critical when it comes to creating a kitchen, the most intensively used room in the home. There's no need to restrict creative impulses, but it's important to be aware that impetuous, headlong decisions all too often result in expensive mistakes.

A gestation period will give you time to review all the options and devise the best layout and disposition of space. In the field of kitchen design, established ergonomic principles recommend sensible work heights as well as distances devised to minimize effort and increase efficiency. This is also the stage where you may well benefit from professional advice to help plan servicing, utilities, lighting and other elements that make up the kitchen infrastructure.

Planning cannot take place in the abstract, however. In this section, five specific kitchen layouts demonstrate a range of solutions, each of which is a response to a particular set of priorities and spatial characteristics. Uncovering the qualities of the space at your disposal is all part of the vital planning and decision-making process.

Another lateral inspiration: a plate warmer sited above the countertop burners benefits from rising heat from the cooking pots (BELOW).

PLANNING FROM SCRATCH

The first of many questions to ask yourself is whether the kitchen is in the right place. Is it easy to reach the dining room from the kitchen? It's a mistake to perpetuate a pattern such as having a full bathroom downstairs when only a guest powder room is needed. By freeing this floor space a new dining room could be built closer to the kitchen or the existing kitchen expanded.

Relocating the kitchen or dining room can give your home a nucleus with a familiar, lived-in feel. Services and utilities need to be redone even if the kitchen stays put. Major restructuring of space – moving the kitchen or knocking out load-bearing walls, windows, doors, chimneys – is not necessarily cost prohibitive. Price will depend on the character and traits of the structure. But it's the fittings and finishes, not relocating gas, electric and water mains, that comprise most of a new kitchen's cost, although drainage and ventilation are essential considerations in the decision-making process. Uncomplicated moves don't have to be unremarkable. It may make good sense to move the kitchen to another area on the ground floor or the laundry room to the upstairs closet.

If a kitchen addition is unaffordable or impractical, then moving a radiator or heating duct, the sink or the location of your existing appliances can improve your kitchen layout and storage capacity with only a little financial outlay. In fact a limited budget often prompts a fresh, non-purist approach that results in some of the best kitchen plans. Money-saving options might include installing painted or laminated cabinets made from wood substrate, molded plastic or MDF substrate instead of solid wood or wood veneer. You can always upgrade later by replacing or refacing the doors and retaining the rest of the cabinet. You don't have to customize the interiors: the more you outfit a drawer or cabinet to accommodate a specific use, the more you'll spend and the less flexible will be its storage performance.

SITE AND SIZE

If you're starting from scratch, rather than remodeling, the first in a barrage of decisions (page 118) is where to situate the kitchen. In a brand-new construction, you can choose which direction your kitchen will face. Orientating the kitchen toward where the sun rises will flood the room with morning light. Aside from its sunny face, the room can be used as a solar collector, pumping heat into the house and lowering energy bills. You will also want the kitchen to blend smoothly with entrances, halls and staircases. Animals and children are constantly going to and fro between the house and the outside world (through the back door) bringing with them dirt and mud. One way to keep old coats, umbrellas and boots out and kitchen heat in is to provide a back-door porch or mud room to mark the transition.

When it comes to kitchen planning, bigger isn't always best. Big kitchens are advantageous only if the appliances are tethered to the principles of ergonomics (pages 122–125). Exploring the design of smaller kitchens, in which either the room is tiny or the "kitchen" is contained in a small portion of a larger room, is not about settling for less or sacrificing style. More and more, small kitchens have come to mean quality over quantity.

WHERE TO START

Begin at home base. It is best to fit in a new or redesigned kitchen without undermining the architectural character of the house or destroying any of the room's existing charms. Think about the factors that are taken for granted and question them. For example, pundits used to put the sink in front of a window. If that is the main window, you will constantly be turning your back on your dinner companions, and you may consider it far better to place the table by the window overlooking the view and to move the working part of the kitchen to the other side of the room.

Lined up against a side wall, a kitchen fitted into a corridor acts as a link between living areas. The design accentuates the unusual layout, the long countertop broken up into distinct working areas, and a continuous display shelf running the full length of the kitchen above a sequence of square windows, which punctuates the wall with views (OPPOSITE ABOVE).

Alcove kitchens with no external lighting can feel enclosed, dark and claustrophobic. Despite its location, this kitchen, with an island unit marking the boundary with the eating area, benefits from the generous natural lighting of the space as a whole. White flooring, walls and ceiling bounce the light around and contribute to the sense of airiness (OPPOSITE BELOW).

Natural light has always been of paramount importance in northern interiors where winters are long and dreary. This Scandinavian kitchen and dining room displays a characteristic love of light, with all of the principal surfaces white or light toned. In such surroundings, contrasts of material and texture are vital to prevent blandness. Here ceramic tiles, matchboarding, plaster, glass and stone supply textural variety. The corner fireplace with open fire draws the eye to the warm center of the room (RIGHT).

GETTING YOUR PRIORITIES RIGHT

There are some universal topics that come up in the initial stages of designing a kitchen. They concern your personality and circumstances, the architecture of your house and your needs when preparing food. You need to ask yourself many questions so you can determine your priorities and anticipate future needs.

THE SPACE

- Is your kitchen properly sited in relation to other rooms in the house, and spacious enough for the activities, appliances and storage required; or does it need combining with other rooms?
- What is the size of your budget?
- Would you feel happier handing the entire project either partly or fully over to the professionals?
- How long will you live in your current home? Is a full-scale remodeling feasible for the value added to the property?
- Can you design a new kitchen without undermining the character of your home? Have you considered the architectural features in the room?
- Do you prefer: open-shelf or closed storage; built-in or free standing cabinets; hood or downdraft ventilation; warm-air, hot water, steam or radiant heating?

THE ACTIVITIES

- Which activities will you do in your kitchen: food preparation and cooking; food storage; everyday eating; entertaining friends, family and business associates; professional cooking; laundry; homework from the office and school; watching television; entertaining your small children or childminding?
- Who uses the kitchen regularly? Do you get in each other's way?
- If you plan to eat in or entertain, do you care about hiding the mess? Is a table important? How large a table and how much room for dining will be sufficient? Is your everyday lifestyle different from your entertaining style?

YOUR NEEDS

- What are your challenges, priorities or preferences: a view from your kitchen; a sunny exposure and more light; food preparation with maximum efficiency; a clear division between cooking and dining areas; use of the kitchen as a family room; safety for children; direct access to outside areas; adaptability for use by the disabled or elderly?
- What are the good and bad features of your current kitchen and of other kitchens you have visited?
- What are your favorite kitchen "looks?" (Start a kitchen-design file or folder to contain ideas.)

THE EQUIPMENT

- Which kitchen appliances do you want: free standing stove; wall oven; separate cooktop; a griddle; a barbecue grill; built-in or free standing microwave oven; refrigerator; freezer; food waste disposer; dishwasher; trash compactor?
- How much storage space will you require for: portable cooking appliances; electronic equipment (e.g. television, computer); bulk foods; fresh food and groceries; wine; cutlery and china; cleaning products and equipment?
- Which other activities would you ideally like to have better space for: sewing; laundry; homework; home office; phone; sports equipment; recycling; preserving foods; toys and games?

SAFETY

Most accidents at home happen to children in the kitchen. Whether you're starting from scratch, remodeling, or just plain revamping, try to make sure these planning precautions are allowed for in the budget and the design:

- Install stoves and burners away from windows – drafts may blow out gas flames and curtains might catch fire.
- Choose a non-slip floor material and always mop up spills straight away.

- Many kitchens have painted walls or cabinets that cross the line from period charm to decrepitude. If paint was applied to a surface in your kitchen before 1978, there is a chance that it contains lead. Use a test kit to be sure or contact your local health department.
- Illuminate work surfaces, storage areas, and the sink, cooking area and floor with adequate lighting (pages 144–145).
- Fire is a kitchen's worst nightmare. Flank cooking areas with a noncombustible countertop material.
- Consider allocating space for a fire extinguisher or fire blanket.
- Line the bottoms and sides of cabinets adjacent to cooking surfaces with steel or metal to prevent fire.
- Round corners on countertops to avoid knocks, bruises and scratches.
- Never trail electrical cords across a sink or stove top. Install electrical switches and outlets away from the water source.

KEEPING QUIET

A kitchen's buzz is part of daily domestic life. What you want is sound control rather than soundproofing. What you don't want is to be forced to shout conversations over a droning dishwasher or to be wary of setting a cup down on a counter above a washing machine for fear that vibration will nudge the cup off. The best way to help your kitchen keep its composure is to impose control over the source of the sound and then cut reverberation.

First, reduce vibration. Try mounting the washing machine on rubber pads and eliminating water hammer by placing air chambers in the water pipes. Top-of-the-range dishwashers are most likely to insulate noise. They are outfitted with noise- and vibration-reducing interior fittings to buffer sound – particularly important if you have an open-plan kitchen.

Exhaust systems in hoods, especially downdraft exhausts built into stoves, are known for being loud. If the fan is located at the back of the pipe, instead of in the hood, it will pull rather than push air, reducing the noise. You can help muffle refrigerator sounds by making sure the refrigerator is level and the defrost collection pan is in position (usually accessible behind the bottom toe panel). Putting carpeting or sound-absorbing ceiling tile on the wall behind the refrigerator can also help. Be sure, too, to allow enough space between the back of the refrigerator and the wall unless the unit is designed as a "built-in." To cut down on the refrigerator compressor's running time, you should vacuum the compressor coils at least twice a year, more often if you have pets. It also helps to keep your freezer at least three-quarters full.

Cutting reverberation calls for measures requiring more compromise. Hard surfaces are the least likely to keep the peace. Tiled floors, steel countertops and shiny kitchen units reflect sound. Wood floors are less noisy to tread on than ceramic tile. Vinyl-backed sheeting is even quieter and work surfaces of wood are the quietest. The contents of doorless cabinets act as sound absorbers, unlike the surfaces of flat, closed doors. Wood paneling on walls or ceilings reflects less sound than painted or papered sheetrock. Acoustic tiles offer more repose for the truly conscious than wood. Unfortunately, the quieter a kitchen the harder it is to keep clean, as texture absorbs not only sound but dirt as well!

An island unit incorporates two different surfaces – granite and wood – at two different working heights to suit different cooking tasks. A suspended *batterie de cuisine* keeps tools and utensils readily to hand and a variety of open storage shelves are organized around basic kitchen activities in an intelligent and attractive way (RIGHT ABOVE).

The lower level of this stepped counter acts as a divider between kitchen and eating area. In an open-plan room, the wall space has been kept free of units, with below-counter storage screened by the U-shaped layout (RIGHT).

DESIGN CHALLENGES

A large kitchen allows scope for equipping it to the highest specification, but requires careful planning to avoid unnecessary journeys between different work zones. Here, abundant natural light and generous countertop areas mean that space does not seem cramped even though the island unit incorporates a seating area. The countertop spans three walls of the room, continuing round to form a divider between the kitchen areas and general living space (RIGHT).

If you have young children, assemble the best-equipped kitchen you can afford, with labor-saving devices and adequate space. While children come for the food, they come back for the love. Whether or not they have a separate playroom, young children want to be where their parents are and can be counted on to be permanent fixtures in the kitchen. Allocate sufficient space for them and their activities.

As children grow up, open kitchens can be tantamount to one-room living, filled with the usual bevy of home entertainment vices. If your children have flown, or you are nearing retirement age, work at home or just anticipate spending more time in the kitchen, you might conceivably invest more in a new kitchen.

Make a tour of your present kitchen. What haven't you got enough room to store? Some cooks encounter serious preparation problems if necessary possessions are hidden away. The solution is often to incorporate open shelves or a walk-in pantry. Other chefs exert a more totalitarian control over appearances. Hiding culinary paraphernalia behind closed doors, so that surfaces are left smooth and clean, is conducive to calm. Narrow cabinet and pantry shelves designed to hold specific items often help keep storage intelligently organized and under control.

Sensibly, you want to store glasses and dishes near the sink and dishwasher, and sponges, scouring pads, garbage bags, etc. nearby. Stow frequently used pots and pans near the sink and stove. You can set the table without getting in the cook's way if cutlery is located close to the dishwasher but outside the work triangle.

PLAN OF ACTION

After outlining your design challenges, and taking into account the work triangle and the concepts that go with it (pages 122–125), the next stage in planning a kitchen is allocating space. You need graph paper, a pencil and tape measure. Choose a convenient scale, for example $\frac{1}{2}''=1'\text{-}0''$, to draw up your plans; every half an inch on the graph paper can represent one foot in your kitchen. Measure the kitchen and draw in the size of any permanent fixtures, such as walls, doors, radiators and windows.

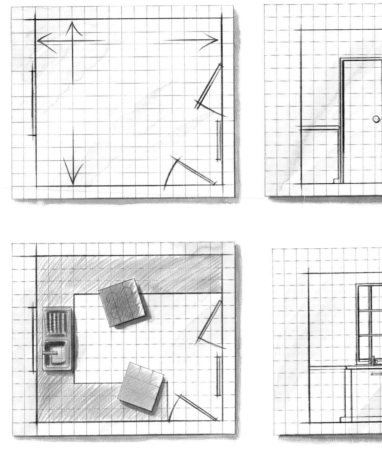

Drawing up an Elevation – Make a scale drawing of each wall in your kitchen and mark in all the relevant features. This will help you to avoid any jarring changes in height and to spot potential problems such as placing the refrigerator or dishwasher in a corner where access will be awkward or ending up with "dead" spaces that are too small for any useful purpose. Fixtures such as a radiator are relatively expensive to move, so if you are on a fairly restricted budget you will have to plan the layout carefully to incorporate such elements into the new scheme (LEFT).

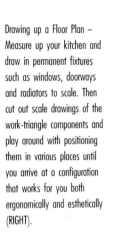

Drawing up a Floor Plan – Measure up your kitchen and draw in permanent fixtures such as windows, doorways and radiators to scale. Then cut out scale drawings of the work-triangle components and play around with positioning them in various places until you arrive at a configuration that works for you both ergonomically and esthetically (RIGHT).

Cut out pieces of paper to scale to represent the sink, stove and refrigerator, and arrange them into a work triangle that you think will work for you. Place the rest of the kitchen on the graph paper. It helps to use tracing paper over the graph paper and draw the emerging floor plan in bold lines so you can see it take shape. You could use a personal computer and one of the many software programs on kitchen design.

Another way to visualize your layout is to draw each wall to scale (called an elevation). Show a front view of the cabinets, stove, sink, etc. With plans and elevations you will be able to see any problems. Usually the final design is a synthesis of the two.

After the design is refined, discuss it with your designer or architect (or a professional cook if you know one). So you can keep track of the cost of various options under consideration, request multiple choices for products and materials. You can more readily scale back to control costs and more easily understand possible options. A useful tip is to label products and materials as "good," "better," and "the ultimate."

There are four basic phases to installing a new kitchen: structure, services, finishes/fittings and equipment. After you have settled on a kitchen plan, the first thing that must be done is structural work. If there is a moisture or termite problem, it must be treated. Then wiring, plumbing and gas installation must be completed. When the room itself is finished, the fittings, equipment and appliances can be introduced.

PERMISSIONS

Despite the fact that the kitchen is often a refuge, it is not exempt from government laws and regulations. If you intend to add a room or alter any part of your home's exterior, you need to check local building codes and zoning laws. If you want to knock down any existing walls, install plumbing or electricity inside or outside the home, or make any additions or alterations other than cosmetic ones, advise the building inspector. He or she is worth consulting anyway. If you hire an architect or interior designer, he or she *may* check permits for you. If not, start with the building inspector and ask to be referred to any other authorities whose permission is required. Do this *before* a hammer is lifted.

ERGONOMICS

In the early 1950s Cornell University researchers conceptualized the notion of the work triangle – the geometry determined by the sink, the refrigerator and the stove, the three chief activity centers in the kitchen. Since nearly all the manual labor done in the kitchen involves laps between the three, the objective was to make the distances between them comfortable. With an eye to convenience and safety, the study established carefully measured distances between these three primary and pivotal kitchen areas. Ideally, an imaginary line joining the sink, refrigerator and stove should measure no more than 20ft (6m), though the legs of the triangle typically range between 12ft (3.5m) and 26ft (8m). If the distances are too far, you wind up doing tiresome trotting between them. If the distances are too short, working in the kitchen becomes cramped.

The most important work space in the kitchen lies between the sink and the stove because that's where there is most activity. Situate the main food preparation area between the two; make it the longest stretch of continuous countertop in the kitchen and large enough to serve up a meal. Neither the sink nor stove should be relegated to the corner of the room. Place them at a distance of at least 16in (400mm) from the corner so you can stand in front without banging elbows or pans on the wall.

BASIC CONCEPTS FOR DESIGN

Obviously, dimensions of the triangle vary, depending on the size and shape of the kitchen, but every design warrants examination of the basic concept. And there are some inherent basics worth adhering to.

- Place a work surface near the refrigerator so ingredients haven't far to travel.
- Since plumbing is the most expensive item to change, start from the present position of the sink in your existing kitchen and plot your layout from there. The dishwasher should be sited near the sink for convenience.

Incorporating countertops at different heights makes good ergonomic sense. An island unit provides a lower-level granite countertop fitted with a grill, so the cook can easily keep an eye on what's cooking; it is also at a good height for kneading dough (LEFT).

- Remember to locate the main wash sink so that the dishwasher can be opened while someone is standing at the sink.
- Try to maintain a comfortable relationship between the stove and the sink, since hot pots and washed vegetables travel frequently between the two.
- The stove or cooktop should be placed along an exterior wall, making it easy to install an efficient hood and ventilation system unless you intend to install an island cooktop with hood.
- The acceptable clearance between an inward-opening kitchen door and the front of a run of cabinets is 16in (400mm).
- Avoid interrupting the elements of the work triangle with tall oven-housing units. It is better to group tall units together at the end of a run of countertops in a built-in kitchen and in an area outside of the triangle.

STANDARD DIMENSIONS

Vertical dimensions are equally important to a kitchen in good working order. Design cabinets, shelves and drawers to minimize bending down and stretching. Bending down is more tiresome than reaching up and you need more space to do it in.

It's generally considered a mistake to plan a kitchen with all the countertops at one uniform height. Delicate, complex

Most manufacturers build their kitchen units to dimensions that ergonomists have calculated will be best for the greatest number of people. The countertop is at a height to suit general food preparation tasks, and it's illuminated by a light beneath the wall cabinet. The shelf inside the wall cabinet is at eye level, although it could be raised to a maximum height of 6ft (1800mm) if desired (ABOVE).

jobs, such as icing a cake, need a higher surface. Heavier tasks, like kneading bread or rolling out pastry, call on upper arm and back muscles, so the countertop should ideally be correspondingly lower. The cooktop can be lowered to the height of a traditional cooking range so that you can see into the pans during cooking. Pastry chefs and professional cooks often lower a section of countertop to 30in (750mm). For most of us, using a tabletop is the old-fashioned, pragmatic contingency.

While it is a plus to have a tailored countertop suited to you and specific tasks, countertops that vary too much in height can create jarring disharmonies and can overly complicate small kitchens. It's worth experimenting to find a height that suits you, but commercially sold kitchen units are standardized internationally. It may be simpler to create a higher work surface by adjusting the bottom plinth or building the countertop up with a thick slab of wood for chopping or with a marble slab.

KITCHEN LAYOUTS

Surprisingly, efficient use of a kitchen space depends more on how it is laid out than how big it is. The layout of a kitchen, both horizontal and vertical, should always be designed around your needs and the architecture of the room. There are six basic layouts that, working within the work triangle, will give you a practical kitchen.

The one-wall (or strip) kitchen allows any room with a 10ft (3m) run of uninterrupted wall space to work as an efficient kitchen. Plan with ingenuity and allocate as much countertop as possible. The entire kitchen can be screened off with doors, shutters or partitions, when necessary.

The corridor (or galley) kitchen provides the most efficient use of space. This is the layout most coveted by professional chefs. The layout is comprised of counters on both sides of the room with a corridor down the middle. The only time this layout shouldn't be considered is if the corridor is open at

ONE WALL

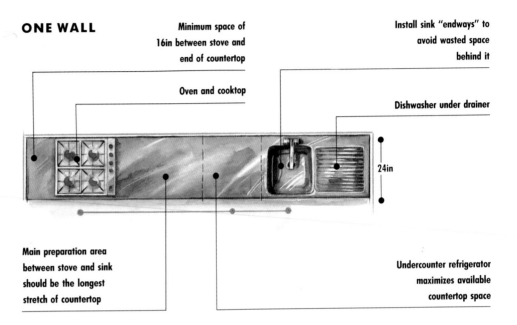

Minimum space of 16in between stove and end of countertop

Oven and cooktop

Install sink "endways" to avoid wasted space behind it

Dishwasher under drainer

24in

Main preparation area between stove and sink should be the longest stretch of countertop

Undercounter refrigerator maximizes available countertop space

CORRIDOR

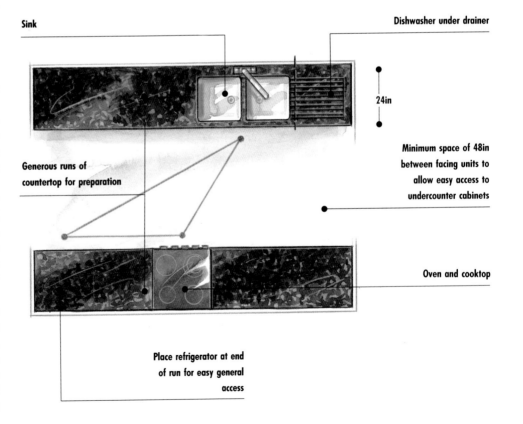

Sink

Dishwasher under drainer

24in

Generous runs of countertop for preparation

Minimum space of 48in between facing units to allow easy access to undercounter cabinets

Oven and cooktop

Place refrigerator at end of run for easy general access

both ends, since it then results in general congestion. Plan to eat elsewhere, unless a pull-out or flap-down tabletop can be incorporated at one end. A window somewhere, with lots of natural light, keeps a galley kitchen from being claustrophobic.

The island kitchen is usually only an option where you have quite a lot of available floorspace. Islands create a separate working area while allowing for a feeling of openness. This layout hungers for plenty of room and careful design to ensure economy of movement. Guests can participate socially with the cook working in the kitchen, but stay out of harm's way seated on the other side of an island, which can also double as a room divider. At its simplest, the island may just be a wooden table around which several people can gather to do the peeling, chopping and slicing.

The L-shaped kitchen is a versatile layout that places countertops along two adjacent walls. It combines well with a sitting area integrated into the same room, overcomes any shortage of wall space, and is most at home in a large or long, narrow kitchen or an awkwardly shaped corner.

The U-shaped kitchen groups units and appliances around three sides of the room. Size is less of an obstacle than ill-sited doorways in creating a U-shaped kitchen. It's safe, efficient, offers maximum storage and work space, and suits large and small rooms. The inherent danger with a U-shaped plan is that separate work centers can become remote and that there are potentially two "dead" areas in the inside corners; it's very hard to squeeze easily accessible storage in here.

The G-shaped kitchen positions fittings around most of the walls. The newest in kitchen layout design, this is essentially an expanded U-shaped kitchen, with a peninsular leg or fourth wall of cabinets and appliances. This shape is extremely efficient, saving the cook many steps; but it can feel shut off or enclosed, particularly if lighting is badly planned.

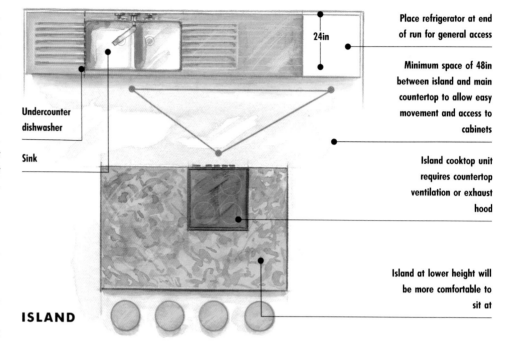

Place refrigerator at end of run for general access

24in

Minimum space of 48in between island and main countertop to allow easy movement and access to cabinets

Island cooktop unit requires countertop ventilation or exhaust hood

Island at lower height will be more comfortable to sit at

Undercounter dishwasher

Sink

ISLAND

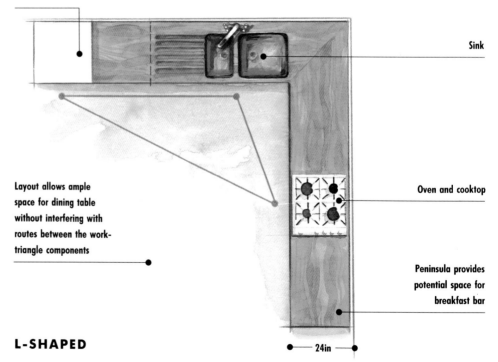

Place refrigerator at end of run for easy general access

Sink

Layout allows ample space for dining table without interfering with routes between the work-triangle components

Oven and cooktop

Peninsula provides potential space for breakfast bar

L-SHAPED

24in

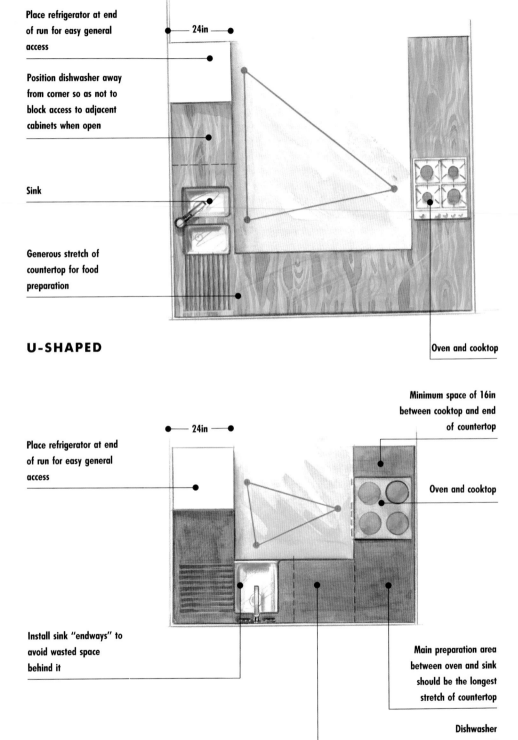

Place refrigerator at end of run for easy general access

Position dishwasher away from corner so as not to block access to adjacent cabinets when open

Sink

Generous stretch of countertop for food preparation

24in

U-SHAPED

Oven and cooktop

Minimum space of 16in between cooktop and end of countertop

24in

Place refrigerator at end of run for easy general access

Oven and cooktop

Install sink "endways" to avoid wasted space behind it

Main preparation area between oven and sink should be the longest stretch of countertop

Dishwasher

SMALL U-SHAPED

BEYOND THE TRIANGLE

Today's kitchens function very differently from those of 50 years ago, when the work triangle was first devised. Homeowners were more panicky about the combination of water and electricity and were still wary of new technology "invading" the home. The work triangle is the best organizing principle around, but it's not gospel.

Ergonomic principles must be considered, but don't forget the human element. Every kitchen remodel has its own quirks and peculiarities, and every chef has his or her own predilections that might mean that elements of the triangle are partly sacrificed. Modifications vary: if you like to encourage friends and family members to pitch in, it may make sense to expand the legs of the work triangle, or to add a second sink and work area. Set the kitchen up as a workshop; use glass-fronted cabinets, put tools out in the open on shelves and hang pots from bars or racks. Visible storage invites guests to find what they need easily and enables them to become genuinely helpful.

However, if you want to prevent guests from becoming co-workers, the kitchen should be laid out so friends are given subtle spatial clues about where they can or can't linger. The easiest way is to incorporate an island with seating at one end, away from the work area.

A mother's priority might be to situate the burners so she can keep her eyes on what's cooking, the back door and the children in an adjoining room all at the same time – even if this means taking a few more steps to the refrigerator.

Of the three activity centers in the work triangle, it's the refrigerator that is the most flexible. You may choose to move it to a more distant place, since many cooks take all the ingredients out of cold storage at one time. Microwave ovens can also easily be placed outside the work triangle without sacrificing the most important ergonomic principles of the layout.

PLAN 1: A FAMILY KITCHEN

The owners of this family townhouse approached Bulthaup kitchen designer Bennie Matharu with a list of specifications for their new kitchen: they wanted the cabinets to be white to match the large connecting door between the kitchen and the formal dining room and so as not to detract from their extensive collection of Asian artefacts; and, although the layout of the kitchen allowed little leeway, they wanted to squeeze into just 118 square feet (11 square meters) a gas cooktop, barbecue grill, electric cooktop, built-in oven, microwave, full-sized trash can, economy-sized refrigerator, undercounter refrigerator and a dishwasher for 12 place settings.

PLAN

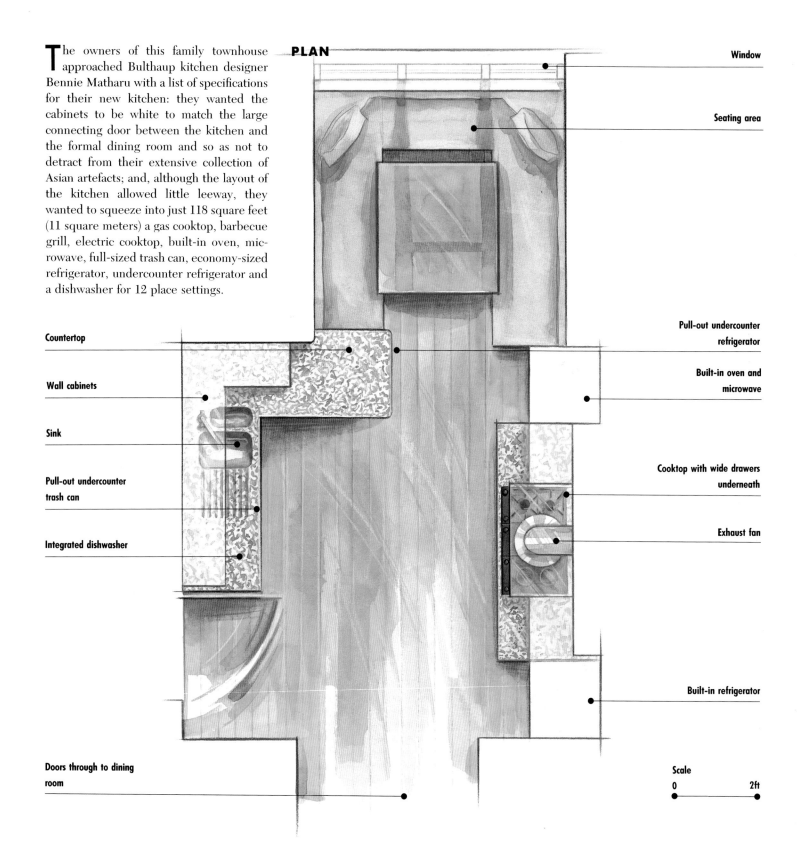

Window

Seating area

Pull-out undercounter refrigerator

Built-in oven and microwave

Cooktop with wide drawers underneath

Exhaust fan

Built-in refrigerator

Countertop

Wall cabinets

Sink

Pull-out undercounter trash can

Integrated dishwasher

Doors through to dining room

Scale

0   2ft

On one side of the kitchen, the sink is inset into an L-shaped granite countertop, with the dishwasher adjacent to it. Cabinets offer ample storage space for bulky items such as pots and pans, and for unattractive cleaning equipment (LEFT).

The second work zone in the kitchen is centered around the countertop which occupies an alcove; to one side of it is a double wall oven and to the other a refrigerator (BELOW).

Building on the clean, cool simplicity of the white laminated cabinets, Bennie Matharu introduced the cultured sparkle of granite countertops, the functionalism of stainless steel and a floor of warm beech. Wire-glass panels (usually used for roofing and safety glass) are an inexpensive way to achieve an integrated look and provide a minimalist alternative to a tiled backsplash behind the countertop areas. The panels also require less maintenance since they wipe clean easily and there are no grouted joints to gather dirt and grease.

The cooking equipment and a powerful exhaust hood (ducted through a dropped ceiling in the breakfast area) provide flexibility for the Thai stir fries and satays that regularly form the family's dinner menu. Bulthaup's gleaming, svelte hood is also the room's focal point: its micro-switch sensor system works on the velocity of steam emitted from food (automatically setting itself to switch on at a low speed for gentle cooking and switching to high-speed extraction for vigorously boiling pots or sizzling cuts of meat on the barbecue grill); this enables the chef to concentrate on cooking and company, without having to worry about adequate ventilation.

Double-stacking cabinets on the sink and food-preparation side, but single-stacking cabinets on the cooking side, give the kitchen plenty of storage space without making it claustrophobic or too perfectly paired. A pull-out, undercounter refrigerator provides a bar of beer, fruit juice and milk close to the breakfast area.

Making the most of available space, the layout tucks the sink into a 90 degree angle without sacrificing utility. A wire shelf, united with a peg rail, is mounted over the sink area to keep everyday dishes, mugs and utensils conveniently to hand. The television is fixed to the peninsular wall on a bracket; it swivels so that the cook can watch while working in the kitchen and the two children can feast two senses at once in the breakfast area.

PLAN 2: OPENING UP THE WORKSPACE

New space is often discovered by thinking laterally. Food critic and renowned cook Fay Maschler approached London-based architect Rick Mather to remodel the ground-floor kitchen and dining area of her Arts and Crafts cottage.

In the old configuration, the kitchen was a self-contained room and, while perfectly functional, it meant that guests unwittingly got in the cook's way. Fay Maschler wanted a new kitchen in which she could work while chatting with family and friends, but without them invading the work space. As a result, Rick Mather laid out the kitchen so that other people are subliminally discour-

aged from entering the vicinity of work. Several ground-floor rooms – the kitchen, dining room/conservatory and sitting room – were combined into a liberated kitchen/living space. Moving the sink and all appliances but the washer and dryer improved the kitchen layout, increasing the countertop area and storage capacity.

The walls of the conservatory were taken down to allow the glass roof to flood the remodeled living space with light. The kitchen walls were knocked down to provide room for an elegant Georgian dining table seating up to 10 people with a view to the garden through the french

windows. The actual size of the kitchen was reduced, shortening the distances between the refrigerator, range and sink, with a larger refrigerator and pantry moved to the outside wall of the conservatory and hidden behind cabinet doors. A 16in (400mm) green slate shelf oversails the countertop at elbow height, anchoring guests in the non-working part of the kitchen.

Dividing the kitchen into two preparation areas has created a space that is manageable for Fay to work in alone, but with room for two or more to work without getting under each other's feet. Tools are well organized, with those not in everyday

GENERAL PLAN

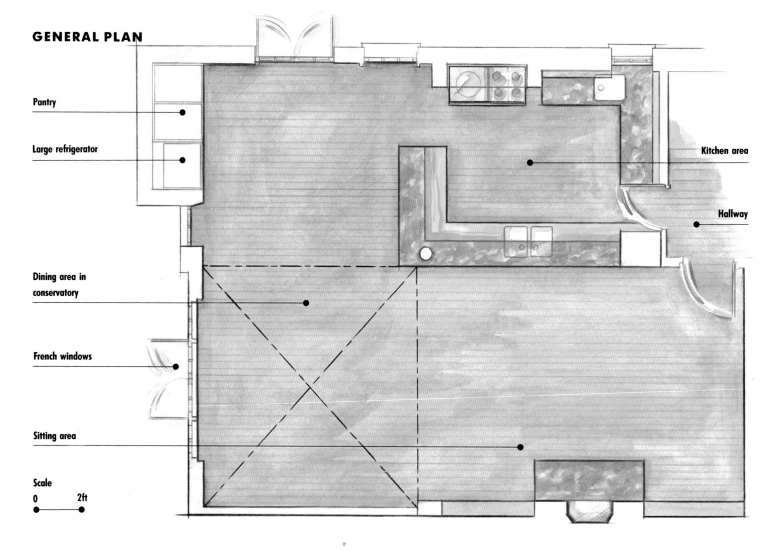

Pantry

Large refrigerator

Dining area in conservatory

French windows

Sitting area

Kitchen area

Hallway

Scale

0   2ft

PLAN

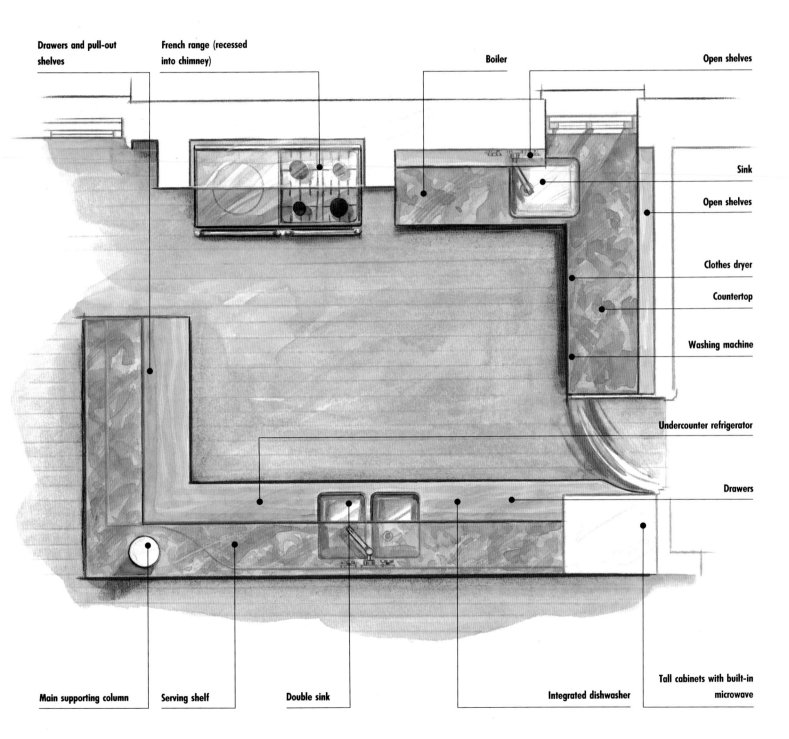

Drawers and pull-out shelves

French range (recessed into chimney)

Boiler

Open shelves

Sink

Open shelves

Clothes dryer

Countertop

Washing machine

Undercounter refrigerator

Drawers

Main supporting column

Serving shelf

Double sink

Integrated dishwasher

Tall cabinets with built-in microwave

The architecture of the kitchen is based around three "task planes": the overhead cabinets; the serving shelf and countertop; and the undercounter cabinets and fittings. The white counter divides the kitchen from the rest of the room, sweeping behind the support column at the outside "corner" (ABOVE).

Wine glasses form a practical and attractive display, catching the light from the window; sleek aluminum cans along the adjacent wall hold tea, pulses and other dried ingredients (LEFT).

use stored neatly in cabinets: small appliances are plugged in at a usable height, concealed in a cabinet which also houses a built-in microwave; utensils and pans are secreted below counters or stashed in cabinets out of guests' reach. Glasses are ranged on shelves close to the sink and dishwasher, and plates stored in a cabinet accessed from the dining-room side of the counter.

Maximizing the available work surface was a priority, so Rick took the full-size refrigerator out of the working triangle. Installing large double sinks so that the longest sides are perpendicular to the edge of the countertop took up much less space than the proverbial double-sink inset with the longest sides parallel to the edge. A new French range was placed in the old chimney recess; the existing flue eliminated the need for an exhaust fan.

White-painted MDF cabinets conjure serenity while allowing the homeowners the flexibility to be able to change the color. The simple character and warmth of reclaimed maple floors is paired with countertops of wood and green slate that are as practical as they are classic.

A glass roof in the remodeled conservatory area floods the kitchen with natural light. Beyond the double sink, an undercounter refrigerator stores frequently used fresh ingredients; the bulk of the food, however, is stored in the pantry and refrigerator at the end of the room (LEFT).

Placing the French-made range in the chimney recess eliminated the need for an exhaust hood. Pots and pans are stored to one side of the oven, and other cooking utensils are suspended from a hanging rail (LEFT).

The green slate of the raised counter makes a handsome juxtaposition with the main timber countertop and acts as a serving shelf, cookbook perch and a shield for kitchen mess (RIGHT).

PLAN 3: A FARMHOUSE CONVERSION

The eating side of the kitchen is dominated by a wall of shelving on which everyday pots, pans and dishes are displayed. The main shelf is made from marble; an angled mirror above it reflects back the bounty of the bowls of fresh produce waiting to be eaten (LEFT).

PLAN

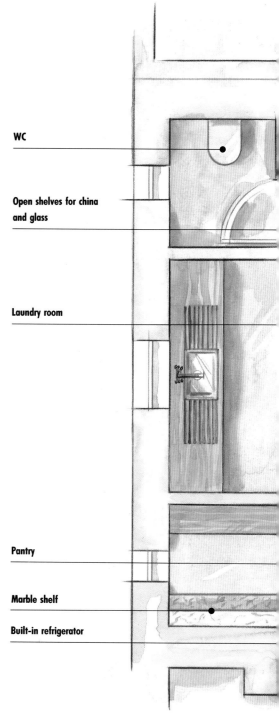

WC

Open shelves for china and glass

Laundry room

Pantry

Marble shelf

Built-in refrigerator

Lying in the south of France, the Conrans' summer retreat is a nineteenth-century farmhouse where Terence Conran has converted one of the barns into a large, light-filled kitchen, laundry and pantry.

The design and layout of the kitchen hinge upon basic principles that Terence Conran has applied to the many other kitchens he has designed: the main cooking and preparation areas are anchored along one wall, so that the cook can work unimpeded but join in with conversations. Along this wall are two Gaggenau ovens and a row of white-painted cabinets filled with cleaning materials, kitchen linen and pieces of kitchen equipment that are seldom used. Above these, a continuous solid oak countertop houses two cooktops – one electric, the other gas – a counter grill with its own surface-mounted ventilation unit, and a pair of glazed stoneware sinks with angled draining boards on either side.

Pots and pans are stored readily to hand on a broad oak shelf above the countertop. A continuous strip of incandescent lights beneath the shelf and shielded from the eye by an oak baffle illuminates the countertop; bevel-edged tiles identical to those used in the Paris Metro increase the level of light, reflecting the glow from the bulbs.

The single most important item is a huge, freestanding work table that divides the working part of the kitchen from the eating area. Made from rough planks of oak, the table is large enough for three people to work at comfortably. Knives slot into a rack at one end, wooden spoons and spatulas are kept in an earthenware pot.

The other table in the kitchen, a fine example of English craftsmanship, is also made of oak and seats up to 14 people at mealtimes. Behind it, on the wall opposite the countertop, is a huge length of shelving. Above the main, cantilevered shelf of white marble is an angled mirror that reflects the bowls of fruit and vegetables on display, a feature that commands attention the minute you walk into the room. Above the mirror, narrow shelves reach up to the ceiling and hold plates, dishes and other daily items. These shelves bulge in the middle of their run to provide a space for larger dishes and soup tureens.

Natural ventilation and light is afforded by the two enormous french windows. At the back of the room, a large refrigerator is recessed into the wall of the pantry beyond it. Throughout, simplicity is the cornerstone of the design in this perfect kitchen for a hot climate.

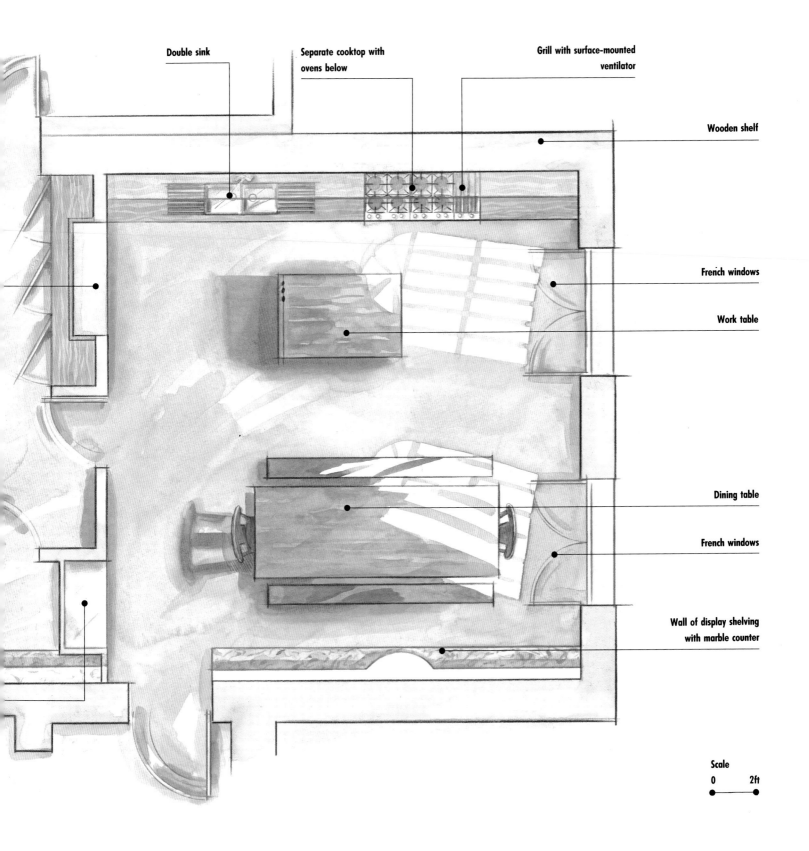

Double sink

Separate cooktop with ovens below

Grill with surface-mounted ventilator

Wooden shelf

French windows

Work table

Dining table

French windows

Wall of display shelving with marble counter

Scale

0   2ft

PLAN 4: NEW SPACE FOR OLD

A young couple in advertising had big plans for their small kitchen in their newly bought apartment. They wanted it all – cooktops, oven, sink, dishwasher, refrigerator, washing machine, clothes dryer, microwave, more floor and work space, and storage – and they wanted it in just under 64 square feet (6 square meters) of space on a maximum budget of $7,000.

Furniture designers Owain George and Merlin Wright reconfigured the original kitchen and ingeniously incorporated space from an existing chimney. The old kitchen's black-and-white tiled floor, gray monolithic cabinets and a tower of appliances stacked in a corner all depressed the homeowners, as did the severely restricted space – only two people could move past one another, and even then they had to be pretty close friends. Though still pint-sized, the new kitchen is big on style and substance, combining form with function, and good design with economy.

The room's narrowness made it impossible to mount standard cabinets on facing and adjacent walls without destroying the airiness of the kitchen and any semblance of traffic flow. The designers built cabinets and carcasses from waterproof MDF, customizing them to look like more expensive timber panel-and-frame units. Only the cabinets under the window use 24in (600mm) units to house a washing machine, refrigerator and butler sink.

The existing chimney provided a place to inset the microwave flush with the backsplash and to recess the oven, reducing the depth of the base units to 14in (370mm), which freed up valuable floorspace. Electric burners were separated from the usual foursome and set in pairs on the countertop diagonal to the sink to maximize the amount of workspace between these two work-triangle components. Notches in upper cabinet cornices house wine bottles, a design feature that makes the most of seldom-used space while taking up much less room than a wine rack.

The old kitchen was poorly laid out and wasted precious space: appliances stacked in a corner partially blocked natural light and the view from the window, while the corner diagonally opposite contained nothing but a useless empty space (RIGHT).

Side-by-side burners, recessed appliances and shallow base units all help to make the most of available space (OPPOSITE ABOVE).

Elevations illustrate the layout along two walls. The oven is partly and the microwave fully recessed into the chimney. Note the notches in the cornices which are used to store bottles of wine (OPPOSITE BELOW LEFT).

Along the outside wall, the refrigerator and sink are positioned below the window; the washing machine in the corner is faced in cladding (OPPOSITE BELOW RIGHT).

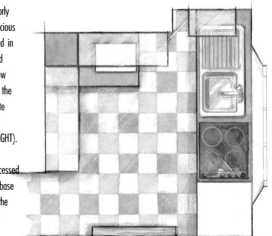

PLAN

Scale

0   2ft

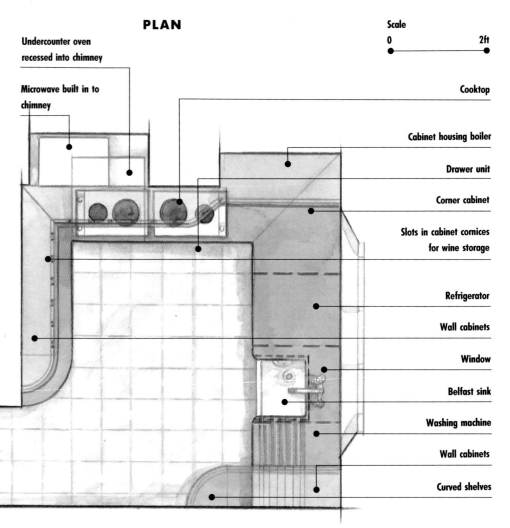

Undercounter oven recessed into chimney

Microwave built in to chimney

Cooktop

Cabinet housing boiler

Drawer unit

Corner cabinet

Slots in cabinet cornices for wine storage

Refrigerator

Wall cabinets

Window

Belfast sink

Washing machine

Wall cabinets

Curved shelves

The two biggest structural changes were minor plumbing moves. The sink was moved slightly to the right to accommodate the refrigerator, and the boiler, originally in the middle of its cabinet, was moved to the corner to create more storage space. Its new MDF door is entirely removable for easy access. Three copper pipes from the boiler were left exposed, cleaned up with wire wool, straightened by the plumber, and incorporated into the design.

There were some trade-offs: the sink is under the window (though not centered); a dishwasher was forsaken; the freezer, infrequently used, was relegated to a spot under the stairs just beyond the kitchen door; and high wall cabinets extend over most of the countertop depth, leading to a greater chance of the owners hitting their heads.

Color, texture and form were used to reshape the room. The texture owes much to the cherry countertop, cherished for its warm hues despite needing more maintenance than most hardwoods.

Selecting the paint turned out to be perhaps the most nerve-wracking decision the designers faced, being more of an esthetic specification than a choice determined by logic or practicality. The color had to fit into an intensely crafted kitchen without making it seem cluttered. Various shades tested on large sample boards eliminated paler colors and paint effects. Magnolia paint inside the cabinets and a creamy tiled floor are cozier and less anemic than white, providing mellow counterpoints to the blue-green cabinets.

Rounded upper cabinets and a trademark S-shaped whiplash curve on the wall units are Owain's solution for smoothing over problems with the layout and minimizing the impact of such a small doorway. The countertop remains squared off: although curves would have added only an inch, the kitchen couldn't spare them. Hand-forged iron door handles, dulled with a zinc coating, maintain the desired balance between futurism and a country look.

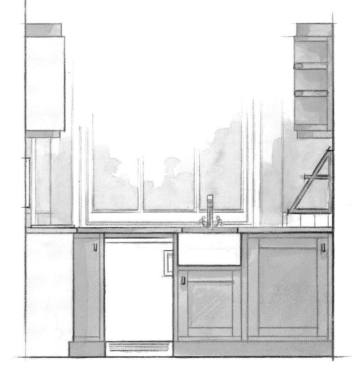

PLAN 5: A COOK'S KITCHEN

From the foyer, steps lead up to the open-plan dining room, while a lacewood and ribbed glass door slides open to lead into the kitchen; a refrigerator to the left and a pantry straight ahead can be glimpsed (LEFT).

The inventory of amenities in this kitchen is equivalent to those found behind the scenes in many top-class restaurants. This is understandable since it is the gracious New York refuge from a fast-food world for professional chef Paul King and associate Walter Jaffe. Rather than fill the kitchen with the predictable built-in units usually dictated by the cramped quarters of a period Manhattan high-rise, they and their architect, Deborah Weintraub, took a more original approach. They still managed to fit three ovens, a baking center, an appliance barn and two refrigerators into just 185 square feet (17.9 square meters).

Since light and space are scarce commodities in city kitchens, space was annexed from a generous foyer and the kitchen was tucked in behind a curved lacewood wall and ribbed-glass sliding door. The interplay of materials in this new architectural focal point coaxes natural light and a modern rhythm into the adjoining sitting room.

The kitchen is also accessible from a swinging door of sandblasted glass and stainless steel that opens to the dining room. Next to the door, panels of luminescent Venetian glass reflect the sun's rays like a prism and amplify light shared by the kitchen and dining room. Both the doors allow Paul King – who prefers to cook in privacy when entertaining – to cordon off his laboratory without making living and dining areas somber.

Planning in tandem, the architect and homeowners decided it was worth tearing down the original wall between the kitchen and dining room to gain a precious 5in (12cm) of space needed to organize storage more sensibly. It was rebuilt to form a wall of cabinets. On the kitchen side, plum-stained tambor doors front an electrically wired 8ft (2.4m) appliance barn: Cuisinart, blender and coffee maker remain plugged in and can be used *in situ* or pulled onto the kitchen counter. Lunstead metal, an etched laminate more typically used in commercial installations, proved an economical alternative to facing the doors in stainless steel. On the dining-room side, the cabinets boast a cherry veneer.

Normally, carpenters don't talk daily with the plumber and electrician, but this innovative wall of cabinets required close co-operation. Carpenters adroitly laced pipes through the plywood frame and crafted a hatch between the dining room and kitchen that incorporates a professional, restaurant-grade food warmer and a gliding onyx door on the dining side.

PLAN

Scale

0   2ft

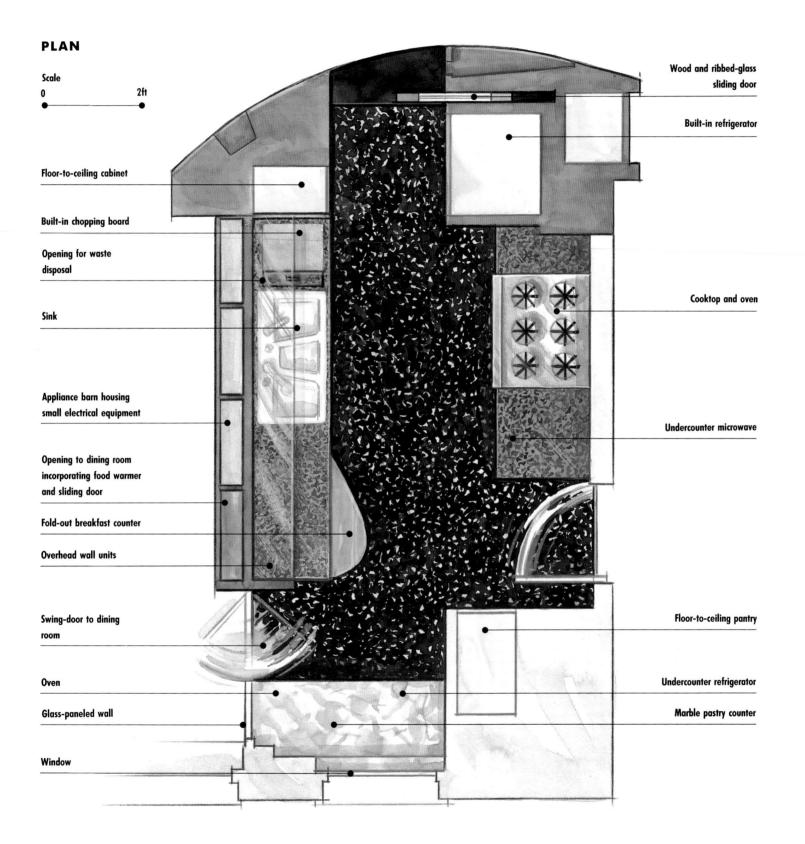

Wood and ribbed-glass
sliding door

Built-in refrigerator

Floor-to-ceiling cabinet

Built-in chopping board

Opening for waste
disposal

Cooktop and oven

Sink

Appliance barn housing
small electrical equipment

Undercounter microwave

Opening to dining room
incorporating food warmer
and sliding door

Fold-out breakfast counter

Overhead wall units

Swing-door to dining
room

Floor-to-ceiling pantry

Oven

Undercounter refrigerator

Glass-paneled wall

Marble pastry counter

Window

The interior of a floor-to-ceiling cabinet has been customized to provide storage for pots and pans (ABOVE).

A six-burner professional range with electric oven adjacent to a built-in microwave for quick heating provide a variety of cooking means (ABOVE RIGHT).

The semi-circular breakfast table-cum-preparation counter folds out from the space between the dishwasher and countertop (RIGHT ABOVE).

Plum-stained tambor doors above the sink conceal an appliance barn into which small gadgets are plugged ready for use (RIGHT BELOW).

Paul King, an expert pastry chef, is a tall man. Hence the countertops in the U-shaped kitchen were tailored to his height. A small commercial salad-bar refrigerator chills the marble pastry counter, and an undercounter convection oven encourages dough to rise.

Industrial-caliber conveniences allow for star-quality cooking. A six-burner professional range with a large oven, a microwave for reheating, a three-compartment sink with an instant hot-water tap and a full-sized dishwasher make up the two parallel work centers. Hidden conveniences include a chopping board and an opening for scraps cut into the Corian countertop; a full-sized refrigerator and pantry concealed behind a lacewood veneer; a commercial exhaust fan and a roll-out butcher block breakfast table. Lighting is brighter than average, as in catering kitchens. The floor, a poured epoxy intended for boiler rooms, is thinner, lighter and cheaper than the terrazzo it resembles in both its good looks and its durability.

Aqua, gray and metal laminates are juxtaposed with stainless steel, glass and wood to reflect the homeowners' taste. Harmony results from the simple lines and the architect's eye for composing surfaces in different, but complementary, textures.

The sliding ribbed-glass door allows the kitchen to become a self-contained haven of privacy in the otherwise open-plan apartment (ABOVE).

The marble pastry counter offers a commanding view of the Manhattan skyline. An undercounter refrigerator and fan oven enable this part of the kitchen to function as a relatively self-contained work zone (RIGHT).

UNIVERSAL DESIGN

For four- and five-year-olds, it's a challenge to scamper up a chair and turn on the hot water behind mother's back and not get scalded. At 70, if arthritis doesn't prevent them turning on the faucet, the elderly may get burned because sensitivity to temperature has diminished. Children don't fit into a kitchen designed for adults any more than aging adults fit into a world designed for children. Those who face additional physical challenges are disabled by a kitchen designed for the fittest.

Universal design, also called barrier-free design, bridges the gap. It is a blueprint of sorts for a kitchen that can be used regardless of flexibility or disability. The basic principle is to amplify ability rather than handicap the less able. Prevailing opinion favors a single work station with concentrated appliances and tasks. U- and L-shaped layouts (pages 124–125) work better than corridors for these kitchens of universal design.

PLANNING CONSIDERATIONS

When planning a universal kitchen, you need to remember that people don't come in one size or have similar physical advantages. Here are some ideas you may want to incorporate into your design:

- Casters turn base cabinets into roll-out units that can be moved under the countertop or out of the way.
- Shallow shelves ensure easy access to items at the back. Pull-out and door-mounted shelves and baskets and swing-out organizers aid adaptable design by bringing stored items forward and increasing usable space.
- A seated area at the sink provides comfort; a shallow sink works best.
- Mount a single-lever faucet with a high-necked swivel arm for filling kettles and pans with ease.
- Electronically controlled faucets, though expensive, turn on without a touch.
- A separate cooktop and wall-mounted oven are sensible for barrier-free living.
- Electrical appliances are usually recommended for those with physical challenges, there's no open flame or combustibles. If gas is a must, choose a pilotless ignition range. Proper installation and maintenance are essential.

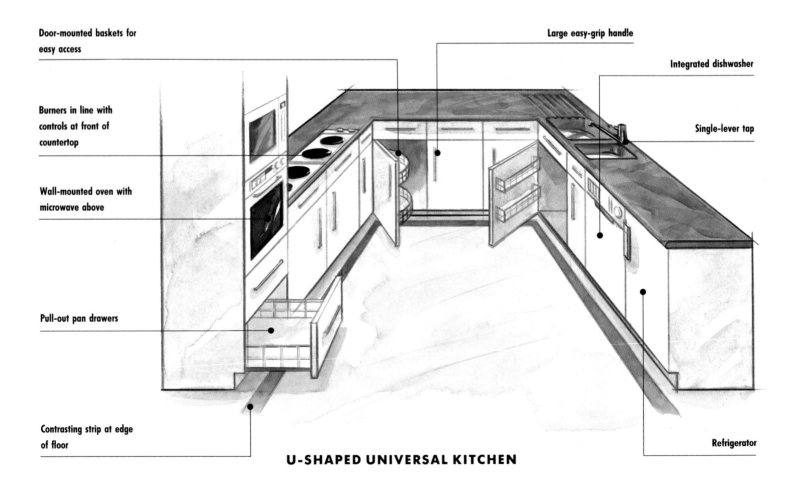

Door-mounted baskets for easy access

Large easy-grip handle

Integrated dishwasher

Burners in line with controls at front of countertop

Single-lever tap

Wall-mounted oven with microwave above

Pull-out pan drawers

Contrasting strip at edge of floor

Refrigerator

U-SHAPED UNIVERSAL KITCHEN

- High degrees of visual contrast prevent accidents. Opt for black heating elements inset on a white cooktop or white ceramic elements in a metal or black cooktop so they are easy to see.
- Front controls for ranges and cooktops and staggered burners make it unnecessary to reach over a hot surface. Push-turn knobs are tamperproof and protective of small children; push-button, touch- and T-type are easier to use.
- Wall-mounted microwaves and ovens at counter level eliminate bending.
- The microwave is an excellent appliance for the universal kitchen; it cooks quickly and it is easy and cheap to operate. A toaster oven is also practical for broiling and baking.

- Side-by-side refrigerators or bottom freezer models are ideal for those who cannot reach upper shelves. Door ice/water dispensers simplify tasks.
- Dishwashers raised about 10in (250mm) off the floor eliminate bending when loading and unloading.
- A non-slip and no-trip floor is a must. Avoid a busy pattern; stick to neutral colors so spills are easily seen.
- Insetting a contrasting stripe at the edge of the floor signals an obstacle to the visually impaired.
- With furniture, universal doesn't necessarily mean industrial design. An antique trestle table generally has the extra height to allow for comfortable wheelchair and leg room.

- Pull-out or flap-down kitchen tables provide extra work space and can retract for wheelchair passage.
- Wheelchair users need a countertop height of 31in (785mm); allow a 24in (610mm) wide space for knees.
- Tables with a center pedestal offer less obstruction than a table with corner legs.
- Make sure drawer handles are large enough so that a good portion of your hand can get behind them as a lever. (If you can twist a knob without gripping or exertion, it is well designed.)
- Push-action magnetic catches don't require the hand strength or dexterity arthritic and rheumatoid fingers lack.
- Lever handles that press open and shut with an elbow offer easy control.

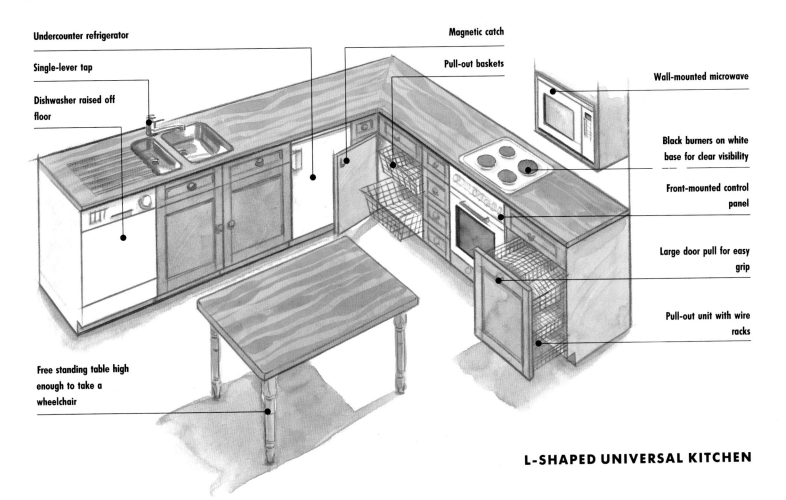

Undercounter refrigerator

Single-lever tap

Dishwasher raised off floor

Magnetic catch

Pull-out baskets

Wall-mounted microwave

Black burners on white base for clear visibility

Front-mounted control panel

Large door pull for easy grip

Pull-out unit with wire racks

Free standing table high enough to take a wheelchair

L-SHAPED UNIVERSAL KITCHEN

ESSENTIAL SERVICES

Expect to see your plumber and electrician twice during your kitchen renovation. On the first visit, pipes and wires are roughed in; on the second, appliances and electrical devices installed. Either hire licensed plumbing and electrical subcontractors separately or a licensed kitchen designer and a general licensed building contractor to do the whole job. If you hire subcontractors, ensure their work is coordinated. Call in a plumber before the sub-floor, insulation, sheetrocking and finishing. Then schedule the electrician's visit – pipe is bigger, heftier and less flexible than wire. Ask your plumber and electrician how much of the old walls, ceiling or floor must be removed or lifted before they can begin (unless you are gutting the kitchen or starting from scratch).

Your most expeditious move would be to make a firm decision on which appliances you are ever likely to need in your new kitchen so that installing all the supply and waste pipes, gas mains and electrical wiring can be accomplished in one economical and convenient operation.

PLUMBING

Most kitchens today require more than water pipes to the sink and dishwasher and a natural gas supply to the oven. Brief the plumber if your plans call for a food waste disposer, hot-water dispenser, water-purification system or gas grill, for example. Here are a few points about plumbing you should consider:

- Drinking-water faucets should branch directly off the rising main. A number of municipalities require that "vacuum breakers" be installed if pull-out, integrated spray faucets are used. A vacuum breaker prevents potential backflow which could contaminate the potable (fresh) water supply.
- Drains from sinks and waste-disposer units should be fitted with a trap to stop unpleasant odors coming back into the room and to provide an easily accessible

stopgap so that any blockages can be cleared from the drain-pipe.
- Lead carries a serious health hazard to both children and adults. If your house or apartment contains lead pipes, always flush the cold-water faucet for 30–60 seconds each morning or after 6 hours of non-use.
- Different areas of the country have different water. Have your water tested by a state-certified laboratory. For most diagnoses, the best filtration method is usually the simplest. If your water leaves a bad taste in your mouth or is foul smelling, a water-purification system at the point-of-use is the best antidote. A carbon filter nets sediment and combats odors. The perfect water-purification treatment provides distilled water and easily fits the cold-water tap.
- The best course of action for dealing with hard water is a whole-house water-softening system. The most labor-saving models are equipped with an automatic cycle and the only maintenance they require is occasional refilling with salt.
- Connect water-softening systems to all taps, except for a separate line to the cold-water faucet for unsoftened drinking water. Hard water generally tastes better. The sodium in softened water is not considered good for the heart by some authorities and can pose a health risk for people with high blood pressure.

NATURAL GAS

Natural gas, because of its explosive nature, is never a DIY installation. Contact a licensed plumber and have the finished installation inspected by the gas company.

ELECTRICITY

Electricity can seem complicated but, put basically, it is delivered through the house by a commonsense system of circuits from a distribution panel to a number of lights or other outlets. Quantity and location are crucial to effective use.

By sharpening your eye, you can identify the telling locations that put kitchen outlets in their most useful and architecturally pleasing location. If you are planning from scratch think about whether or not you want dimmers, two-way switches, track or recessed lighting. The challenge is to locate electrical outlets into your plan before the electrician embarks on the business of installation. Wiring is cheap and easy when the walls are just framed, difficult and more expensive after they have been sealed.

- For the kitchen, a minimum of four socket outlets should be included for portable electric appliances, such as the coffee-maker and toaster.
- Stoves and water heaters, if totally electric, are high-wattage appliances and must be connected to the service panel on entirely separate circuits.
- Electricity and water are a dangerous combination. To ensure electrical safety in the kitchen and throughout the house, a ground fault circuit interruptor (GFCI) should be installed in the circuit breaker or, if that's not possible, in outlets near water sources. GFCIs may not completely prevent a shock, but they will prevent a fatal one.

CHOOSING FUEL

The choice of fuel for home heating generally boils down to gas, oil, electric or solar. If you have an existing system, it may be worthwhile to investigate changing fuels. The cost of conversion could be offset by energy savings.

For heating, while you can't see warmth, you certainly feel its absence. Even though the kitchen heats up considerably when you are cooking, you still need an effective heating system that will see you through cold winter months.

For cooking, the choice is typically gas or electric, though neither has a clear advantage. The ideal solution is to use a rangetop or cooktop that features gas-fueled burners, and an electric oven (pages 190–195).

WHAT TYPE OF SYSTEM?

A major kitchen remodeling often necessitates modifications to the existing heating or heating-cooling system. If you are contemplating major changes, consult with a heating-and-cooling contractor.

Underfloor heating is the neatest source of heat for a kitchen. Warm water whirls through plastic tubes laid in a loop pattern. These plastic pipes can be mounted beneath existing joists, built into a plywood overlay or embedded in a concrete cap.

With underfloor heating there are no hot or cold spots, no drafts to dampen the spirit or chill the skin, and no wild swings in temperature. It's invisible, which makes it more aesthetic than most heating systems and frees up valuable space. It's also an energy-saving system, delivering more of the heat you're paying for to where you want it. It's quiet, too, since the plastic pipes don't expand and compress noisily. The temperature is thermostatically controlled so different rooms can be set to individual temperatures.

Underfloor heating is more expensive to install but it can sometimes be operated by solar energy sources. This heating system works under any flooring material, and is particularly effective under wood, vinyl or ceramic tile. It does take a day or two to heat up (and cool down) making it less suitable for weekend homes.

If the house is heated by warm-air ducts, it's simple to run a duct into the kitchen and fit a grille in a convenient spot. However, warm-air heating can have the disadvantage of stirring up dust and pollen.

Combined range/boilers run on oil, gas or solid fuel and recall old-fashioned charms. As well as heating the kitchen, many models also heat hot water and a number of radiators.

Individual gas heaters give out a fair amount of heat for their size. Set them on an outside wall so that flues can be easily routed. If gas is fueling the stove, it can be an economical heating source.

A slimline electric radiator, specifically designed for the kitchen, provides a good source of heat and also ample space for drying tea-towels and dishcloths (RIGHT).

Electric heaters are clean and easy to operate. Fit them so that they are angled to eliminate drafts of cold air. An electric rail dries dish-towels. These electric kitchen radiators are perfect for those who want to avoid the turmoil of employing a plumber but want something to turn on for instant warmth during months when the central heating is switched off.

SOLAR HEATING

In hot climates you don't necessarily need fuel as intense and muscular as gas or oil to heat water. Solar panels absorb the sun's direct and diffused energy. This solar energy is then transferred into a pumped circulating liquid, usually water mixed with anti-freeze. The quantity of hot water generated depends on the hours of sunshine. The problem is that solar heating isn't available when you need it most.

CUTTING COSTS

A simple way to reduce bills is to ensure your central heating boiler is operating at peak efficiency: make sure it's serviced once a year. A modern efficient, boiler and automatic controls, coupled with weather stripping and insulation, will significantly cut heating costs. Insulating your hot-water heater is most important; a truly thick jacket saves the cash equivalent of roughly 32 dishwasher loads a week.

Since the kitchen isn't a place for heavy, lined drapes, double glazing windows is a sensible way to reduce fuel bills. Double glazing reduces condensation and the cold zone that you get near windows. DIY double glazing may be less expensive than professionally installed glazing panes; both methods are sensible if you plan to stay in the same place for many years.

KEEPING YOUR COOL

The ideal air-conditioning system keeps you cool in summer, warm in winter, and both cleans and humidifies the air in the process. There is a wide range of air-conditioning equipment, of varying degrees of sophistication, that can achieve a temperate indoor climate. Some systems extract only part of the warm air to the outside and recirculate the rest to maintain the desired temperature. Even if you have air conditioning, it is important to fit a separate ventilation fan above the cooktop.

KITCHEN LIGHTING

Even if the kitchen is your retreat from the cares of the world, its primary purpose is hardly sedentary. While it may be a place to be at ease, it's still the work-room of the house. In a kitchen, you need general lighting to see by, focused task lighting to work by, and ambient light to dine by. Light sources in a kitchen should always be in front of you, rather than behind, to prevent your shadow coming between you and the task at hand.

The quality of light counts as much as the quantity. The colors and textures of finishes, surfaces and materials in the kitchen affect the quality of light. Pale colors reflect light and dark colors absorb it. If your penchant is for dark woods and a rich palette, compensate by allocating more lighting. Matt finishes, such as milk-glass globes or sandblasted aluminum surfaces, diffuse light. High-gloss surfaces pick up reflections causing glare and tired eyes. The best kitchen lighting design is one that doesn't require the eyes to cope with abrupt, drastic changes in the level of brightness.

All light sources emit some degree of ultraviolet light, but the amount of ultra-violet light kitchen fixtures give off is very minimal compared to daylight. Although there have been news reports linking various types of artificial lighting to skin cancer and eye disorders, solid scientific evidence to support these claims is still lacking.

Aesthetics comes into consideration here, as it does with other kitchen fittings. Light is the commodity; fixtures are the technical tool that give you the right effect. But whether you plug into sleek, avant-garde styles or tap into the more vernacular period look, all kitchen lights must suit their assigned task, be easy to clean and have easily replaceable bulbs or tubes.

Lighting can disguise the dimensions of the room. Pendent fixtures help to make ceilings appear lower. In a small kitchen, flooding a pale-colored wall with an even amount of light broadens the room.

BRIGHT LIGHTS

Whether you choose fluorescent, incandescent or halogen bulbs, each type has its own characteristics and advantages.

Fluorescent tubes –
- are efficient, using one-fifth to one-third the electricity of an incandescent lamp of the same brightness;
- have an average life of 10,000 hours or more, compared to 2,000 to 5,000 hours for halogen and between 750 and 1,000 hours for incandescent;
- come in new varieties that shed a soft, diffused light excellent for shadowless general lighting;
- are cool;
- can be dimmed only with equipment that's relatively expensive. (Recently developed gear has largely eliminated flicker.)

Compact fluorescent bulbs can be as small as 6.6in (16.5mm) long. Offering color that nearly equals incandescent and superior energy efficiency, they can easily be used in many household fixtures. Though they can't be dimmed and require a different electrical connection, they're economical and can be found in local stores.

Standard incandescent bulbs –
- have a shorter life and are more expensive than fluorescent;
- emit a fair amount of heat;
- give a warm, reddish light that is flattering and resembles natural light more closely than fluorescent tubes.

Mitigate the cost and lifespan of incandescent bulbs by putting them on dimmer switches and ritually turning the lights down when you aren't preparing food and off when you're not in the kitchen.

Natural light is the cook's ally. Cheerful and uplifting, it enables colors and textures to be judged accurately while cooking and helps to maintain a sense of openness and connection with the world outside. A horizontal window with small panes has been fitted under the gable in a sympathetic conversion (LEFT).

A kitchen in the alcove of a dining area is fitted with eyeball downlighters that can be angled to target work areas precisely. The outer wall features more decorative uplighters which provide elegant illumination when the kitchen lights are switched off and the room is used for entertaining (LEFT).

Halogen bulbs –

- emit brilliant, intense light;
- are arguably "cleaner" because they blacken less than standard incandescents;
- are smaller, so it is easier to add light to, say ceilings, without being obtrusive;
- are easy to use with dimmers;
- are excellent for accent lighting and supplementary activity lighting.

Halogen is the gas that the lamp is filled with and within which the filament burns. Its envelope is a heat-resistant quartz tube instead of glass, enabling halogen lamps to reach much higher temperatures. This makes halogen light the whitest and brightest, literally "white hot." A halogen bulb consumes about half the electricity and lasts up to seven times longer than a standard incandescent light bulb.

Halogen with dichroic filters instead of aluminum ones are a shining example of technology from the professional cook's kitchen shedding light on the home front. These halogen lights were developed for commercial use to produce less heat. In these cool customers, a dichroic coating stops infra-red light from passing beyond the bulb. Fiber optic fixtures are as yet too expensive and experimental to be plugged into most kitchens.

GENERAL LIGHTING

The kitchen has a mood, like any other room in the house. If it's open to the living or dining room, include subtle, mood lighting as well as bright lights. Don't rely on a light in the middle of the room as a single source; it will cast shadows and won't always provide sufficient light. Instead, install movable or adjustable fixtures, such as pendent lights, inset downlighters and track lighting which will "wash" walls and surfaces with light.

Recessed lights, which fit flush into the ceiling, provide directional light. The downside is that these "canned" lights are minimal on decor and can be somewhat inefficient since they cut out all side lighting. Track lights are inexpensive and flexible, though they need regular wiping to eliminate the grease and dust that accumulate. A low-wattage lamp yields diffused and even light; use several rather than a single large light as an alternative to recessed ceiling lights. If the ceiling is decorative, opt for a series of wall-mounted side lights. Ceilings can be inexpensively lit by lights hidden on the tops of wall cabinets, or with wall-mounted uplighters.

cabinets. A hanging rack positioned above a central island acts as a lighting gantry as well as a resting place for pots and pans. Clamp-on work lights are basic, considerably less costly than fully integrated fittings and achieve comparable and manageable lighting results.

Sinks need light reflected directly on to bowls and draining boards. Many manufacturers build lighting into exhaust hoods and equip stoves with interior lights.

If feasible, fit lights to the inside of storage cabinets. The best type of pantry and cabinet lights are automatic interior lights; these are operated by a simple switch that automatically turns on and off as the door opens and shuts.

LIGHT ON EATING

A change of lighting between the cooking and eating areas helps differentiate the dining space from the kitchen's work zones. Low-hanging pendent fixtures that rise and fall will adjust to the varying eye levels of a growing family. Alternatively, a cylindrical downlighter, which can be surface mounted or recessed into the ceiling, low-hanging halogen fixtures, or a traditional chandelier can provide general ambient light. Lights hovering over tables are best put on dimmers, so they can be turned up for work and turned down for a family meal, or turned off for times when a candlelit supper is the soul of a quiet evening.

SWITCHES

Installing light switches at elbow height will make it easier to flick them on and off when your hands are full. If the kitchen has more than one entrance, opt for two-way switches. Ideally, each different lighting area should have its own switch for maximum flexibility and economy. General lights should be fitted to a dimmer switch although there is no point in dimming fluorescent lights; this is a costly and unnecessary process requiring extra equipment and wiring.

Concealing the light source is often important in the kitchen where there are many hard, reflective surfaces to catch the glare. Bright, even lighting is provided by these concealed uplighters which bounce light off the ceiling and wash the wall with a soft glow. Natural light is controlled by the venetian blinds (ABOVE).

FUNCTIONAL LIGHTING

Under cabinet lighting is the most efficient way to make sure there's lots of shadowless light on counters from back to front. Mount a shallow fixture underneath each cabinet, as close to the front of the cabinet as possible so that the counter is evenly lit. You can use a twin-tube compact fluorescent bulb or a standard fluorescent channel shielded by an opaque strip on the bottom of the cabinet to subdue glare. The rule-of-thumb is to use two watts of electricity for every linear foot of counter.

Choose rise-and-fall fixtures or recessed, concealed or surface-mounted downlighters to illuminate island countertops and areas where there are no wall-mounted

Recessed downlighters create overlapping pools of light on worksurfaces, and are safe and practical without the sterility of a glaring overhead fixture (ABOVE).

No one could seriously recommend cooking by neon, but a collection of shop signs brings a touch of street life into an urban kitchen. The glass-fronted refrigerator with internal light keeps contents on view (RIGHT).

Two forms of pendent lighting distinguish between dining and cooking area. The single pendent fixture, on a dimmer switch, provides atmospheric light to eat by, while spots on a suspended track can be adjusted to a variety of positions to suit specific kitchen tasks (ABOVE).

"Metro"-style white wall tiles reflect the light concealed behind a deep eye-level shelf, providing even, comfortable illumination for a worksurface (RIGHT).

VENTILATION

Kitchens need breathing room, and kitchen ventilation systems do more than just clear the air. Cooking produces steam, grease-laden fumes and lingering smells. Heat and moisture cause condensation, which can wreak havoc with both your decor and your health. The atmosphere in the kitchen needs to be pleasant and controlled if it's to function properly.

Work out the volume of your room. This cubic measurement will be used by the supplier to calculate how much ventilation you need. Both foreign and US manufacturers label fans, hoods and exhaust systems with CFM (cubic feet per minute) measurements. In Europe, ventilation draw – how much air a fan must draw in a given time – is measured in liters per second (L/S), but requirements vary by country. Check with an appliance store.

CONDENSATION

Cooking with gas has its advantages but it requires proper ventilation to prevent indoor air-quality problems. Natural gas produces warm moisture-laden air that condenses on contact with cold surfaces. It becomes vapor that spreads throughout your home, clinging to cool walls where it turns to condensation. Vapors lead to dampness which leads to spores and microorganisms – not exactly desirable house guests. Condensation also causes wood to rot, wallpaper to peel, plaster to crumble and black mold to grow.

The best way to avoid condensation, endemic in kitchens and bathrooms, is to extract water vapor at the source and keep walls and ceilings warm. Insulating outside walls is elementary; the kitchen will be cheaper to heat and less likely to perspire.

CHOOSING THE METHOD

Exhaust fans expel smoke, steam, smells and heat outside through the roof or walls via aluminum or galvanized steel ducts or up disused chimneys. An internal fan mounted inside the hood or an external fan mounted outside the house will inhale the steam and odors from cooking. Another ventilating unit is a grill inset into a cooking surface with an internal fan that swallows smoke and fumes before they waft upwards or outwards, eventually venting them into the open air. These are popular for island cooktops. Disadvantages are noise, and the fact that downdrafts must overcome the laws of physics (hot air rises).

A less-effective type of ventilation uses a filtration system instead of ducts. Dirty air with vapors and combustion gases is refreshed then recirculated, a charcoal screen filtering out odors and grease. Ductless systems suit light-duty kitchens.

The sheer power of the blower; the length, size and directness of the duct system and the location and size of the hood or grill determine how effective your exhaust system is. Long, winding ducts are less efficient than short, straight runs.

Ventilating systems work best when fixed to an outside wall. Adequate ventilation for a stove or cooktop set on an island or peninsula requires more work. The depth of the hood determines how high above the cooking surface it should be mounted; for example, a hood 16–17in (40–42.5cm) deep should be 21in (52.5cm) off the surface. No hood should be mounted more than 30in (75cm) from the surface.

Conventional hoods are cabinet mounted and should extend 3in (75mm) past the range on each side. A pull-out visor extends the depth to extract cooking fumes and steam from the front two burners. Some are see through. Enclosed, metal canopy hoods are large and efficient. Integrated, retractable ventilating devices can be installed behind a hinged door or fascia panel to blend in with a built-in kitchen. Slim and flat telescopic hoods (about 20in/50cm deep) slide out when in use.

In older houses, the cooker is sometimes placed in the chimney recess to take advantage of the existing flue and thus make a ventilation fan unnecessary.

As a general rule, the sleeker the design the higher the price tag: this elegant exhaust hood is programed to increase the rate of ventilation automatically, according to the amount of steam and heat being produced by bubbling pans on the cooktop (LEFT).

Built into a concrete hood above the cooktop area of an island unit, this heavy-duty exhaust hood is ducted through the kitchen ceiling to an outside wall, expelling smells and heat outside (RIGHT).

WASTE DISPOSAL

Waste is an unavoidable by-product of human existence. The problem is that there is much too much of it. Even the smallest household produces a staggering abundance. How you get rid of it depends on where you live. In Germany, residents are required by law to separate garbage. In the United States, recycling mandates vary from city to city, state to state. In a high-rise building, residents are likely to rely on a combination of the chute, waste disposer, incinerator and can. Homeowners tend to use trash compactors, waste disposers and trash cans. The enlightened, with a garden or field, recycle a mound of accumulated food waste via a properly built compost heap.

FOOD WASTE DISPOSERS

An electric waste-disposal unit fitted underneath the sink waste outlet will noisily chomp food scraps, including bones, fruit pits, cardboard egg cartons and waxed food boxes. Everything is washed down with continuous cold water and converted into a fine slush that goes into the drains. Waste disposers use little electricity and are low maintenance. Check local codes allow this appliance; some high-rise condominiums and municipalities do not.

There are two basic models: with a continuous feed the machine is always open, controlled by a switch on the wall; a batch-feed is safer for small children because it can't be in operation unless the lid's in place, but it is costlier – waste goes in and a safety plug goes on which, when turned, starts and stops the grind. Waste disposers should not be used with a septic tank.

TRASH COMPACTORS

These machines reduce waste to less than one-quarter of its bulk and compress it into tidy square bundles wrapped in paper bags inside a removable container that pulls down or pulls out. Compactors come in sizes that allow them to squeeze under the countertop and take up no more room than

An arrangement of double sinks includes one bowl with a batch-feed food waste disposer: the chopping board sits above the sink and has a slice cut from it, enabling the cook to sweep vegetable trimmings and peel directly into the bowl (LEFT).

A sliding cutting board on a kitchen countertop is designed so that a plate or dish can be slipped underneath. At the end of the countertop a lidded cut-out is positioned above a trash can so that food scraps can be disposed of with a minimum of fuss (ABOVE).

a stack of drawers. Homeowners with large families or a lot of household garbage like them. Compactors are generally used to compress non-biodegradables and packaging materials such as cardboard wrapping and plastic containers.

They can play a role in recycling if filled with one category of garbage, just aluminum cans or newspapers for instance, compressing and reducing their volume.

Some environmentalists disdain them due to the length of time it takes compacted trash to decompose. They can be expensive, require special paper bags, and can contribute to kitchen smells. Their loads, while compact, tend to be extraordinarily heavy to lift. The best models are activated only when the drawer is pushed in, and come with a charcoal filter (to minimize and localize odors) and a safety lock.

COMPOSTING

Composting is a simple way of recycling kitchen (non-animal) food scraps, enriching your garden, and demonstrating an active concern for the environment. Composting does not necessarily require a lot of space. You can start a compost pile in your backyard by simply alternating layers of kitchen scraps, leaves, and grass clippings with shallow layers of soil.

RECYCLING

You can feel properly virtuous if you recycle. Many households are already required to separate waste into four broad categories – paper, biodegradables, glass and metals – and many more local authorities are considering mandatory recycling policies.

The key element to separating rubbish is having the room to do so. You need designated places to store recyclables. First, find out what the most convenient recycling mode is where you live. The waste may be collected on a designated day, or you might have to take it to a depot.

Stacks of newspapers and boxes of glass grow heavy quickly. It's wise to dump recyclables into mobile containers close to the door. Sensible and affordable storage alternatives include cupboards with adjustable shelves for non-odorous items such as glass or newspaper, or a pantry closet. Many homeowners opt for plastic bags or bins fitted with wheels and a hinged or flap-down lid, each allocated to one category of rubbish. These can be stored in the garage, back porch or yard. Costlier and harder to keep pristine are a series of hatches in the kitchen that discharge waste directly into dustbins in a vented area (basement, garage, outside); the advantage is that you have no need of indoor bins.

Separating garbage into different categories ready for recycling is environmentally responsible; this pull-out waste unit is sub-divided into smaller units for separate materials (ABOVE LEFT).

Trash compactors alleviate the storage difficulties caused by bulky materials waiting to be recycled. Trash made from the same materials is compressed into a compact form that can then be disposed of more easily (ABOVE).

Fitting

Kitchen character comes across in the choice of surfaces, finishes and fixtures with which you outfit the room. In the working kitchen there is a natural emphasis on practicality and fitness of purpose, but there is absolutely no need to be bland or strictly utilitarian – practicality doesn't have to be achieved at the expense of a pleasant working environment.

Recent years have seen an astonishing variety of materials adopted for kitchen use, each with its own stylistic stamp. The modern kitchen embraces a dynamic range of colors, patterns and textures that bring a whole new decorative dimension into play. But choice cannot be based on looks alone. Different materials deliver different advantages, and suit different applications, lifestyles and budgets. Sifting through the alternatives can be a bewildering process for the uninitiated.

The following section aims to take the hard work out of kitchen research. Presenting all the contemporary choices for flooring, walls, countertops, built-in and unfitted storage and kitchen furniture, it provides all the information you need to transform a basic shell into an attractively furnished room.

A successful contrast of old and new is achieved by combining different elements in the same basic material. The built-in storage wall and kitchen counter in pale new wood work admirably with the rustic refectory table and chairs that display equal strength of line (LEFT).

Kitchen floors need to be warm, practical and easily maintained. Stained wood in a checkerboard pattern offers an ideal solution (BELOW).

The best kitchen storage achieves the right balance between concealment and open display. Base cabinets take the clutter while an arrangement of open shelving at top level allows the expression of decorative aspects (LEFT).

The color and finish of basic surfaces serve to define and articulate kitchen areas. Brilliant scarlet makes a dashing contrast with the sea-green tiles in a playful expression of kitchen geometrics (ABOVE).

FLOORING

Before choosing a flooring color or design, choose the proper material. The ground rules are price, wear and tear, maintenance, comfort and the type of atmosphere you want to give the kitchen. Terra cotta, granite and wood acquire the lovely patina of use and age. Ceramic tile and marble are popular today, but heavier and less sound insulating than vinyl, which is easy to lay and cheaper in price.

Take into consideration the kitchen's relationship to its surrounding spaces. If there is a view into other areas with different floor coverings, do you want to separate or unite the kitchen? Wood and stone link indoors and outside. If you're remodeling a small or open kitchen, continuing the same flooring material into the kitchen will convey unity and spaciousness.

WOOD

There really is no substitute for the warmth and beauty of real wood floors. Wood is also resilient, so it gives, making it kind on your legs and kinder on things you may drop. For centuries, wood was one of the most popular flooring materials, even in kitchens. It fell out of favor for a while due to its sensitivity to moisture and staining. Now, thanks to new penetrating sealers and plastic finishes and advanced engineering techniques, wood is a viable flooring material for kitchens and very much in style. Wood flooring comes in prefinished and unfinished planks and tiles. Prefinished floors have a durable penetrating sealer applied at the factory, so the messy stain-and-sand process that can take up to three days with unfinished wood flooring is eliminated. Available in ⅜in (9mm) thick strips, they can easily be installed over existing floors without blocking door bottoms – an advantage if you're remodeling. Prefinished wood with urethane finish is recommended for kitchens. Experts caution that extra vigilence must be taken with prefinished floors to quickly wipe up spills because prefinished tiles and planks do not

1

provide a completely sealed top surface. The joints between prefinished pieces aren't sealed, whereas with unfinished floors they are once they're installed and multiple coats of urethane have been applied. Oak is the most popular wood flooring for residential use, followed by maple; other exotic woods, such as pecan, teak, kumbac, and ebony start at roughly twice the price.

CERAMIC TILE

It is little wonder that ceramic tile is a favorite flooring material for many kitchen designers and homeowners. Made from clays, porcelain, shales, or baked earth, ceramic tile is a long-lasting, versatile material that offers many design possibilities. It resists water, heat, and most household chemicals, and it is easy to clean and never needs waxing. But it reflects sound and is therefore noisy. It is also harder on the feet and ankles than softer materials. If you drop a plate on a tile floor there's a good chance it's going to break.

There are three common tile types for kitchen floors: glazed, quarry and ceramic mosaic. Glazed tiles have a glass-like surface which may be glossy, matte or textured. There are also tiles with slip-

2

3

1 Terrazzo tiles in various
   shades
2 Chestnut floorboards
3 Brick paviors
4 Manufactured terra cotta
   tiles
5 Hand-made terra cotta
   tiles
6 Ceramic tiles
7 Marble slab
8 Flagstone (with floorboards
   in the adjacent room)

4

5

6

resistant glazes and extra-duty glazes for heavy traffic areas. Quarry tiles are unglazed tiles which maintain their natural clay color throughout the body of the tile. As they age, unglazed tiles develop a rich patina which glows with a quiet fire. But within this broad category of tile, which includes Mexican tiles, there are wide variations in quality. Some are very soft and irregular in shape; others must be stained and sealed because they are so porous. What distinguishes ceramic mosaic tile from other tile is its small size, which ranges from less than 6 sq. in (2.45×2.45in if square shape) to the newest 12 inch sq.

7

8

1

2

3

4

5

MARBLE

Cool, elegant and expensive, marble is in demand today for kitchen floors. It comes in slabs or tiles, including a stunning selection of inlaid tiles. Marble is graded A, B, C, or D based on its fragility; A and B marbles are the most solid, C and D marbles are the more delicate, but also the more colorful, decorative and costly. The drawback of marble is that it is soft and porous. This means it scratches and stains easily. Marble must be sealed when it is first installed with at least two coats of a penetrating sealer, and frequently re-sealed. Unless it has an etched, honed or pummeled finish, making it slip-resistant, marble is slippery when wet.

GRANITE

Granite's popularity as a kitchen flooring (and countertop material) is growing steadily, as more and more people with the means to afford it discover its virtues. In the same price range as marble but much less prone to staining and scratching, granite combines a sense of lasting beauty with high durability. For ease of laying, granite is now available in thin tiles. It comes in 50 different colors. Although a matte finish is skid-resistant, polished surfaces show off the stone's color.

TERRAZZO

This smooth aggregate of marble chips and concrete is durable and requires little up-keep. It is available in field and decorative border tiles in dazzling patterns and colors.

MASONRY

Stone split into thin slabs, generally known as "flagstone," makes an attractive kitchen floor. The most common types are blue-stone and slate. Both are heavy and may require extra support. Installation must be done by a stonemason. Brick floors can also be striking, particularly when laid in unusual patterns.

VINYL

Vinyl is having a renaissance. No longer the drab and brittle material found on kitchen floors years ago, vinyl is available in bright, crisp colors and more interesting patterns, including ones that closely mimic the look and texture of flagstone, granite, wood, marble, and ceramic tile. These factors, coupled with vinyl's durability and affordability, have made vinyl a popular choice.

Vinyl has been dubbed "resilient floor-ing" because it cushions your feet and has good traction. It is manufactured in two basic types: sheets – some wide enough to fit seamfree – and tiles. All vinyl is

6

7

8

9

susceptible in varying degrees to denting and scratching. That's why it's important to shop carefully for vinyl that matches your needs. Generally, the thicker the vinyl the more durable the floor. "Inlaid" sheet vinyl refers to vinyl that has the pattern extending throughout the entire wear layer. It is generally more durable than "rotogravure" vinyl, which has the pattern printed on it. Cushioned sheet vinyl is extremely comfortable underfoot and has good sound-absorbing quality, but can be cut by sharp objects. Some types of sheet vinyl can be laid over existing floors. Vinyl tiles are the perfect DIY project, and there are now some sheet vinyls marketed specifically as a DIY installation.

1 Slate tiles
2 Terrazzo tiles
3 Granite tiles
4 Linoleum
5 Mosaic
6 Vinyl tiles
7 Cork tiles
8 Rubber sheeting
9 Concrete

CORK

Warm, comfortable, lightweight and quiet underfoot, a cork floor's patina can improve with use. Its palette is narrow, limited to natural colors. Made from natural cork, compressed with binders and baked, it is easy to fit (with glue) but needs sealing to prevent wear and staining.

RUBBER

If you're after a synthetic, space-age look, rubber comes in wetsuit finishes, primary and pastel colors, and in industrial studded sheets or tiles. More expensive than vinyl sheeting, it can be glued to any sound, dry floor and only requires a metal edging or cap for protection at the edges.

CONCRETE

A centuries-old mixture of cement powder, sand and water, concrete is affordable, sensitive to site and climate. It has an austere quality in slab form, much less so as tiles, or when waxed or stained. Concrete floors can be economical for new homes, kitchen additions, or kitchens requiring new screed, although special finishes can make it very expensive. Concrete is susceptible to chipping and cracking and must be sealed against oil and food stains.

WALLS

1

Color and texture can turn both walls and backsplashes into the perfect kitchen background. However, kitchen walls do predominantly suit white. White forgives battered old surfaces and has an inherent illusion of cleanliness. But design options are infinite, most relying on taste and architecture. If the kitchen is all light toned, one wall might be set apart with a deep color to give you a sense of traveling between worlds in an otherwise small space. In a tiny or oddly shaped kitchen, consider pulling the space around you like a

cloak with a dark color. Pale wall finishes reflect light and make you less aware of the kitchen's confines. When in doubt, you can always give the whole room a once-over with white paint and live with it until you develop a comfortable design scheme.

The backsplash is the wall area between the base units and the upper cabinets. For backdrops to the stove or cooktop, you are best served by heat-resistant surfaces, such as ceramic tile, metal or stone. Recesses can be cut into backsplashes to accommodate small appliances or extra storage.

PAINT

The power of paint is its immediacy and color. It is cheap and can always change. Mixing paint enables you to have any colour you've seen and loved, from the yellow brown of thatched roofs to Shaker blue.

Latex and oil-based paints come in five finishes from dull to shiny: flat, eggshell, satin, semi-gloss, high-gloss. Modern additives speed drying, reduce mildewing and improve the surface appearance. Eggshell and gloss finishes come in both oil-based and latex forms; in general, oil-based paints

2

3

4

5

6

1 Paint (and breeze block)
2 Paint
3 Hand-painted mural
4 Paint, stencils and gold
  leaf
5 Granite tiles
6 Stainless steel

are more washable. Gloss and semi-gloss are recommended for steamed-up kitchen walls and high-usage doors and trim. Latex is the least durable, but has the advantage of easy clean-up for painters. Eggshell and flat finishes hide blemishes, whereas high-gloss paint makes the most of flawless walls by refracting light and energizing the room. A white pickling stain can bring a warm white-wash look to bare wood.

Proper preparation can add years to your paint job. Make sure walls are cleaned and sanded, and uneven surfaces patched before they are primed and lightly sanded prior to the final coat. Professional decorators recommend sanding between coats.

WALLPAPER

Vinyl wallpaper is the most durable type of wall covering currently available. However, its finished appearance can only be as good as the walls under it. A transparent plastic coating on washable wallpapers makes them water resistant. Not as hard-wearing as vinyl, they have a pleasanter matte surface.

Technology has brought increased sophistication to printing, and wallpapers now match textiles in scope of patterns. Before ordering, it's wise to bring samples home to view in your kitchen's light.

PANELING

Not the least of paneling's appeal in a kitchen is that it rarely if ever needs painting, it's easy to clean, and it's dirt-resistant. The types of paneling best suited for kitchen use are: wood (prefinished and unfinished), particleboard (available in a wide

1 Painted tongue-and-groove
2 & 3 Slate tiles
4 & 5 Ceramic tiles
6 Ceramic tiles with detail insets
7 Handmade ceramic tiles with mosaic
8 Broken-tile mosaic

1

2

3

4

variety of surface finishes), hardboard (with plastic laminate, lacquer, and baked-on finishes), and other kinds of wallboard (with many different finishes). Prefinished hardboard comes in a variety of wood grains and is treated to be stain-resistant; solid wood paneling needs to be sealed and finished.

CERAMIC TILE

With tiled walls and backsplashes, there are rich possibilities in size, hue and finish in incarnations including glazed and unglazed porcelain, vitreous glass, terra cotta and clay, not to mention antique tile salvaged from old houses and one-of-a-kind handcrafted pieces. Tile is manufactured in batches and can be subject to wide color variations; buy extra to use as replacements later. Grout joints are subject to dirt accumulation though new mildew- and stain-resistant grouts are available. Unglazed tiles such as terra cotta must be sealed. Handmade tile is uneven and looks best if grout joints are not too tight. Since tiles can last for generations, you may want to choose neutral hues for large walls. Neutral colors can be easily coordinated with appliances and accents, and you aren't liable to tire of them as quickly. To add interest, use colors and decorative designs in smaller areas.

5

6

7

8

COUNTERTOPS

1

A kitchen countertop sees a lot of living. Necessity demands a countertop that cleans easily and wears well, and the best can take the heat of pots and pans, wipe clean with soapy water, withstand the abrasive effects of scouring, resist the cutting edge of a sharp knife and not absorb the stains from food, vinegar and steel pans.

Sadly, there is no ideal, all-purpose material. While wood, laminate, or Corian and its ilk are more easily cut and spliced to accommodate sinks and cooktops, you'll find that it's granite, ceramic tile and stainless steel that make especially good accompaniments to both cooktops and stoves.

Materials that show wear and do it in beautiful ways (like butcher block, soapstone, stainless steel and zinc) have an appetizing quality. Some people prefer their scratched and stained surfaces to, say, granite, which will have changed little in ten years' time.

COMBINING MATERIALS

Connoisseurs match their kitchen countertops to different materials according to the intended purpose: for example, a butcher block chopping board, an area of smooth marble for rolling pastry, and water-resistant steel or laminate surrounding the sink.

If you want and can afford to vary height and materials, limit the surface of a specific self-contained work area to one material and one level. Loose cutting boards – of wood or marble, for example – move items from one place to another and wash easily. By contrast, cutting boards, marble slabs, etc. that are mounted on countertops are less versatile and, like drainage grooves cut into the countertops, might become annoying obstacles if you are rolling out dough or setting out plates. Keep the working surface between the stove and the sink at the same height; it's safe and pragmatic. Careful planning is required.

2

3

1 Terrazzo island and
  stainless steel counter
2 End-grain butcher block
3 New maple
4 Marble slab
5 Genoa marble tiles

WOOD

Wood is a living material, and as such it matures; the conditions in which it lives determine whether it ages gracefully or turns to expensive firewood. Dry air may make a wood countertop contract. If not properly treated, water and other fluids will then seep through causing warping. To avoid excessive shrinkage it is important to keep wood inside for a few months so it shrinks before being cut and installed.

Wood countertops are best when top and bottom are protected by a coat of lacquer or linseed oil-based sealant. Constant wear from hot and cold water and other fluids eventually breaks down lacquer, which should be reapplied annually. Oiled wood tends to improve with age (it's matte to start with) and is more resistant to heat rings from pots and mugs than lacquer. Don't allow wet metalic kitchen implements to linger; they leave rust spots.

Butcher block turns the preparation area into one long chopping block. Wood cut across the grain ensures the chopping block will wear evenly and also discourages warping. Butcher block is usually made from end-grain maple, a dense, strong wood that won't flavor foods.

For sink countertops, consider durable, farmed rainforest timbers, accustomed to

getting wet. Make sure they're certified as harvested in ways not detrimental to forest ecosystems. Durability is determined by the chemical content, as well as the density, of wood. For example, ash and sycamore are tough woods capable of sustaining great weights, yet they can decay through daily dousing or a burst pipe. Oak is also unsuitable around sinks, since tannins, which stain, run out when the wood comes into contact with water. The most familiar durable wood is teak; it's water-repellent and ideal because it scarcely expands and contracts with moisture.

Avoid endangered woods. Contact the Rainforest Alliance (see page 218): this association identifies and certifies companies that produce and sell tropical hardwoods using ecologically sound techniques.

MARBLE

Old World richness is evoked by marble. Cold and hard, it is ideal for pastry-making. But marble also wears; sugar, alcohol and lemon juice stain it. You can maximize its use by honing the surface, choosing darker colors (which hide stains better) and using at least two coats of sealant. Simpler and less expensive than a complete work surface made from marble is to have a block of marble inset into the countertop.

4

5

1

1 Granite
2 Slate tile
3 & 4 Ceramic tile
5 Terrazzo
6 Glass mosaic tile
7 Corian

3

2

GRANITE

The polished, stony good looks of granite have made it fashionable and its functional properties – inert to food acids and flame, immune to stains, spills and marks – maintain its popularity in up-scale kitchens. Cutting on granite will deaden the blade of your knife long before the granite loses its sheen. On the down side, granite is icy-looking, among the more expensive countertop materials, it is often noticeably seamed with concrete, and it is heavy. Base cabinets may have to be reinforced to take the weight. Flecked granite is less expensive and is a neutral foil for food.

SLATE

This is a dense, basically nonporous stone available in black and subtle shades of blue, green, gray, purple and red. It is hardwearing, precision cuts easily, handles hot pots, and wipes clean with a damp cloth. Less expensive than marble and granite, slate is also worthy of attention because it is waterproof, although it can water spot. Surface scratches and stains erase with sandpaper. Choose natural (cleft) or smooth (honed) finishes for countertops; they'll give you a clean, smooth surface for food preparation. Slate holds up well untreated or it can be polished with a protective coating of vegetable oil or olive oil (which slightly changes its appearance).

TILE AND MOSAIC

Ceramic tile has an unstuffy charm, is easy to care for, and works well on kitchen countertops. Choose acid-resistant porcelain or glazed ceramic tile with a textured or matte finish, and buy grout in a color to blend with the tile. Before you buy any tiles, be sure to check the manufacturer's recommendations for countertop use. Quarry tile may be more absorbent than porcelain or ceramic tile, making it subject to grease stains. Tiles are fireproof, durable, moisture resistant, stain resistant, and will not blister, burn, stain or discolor. Tile has excellent abrasion resistance; grout is fair unless it's been sealed.

Tile can withstand the heat of a stove or a pan of hot water, but not the thermal shock of a very hot pan of fat. Water rolls off tile, but can loosen grout, and as the grout wears, tiles will lift. Surfaces must be flat or tiles will crack. Buy extras so replacements are from the same dye lot.

Tiling a countertop with wider grout joints makes installation and cleaning easier. New acrylic latex additives have improved grout, and are more resistant to cracking, loosening and staining. Use a waterproofing grout sealant every six months, and use a toothbrush to remove the stains that form in crevices. Seal quarry tile with a penetrating oil after it has been laid to build up its immunity to stains.

Special nosing tiles can be fitted along the front of a countertop, while special trim tiles used at the back edge will meet the wall neatly. Accent, trim, handpainted and decorative tiles make design choices limitless. Tiles and mosaics can be bedded into concrete, or stuck directly to a base board and grouted in. Use an insert-type sink with a good sealed rim clamped over the tiles, or overlap the sink's edges with curved tiles to prevent seepage.

4

5

TERRAZZO

This is a mixture of marble chips set in concrete and can be pre-cast to form a countertop. It is hardwearing, waterproof and esthetically rich. Terrazzo is available in decorative tiles that, like laminates, needs a plywood girdle for support. Countertops made from terrazzo are fairly heavy and sinks should be fixed to the underside of a terrazzo slab.

SOLID SURFACES

These special kitchen materials are made up of mineral fillers combined with polyesters or acrylics and they have a smooth, opaque quality. Du Pont, Corian, Avonite and Durcon are supremely practical. They are nonporous, renewable – since they're solid, blemishes, burns and scratches are easily sanded out – and as malleable to cut, shape and carve as wood.

Chief among their merits is that, when properly fabricated, the seams between pieces are barely visible. Design options for most of them are diverse: they can be inlaid with alternating colors of the same material or with steel rods (for a built-in pot rest) and can also be molded into integral sinks and countertops that flow together. Kitchen suppliers use them to fashion breakfast bars, draining boards, windowsills,

6

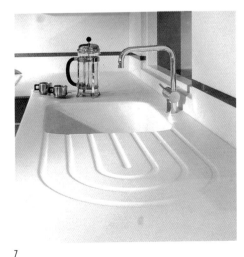

light fixtures and wine racks. All of them are extremely resistant to unsightly permanent marks, and actually find household abrasives refreshing. Even nail varnish wipes off quite easily.

The disadvantages are that they look artificial and somewhat pedestrian and are heavy, expensive and must be installed by certified or approved fabricators to align seams perfectly: they are definitely not a DIY job. However, Avonite poses the least problem of them in terms of weight, and unlike either timber or stone (countertops from which must be pre-cut to specification), it can be milled at the job site.

7

1

LAMINATE

Laminated countertops comprise a thin, plastic laminate bonded to chipboard, plywood or medium-density fiberboard (MDF) which gives it great stability. Economical, easy to clean and cut, laminate comes in thousands of colors and patterns that are continually growing. Laminates are not surface materials you'd be afraid to put a glass on or let children spread their own gooey sandwiches on. Simple washing-up liquid erases fingerprints and grease. Laminated countertops can withstand a certain amount of heat, knocks and scratches – if not used as a chopping board. New plastics are easily contoured over rounded edges, and can be installed flush to the wall and sinks. Laminates can come unglued at the corners and peel at the seams if surface moisture seeps through joints.

CONCRETE

Mixed with additives, concrete is less susceptible to chipping and cracking than the cement that's mixed in trucks and poured on pavements. Concrete can and should be sealed to be impervious to oil, food stains and water. Concrete countertops can be measured, then crated and shipped or poured into forms on site. It takes 28 days of curing for concrete to be truly hard.

2

3

4

5

6

7

RUBBER

Naturally tough and waterproof, rubber countertops, like tires, can take a pounding and are less likely to suffer a burn mark than butcher block. Smooth rubber flooring material comes in a roll and is available in a variety of hues. Rubber is glued to a plywood or particleboard base. It needs a hard edge, like chrome or wood, or can be wrapped around a curved edge.

STAINLESS STEEL

Domestic stainless steel brings its industrial strength to the kitchen countertop. Stainless steel can be matte, polished, patterned or sandblasted. Commonly used for sinks and draining boards, it is also available in sheets which form a whole counter, including sink, drainer, countertop and cutout for a cooktop. Opt for good-quality stainless: it wears well, handles heat with aplomb and is exceptionally hygienic.

Stunning when new, it is hard to keep stainless steel shiny and unmarked. Watermarks, scuffs and fingerprints recur. Use a fine abrasive cleaner, rub in the direction of the grain, and use only cold water to wipe and rinse; hot water evaporates and leaves spots. Steel is an inherently noisy surface but insulation board glued to the undersides of countertops should significantly reduce noise. Stainless steel scratches (though there's no corrosion of the material, and minor nicks blend over time) and becomes pitted if left in contact with bleach (remember washing liquids etc. contain chlorides). Don't leave carbon steel objects, such as kitchen whisks and knives, standing on its surface for long periods: they will rust and mar your countertop's beauty.

ZINC

Roofing zinc is available in thin sheet form and can be glued to a base of particleboard or MDF. The zinc is then wrapped around the front edge of the board and the joins should be soldered. Zinc scratches and stains, but this adds to its charm.

8

1, 2, 3 & 4 Laminate
5 Durcon
6 Syndecrete (pre-cast lightweight concrete)
7 Zinc
8 Polished steel

CABINETS AND UNITS

Some 300 years ago a "china cabinet" might have been nothing more than a few small shelves covered with oilcloth and fixed to the wall with brackets. Now, we've grown accustomed to boxing things in and to organizing and hiding kitchen chaos behind closed doors.

In a built-in kitchen, cabinet units are permanently fixed, planned to fit the room's dimensions. An unfitted kitchen, with some or all of the cabinets designed to resemble furniture, can be an antidote for those tired of the controlled, rectilinear run of cabinets with little variation.

Built-in kitchens use three basic units: base, tall and wall, plus those for special purposes such as a swing-out pantry rack. Unfitted kitchens use these as a starting point, looking back to sideboards and hutches for form.

For either look you can use stock units, mass-produced in a factory, or custom cabinets, hand-built for a particular kitchen. Stock kitchen units are less expensive, readily available, and offer consistency of quality from large, reputable manufacturers. However, stock cabinet makers tend to stick to more saleable sizes and features, finishes and colors. You'll find stock cabinets in oak, maple, ash and a few other species, and melamines and laminates in popular colors. Generally speaking, you will get your best value for money with stock cabinets. If you aren't keen on choosing products from catalogs, think about buying stock units and commissioning doors from either a carpenter or kitchen company to avail yourself of less common woods or of a broader selection of the laminated finishes now available.

An advantage with custom-built cabinets is that you are not limited by precedent. Custom-made units more precisely accommodate the individuality of you and your kitchen. Countertops can be lower or higher than average, even adjustable. Wall cabinets can reach new heights, built to the proportions of the room or to accommodate

prized china. Difficult spaces can be designed for a special purpose, a towel rail fitting or pull-out bread box. Custom-built kitchens maximize usable storage space and make it easier to tuck in appliances.

Certified kitchen designers plan and specify, and may sometimes order and supply, your kitchen and can work with the manufacturer you select. A designer working with a building contractor/installer can do remarkable things to create more interesting cabinet systems and fittings than may be available from the advertised line.

CONSTRUCTION

The importance of the material behind closed doors is a question of stability, preference and cost, coupled with ulterior motives to make a kitchen healthy, natural and of long-term value. Most kitchen units consist of a basic cabinet box and shelves, or a box on adjustable feet or wall brackets, made of flat sheet materials. Particleboard followed by plywood are the most widely used core materials for cabinets today. The finest type of particleboard is medium-density fiberboard (MDF). Cabinets mounted on adjustable legs make leveling the cabinet simple. Once level, toe-kick molding can be installed to conceal the legs, or the legs can be incorporated into the kitchen design.

Cabinets put on one of two faces, either framed or frameless. With face-frame cabinets, a rectangular frame outlines the cabinet box, strengthening it and providing a mount for overlaid cabinet doors. Face-frame cabinets engender the spatial awareness and look of furniture. With a frameless cabinet, the door fits flush with the cabinet box. Frameless cabinets have a modern look and are easy to hang and clean. When choosing door styles, simplicity and price usually go hand in hand. Careful selection is important not only from a design point of view – cabinets can set the tone for the whole kitchen – but also because your choice must be durable.

1

2

3

4

1 White oak
2 Marine plywood counter
 with stainless steel
 countertop
3 Poplar
4 Laminated particleboard
5 Painted wood

5

NATURAL WOOD

Since wood expands and contracts with fluctuations in temperature and humidity, solid wood cabinets must be constructed to compensate for this. You will need kiln-dried timber or boards that have been acclimatized over a period of months to indoor living, otherwise cabinets will warp regardless of species. Wood doors are either built from narrow strips of wood glued together or from four pieces of wood used for the door frame with a center panel that "floats" within the frame enabling it to withstand temperature and humidity changes much better.

1

2

3

1 Baltic pine with wire mesh panels
2 Beech
3 Exterior-grade plywood
4 MDF sprayed with Hammerite
5 Polished steel
6 Stainless steel

4

5

6

Staining woods is very popular today. Stains are used to bring out the ornamental quality of the grain and to emphasize the color of the wood. They are also employed as a way of creating different higher-priced looks more economically using less expensive grades of lumber. For example, a white-wash stain wiped over oak gives it a subtle pink tone. Wiping a cherry stain on oak doors is a common way of creating the prized, reddish look of cherry. Among the other commonly used stain colors are oak, maple, mahogany, and walnut. Stains are not ordinarily used on veneers or richly colored woods, such as cherry, teak, or walnut. Keep in mind that because stains are not finish coats, finishing coats have to be applied over them.

Applying pure linseed oil with an equal mixture of turpentine to freshly sanded and smoothed wood is a way of enhancing the natural color of wood. Colors produced in this way range from shades of yellow to reddish-brown. Light-colored woods that lend themselves to finishing in their natural color or staining include: beech, birch, elm, oak, maple, chestnut, and Phillipine mahogany. Nothing more than a clear finish should be used on such naturally beautiful woods as butternut, cherry, rosewood, teak and walnut.

The one general caveat about natural wood cabinets is that variations in color are not uncommon due to different porosity levels and other natural characteristics of wood. If you are after wood cabinets that are consistently colored throughout, you are better off with "wood-like" man-made substitutes.

VENEERS

A veneer is a thin slice of wood adhered to a structural core of warp-resistant plywood, particleboard or medium-density fiberboard (MDF). MDF gives it great stability, and when veneer is made by peeling thin layers of wood from a single log, cabinet doors have a uniformity. In high-quality laminated wood veneers, the grain, tone and color are consistent. Using veneer panels is an inexpensive way to incorporate wood in the kitchen, especially species with limited availability.

Veneers increase design flexibility: they can be finessed into S-shaped and curved cabinets, whereas it is very difficult to build curved cabinets from solid wood. Inlaid veneers are distinctive.

STEEL

No longer relegated to laboratories and industry, steel – polished, oxidized, sand-blasted, brushed or imprinted – brings industrial strength to kitchen cabinets. The results are simple, structural and stream-lined. High-grade stainless steel kitchens are not only durable, but offer mainten-ance-free service. Steel has a unique qua-lity of light and a clean, reflective surface that evokes the precision of surgical instruments.

GLASS

Transparency gives a sense of depth to the room, especially in confined surroundings. Clear glass mounted on the front of cabi-nets allows the cook to survey the contents of each cabinet at a glance. Sandblasted, frosted and etched glass all capture the play of light from bulbs and windows while hiding clutter behind a veil of misty trans-lucence. Ribbed-glass panels provide a sense of movement; dishes seem to undu-late behind the cabinet doors as you move across the kitchen. Panes of glass in grid-work patterns and opaque, stained and opalescent glass help overcome the mono-tony of machine-made appliances that can all-too-easily dominate. Translucent glass romanticizes cabinet contents, since scar-cely all you see are shadows. Always use toughened glass in interiors to reduce the risks of breakage and accidents.

1 Painted custom
   cabinets
2 Laminate
3 Painted tongue-and-groove
4 Stained wood
5 Paint
6 Painted tongue-and-groove

1

2

3

4

5

6

LAMINATE

The use of laminate panels, particularly with European-style cabinets, has become very popular. Laminate is an easy, cheap, often colorful cabinet solution. Laminated surfaces clean easily but quickly smudge when touched, which means they need cleaning more often. Keys, knives and daily use can scratch the surface, but most high-pressure laminates have superior scuff and wear resistance. Cover the front and back of doors with laminate for strength and to prevent twisting and warping. Laminates are available in a wide range of patterns, colors, thicknesses, performance characteristics and prices. White looks clean, gives a room depth and intrigue, and color on walls and in foods looks fresh against it.

PAINT

Kitchen cabinets in the nineteenth century came with a few coats of paint. Painting MDF or wood cabinets today adds charm and constitutes a marvelous naive evocation of that earlier time. Lacquered cabinets, in which a high-gloss transparent finish is sprayed over a color undercoat, are sleek and give a reflective surface.

Paint must be able to hold its own against moisture and grease. For a durable finish stick to good-quality paints. Oil-based paints are messier and harder to handle than latex paints, which must be carefully applied so brushstrokes and roller dimples don't show.

MAKING THE MOST OF YOUR CABINETS

- Always buy good-quality units; they justify the investment. Two or three overhead units and a bank of base cabinets can be supplemented with additional wall units and a pantry later.
- Keep units simple. Nearly every stock base unit comes with one drawer at the top, leaving you with too many scattered, unsightly and inefficient drawers. Order cabinets without them and put four or five drawers in one base cabinet. It's less costly and more convenient if all the drawers are stacked together.
- Use second-hand items: convert a sideboard or large, strong table into a sink unit; adapt a chest of drawers for a hutch base with shelves above it; form a pantry or larder from a room or screen door. Blend architectural salvage remnants – corbels, banister rails, tiles – with new wood for islands and cabinets.
- Reface existing cabinets for maximum effect and minimum cost. Strip, sand and restain. If your imagination is less restricted than your budget, painting or stenciling them yields quick and easy results. Painting over laminated cabinets is easy if you first sand and prime the surface with a bonding agent, then brush or roll on acrylic paint. High-gloss oil-based paint makes for a tough, reflective cabinet surface.
- Consider the merits of open shelving in lieu of wall cabinets.
- Combine design and function with economy by scavenging for utilitarian materials: look out for things in flea markets, junk shops and small industrial plants. For example, cabinets have a fresh face in translucent fiberglass typically employed for factory skylights; set in an aluminum frame or used as insets with wood frames, fiberglass is strong, won't warp in humidity, cleans easily and poetically diffuses the interiors of cabinets. Rustproof metal cabinets from hospitals and dentists' offices can be adapted by insulating them with wood to deaden sound.
- Stain and seal basic stock particleboard cabinets: the texture is quite interesting.
- Laminated doors come in standard sizes. Don't feel obliged to stay with the ones that come with your units: you might find good second-hand replacements.
- Cheer up dull cabinets with pulls and door knobs – old spoons and forks used as handles look unusual but fitting.

STORAGE

Pots and pans for everyday use hang from a rail, so the cook can quickly and easily find the right equipment. Heavier items such as the casserole are kept on open shelves beneath the countertop, adhering to the same principle of easy access (ABOVE).

Storage can marry utility with decorative display. The tiled walls, old-fashioned refrigerator and marble-topped table all recall the charms of a dairy, and details such as the drying herbs and pottery storage jars further enhance this impression. But the items on view not only look good – they also serve the primary functions for which they're intended (ABOVE RIGHT).

In a kitchen, storage is fundamental. Making every inch count is less hindered by a lack of space than by lack of good design. And no matter how big the kitchen, you can never have enough storage space. Whether for displaying wares, hiding clutter or just storing "stuff," producers of stock, semi-custom and custom cabinets are finding more ways to inject storage into the kitchen. Pull-out trash cans or recycling centers, swing-up shelves, aluminum-lined bread boxes and retractable towel racks are a taste of available options.

In order to organize storage successfully, you have to be ruthless. Decide what you want readily visible as opposed to readily accessible, then assemble storage so that equipment and accessories reside where they are most needed. Only objects used every day, or at least once a week, deserve prime storage space – within easy reach, somewhere between knee and eye level. Even undecided minimalists stash things used once a year, such as party platters, in the back of low cabinets.

Logically, pots and pans should be stored near the stove or cooktop with their lids off so that air can circulate, and in a position

where dust won't collect inside. They are best in slatted drawers or hanging upside down from a hook by the handle.

You'll bend and hunt less if herbs and spices, rice, pasta, sugar and essential condiments are given permanent resting places close to the food-preparation area (spices become unseasonably bland when stored too near heat). Avoid the pitfall of keeping things you use once every couple of months in a key space. Finding a home for old plastic or paper shopping bags close to the trash can enables them to be recycled as trash can liners. Everyday dishes can be stored on plate racks above the sink or in cabinets one or two steps from the dishwasher. Don't store bulky and heavy items, such as bags of dog food too high up, too low down, or at the back of cabinets.

CLEVER OPTIONS

Often the best hoarding devices owe more to cleverness than finance. The leftover narrow space under base cabinets turns as easily into drawers for flat storage of linen, placemats and baking pans as it does into decorative plinth panels. Stock cabinets sometimes leave an odd vertical space. Ask

Successful storage is about having what you need on hand. A magnetic knife holder is screwed to the wall above the countertop; shallow shelves allow flexible organization of easily located pots, pans, dishes and ingredients (TOP).

your carpenter to fit it so that it's perfect for squeezing in cookie sheets, cutting boards and trays. Spare bits of wall that are too small for conventional cabinets can be used for peg boards for utensils, a messageboard for writing *ad hoc* memos, or a pinboard for recipes, take-out menus or bills.

Try to avoid corner cabinets. When they suit the design or fill a hole, opt for plain shelves behind an angled door. Lazy-Susan rotating shelves use only half the allocated space and break down. Better to put unloved wedding gifts in the back and useful items in front; better still, get rid of the wedding gifts!

SHELVES

These can be used to hold collections in rows; they can span the length of the kitchen as a visible catch-all for dishes and cookware, at picture height like traditional pot shelves; or they can blend into the room by filling in unused areas.

Cabinet shelves, like drawers, can be put on runners, which turn them into giant pull-out trays. Shelves on runners make it unnecessary to stoop: even relics at the back can be brought to the fore without it

being necessary to get down on your hands and knees.

Melamine shelves come pre-finished and clean easily. Wooden shelves look terrific, but must be sealed; painted wood may chip and need repainting. Glass shelves add depth and reflect, but are difficult to keep clean. Metal-grid shelves encourage circulation, offer less surface for dust and dirt to gather, and allow things to dry off. Despite water spotting and a high price tag, professionals opt for stainless steel's tough character and hygienic surface.

Pull-out and swing-up shelves neatly store appliances out of sight. If planned in advance, outlets can be inset into the rear of low wall cabinets so appliances are always plugged in. These fittings take up entire cabinets and so are best suited to larger kitchens where space is not at a premium. Utility or broom cabinets consist of one tall space for mops and vacuum cleaners, with cleaning supplies housed on specially abbreviated shelves.

Shelves must be firmly secured to the wall studs. Attaching them to fiberboard walls is risky, especially for those shelves that will be bearing heavy loads.

A number of storage options allow you to prioritize what you keep where. Glass-fronted wall cabinets hold decorative dishes for display, with more utilitarian objects stashed away behind closed doors; a hanging rail above the range and small shelves beneath the run of countertops keep pots and pans and ingredients on view close by (ABOVE).

Plate racks above a double sink perform two tasks in one, providing a place for washing up to drain and practical storage for everyday dishes (ABOVE).

Glass-fronted wall cabinets keep china and glasses free from dust whilst still on view, with cookbooks and condiments neatly ranged on shelves. Bulkier items can be stored in base cabinets, while the peninsular counter allows the countertop along the wall to hold items such as the coffee-maker (LEFT).

Pull-out wicker drawers with easy-grip handles provide practical storage for fresh produce (BELOW LEFT).

Fitting undercounter storage with casters increases flexibility. A chest of drawers can be pulled out to form an additional countertop at a lower height; the stainless steel trolley holds pots and pans, but could be used to serve food (BELOW CENTER).

Slide-out shelves afford easy access to items stashed away at the back of a deep cabinet (BELOW RIGHT).

DRAWERS

Drawer runners vastly improve the quality of life. The best drawers can glide shut with a push from your hip (useful when both hands are full) and close silently. The most expensive are made of wood with dovetailed joints and slide on waxed wooden runners. High-quality drawers have a solid compartment with a decorated front and runners that extend the entire length of the drawer to provide stability. Glue and staples, and runners that go only a part of the way back in the drawer are signs of lower-quality construction. Drawers with two runners on ball-bearing rollers are smoother, quieter and less likely to break or jam than those with single runners.

PANTRIES

A pantry or larder is an indispensable housekeeper, a curator that allows you instantly to know the location, often obscure and sometimes arbitrary, of each of its exhibits. Nothing is as cost effective as this singular old breed of storage – no more overcrowding, no more guesswork to visualize stock. A true pantry or larder is usually a walk-in room or closet with shelves where canned goods or other provisions, or china, serving pieces, small appliances, etc. are kept. Today, with all the ready-made shelv-

ing and organizers available, it is cheap to convert a closet or small room near the kitchen to a pantry. Depending on its size it can double as a laundry, sports equipment storage, or a place for recycling containers. It can be vented to the outside for air circulation or maintained at temperatures lower than the kitchen for wine, say.

A popular supplement or alternative to the old-fashioned, walk-in pantry are today's pantry cabinets, located within easy reach of the refrigerator/storage area. These units range from the ready-made, deluxe "Chef's pantry" cabinets – tall cabinets, 36in (900mm) wide and 84–96in (2130–2500mm) tall, replete with vertical swing-out units and interior lights – to more modest pantry wall cabinets with slide-out canned goods and spice shelf units accessible from both sides.

If you're planning on designing your own pantry cabinet, it should be 24in (600mm) deep. Before beginning, investigate the choices. If you like pantries, buy one or get its measurements so that you can incorporate it into your design. If you decide that you want pantry door shelves, be sure to use piano hinges along the entire length of the door to support the weight. A cabinet 48in (1200mm) wide or more will also need center supports.

Air-tight storage for food such as garlic and loose tea is cunningly organized in small pull-out compartments beneath a glass-fronted wall cabinet (RIGHT).

In terms of space alone, a pantry is a luxury for most homeowners, though the principle can be adapted to fit out a tall cabinet. Thick stone walls keep this walk-in pantry cool, making it ideal for storing fresh fruit and vegetables whilst also leaving plenty of room for dry ingredients. Lighting is essential for locating items at a glance (ABOVE).

Cabinet doors in frosted glass harmonize with the predominantly woody kitchen, a mellowing contrast to the black laminated refrigerator and countertops (ABOVE).

A square hanging rack suspended above the countertop provides a convenient space to store oils and vinegars (LEFT).

A long kitchen workbench is fitted out with shelves beneath; a high-level storage unit above that incorporates an exhaust hood above the built-in cooktop at the far end of the bench. Planning a kitchen from scratch frees you to incorporate more unusual storage solutions (LEFT).

A combination of storage and display softens the impact of the starkly rectilinear shelving, resulting in a look that is comfortably cluttered (BELOW).

Modular storage is more commonly associated with the living room but works well in this kitchen, ensuring a place on view for almost everything. Unattractive necessities such as cleaning fluids and garbage bags can be kept hidden in the more conventional cabinets beneath the countertop (LEFT).

Apothecary drawers add an idiosyncratic but practical additional source of storage in an island unit, and the marble top an excellent worksurface. More conventional storage is provided by the base and wall cabinets; bulky pots and pans sit on or hang from the hanging rack (BELOW).

SCREENING AND DIVIDING

The open-plan kitchen enjoys popularity, working especially well for daily family get-togethers or for potluck meals. But sometimes the cacophony of dogs, television and the whirring food processor in that open arena brings back a love of walls. Enter the intimate alternative – some type of screen, divider, partition or wall – which makes it safe to go back into the kitchen.

Different work areas can be separated by function – office, breakfast room, sitting room, laundry center. Deciding whether or not you want flexible or permanent divisions to open or close off the kitchen will help determine the best solution. Your recipe for comfort might lie in forgoing the open plan for a cozy suite of inviting rooms or smaller functional niches. The most important ingredients in these are doors that can be closed for solitude and private conversations, for a kitchen out of earshot and eye contact. Screening off the laundry center into a utility room shuts off noise and often becomes a place where mess is allowed to accumulate.

For visual or auditory privacy, the kitchen need not be reorganized or walled in. For chefs who prefer not to be seen, large hatches keep diners and cooks on speaking terms. A common, functional way to shield cooks in an open kitchen is to add a shelf to an island or a backsplash that is high enough to cover the mess. It gently separates, instead of brutally segregating, the business end of the kitchen while adding storage and extra serving space. This is a particularly good remedy if a wall or partition would close off the kitchen to views, light and conversation. The island can be a "living" space for stools, a breakfast bar, or a message center.

Cabinets accessible from both sides contribute storage and screen off the dining area from the cooking center, or the servicing center from the food preparation area. Another option is to continue wall cabinets beyond the wall, mounting them on "legs" so they sit on the countertop.

A heavy pivoting solid wood door fitted into a wide opening between kitchen and dining room makes a versatile space divider, controlling traffic flow, screening views and providing the opportunity to segregate the rooms completely. The thickness of the wall, roughwashed in bright terra cotta, is accentuated by this means of partitioning (LEFT).

This kitchen counter ends in a gentle curve taken up to a sufficient height to screen from general view the area of the work surface where dirty pots and pans inevitably accumulate (ABOVE).

French doors close quietly to muffle sound while bringing in natural light from adjoining rooms. Fiberglass panels, glass-block partitions and interior windows are just as good insulation and can be back lit for atmosphere. Another sound solution is to create separate, but not equal spaces which promote intimacy without noise pollution. A layout in which the kitchen opens on to a dining area then flows to a small, more distant sitting room means television sitcoms watched by pre-teens will no longer intrude into the kitchen, an unnerving counterpoint to settling bills, cooking and general conversation.

Vertical or mini-blinds, shutters and accordian doors are responsive, relatively inexpensive visual partitions, which, along with sliding door panels, have the flexibility to open up or close down. These are available in plastic, wood, metal, mirror, and a wide range of colors and finishes, but are probably best if custom made to complement your domestic architecture.

Subtly defining the transition from one area to the other, suspended wooden shelves provide room for storing glasses and for a display of favorite objects, which can be appreciated and enjoyed from either side of the arrangement. The wooden countertop is raised above the work surface to screen kitchen clutter (RIGHT).

Narrow slitted apertures divide off this kitchen area from the rest of the living space for a more permanent form of partition. Small halogen lights in the gaps stripe the wall with light when viewed from the other side (RIGHT).

A long internal window incorporated into the partition wall between kitchen and eating areas adds a sense of openness to a small kitchen. Venetian blinds allow the areas to be separated to a greater degree when required; glassware racked at eye-level catches the light for a sparkling display (RIGHT).

Kitchen clutter disappears behind closed doors in this compact arrangement. Louvered doors fold all the way back to reveal a built-in kitchen tucked into an alcove of an apartment (RIGHT).

The kitchen area of this Italian farmhouse room – with tiled floor, rustic beamed ceiling and large windows set in deep recesses – retreats from view behind a wooden palisade. Curly metal shelves carry a selection of glassware and ceramic bowls for the table (BELOW).

KITCHEN FURNITURE

Versatile kitchen seating combines bar stools for countertop eating with classically plain kitchen chairs arranged around a glass table top ingeniously suspended from the ceiling on a steel support. Furniture plays a simple and unobtrusive role in an elegantly understated space (RIGHT).

Brightly colored Butterfly chairs by Arne Jacobsen ring the changes around a slice of glass table top, built in to the side of polished steel kitchen units (RIGHT).

Akitchen poses a distinct furnishing challenge. In small kitchens, where space is at a premium, it's often a matter of soul searching before fitting in ample storage and a dining area. Even big kitchens must reconcile comfort, individuality and efficient organization. The right table, seating and hardware are to a workable kitchen what the right spices are to fine food: they accent the key ingredients, help define the personality of the room and of the chef and provide stimulating ambience.

It's best to keep kitchen decor less dense and less complicated than in other rooms. Practicality, a lack of fussiness and classic design lie at the heart of chairs and tables that will stand the test of time. Think robust, simple and easy to clean; pieces that are mobile are more flexible than those that aren't – mopping up around a mass of legs will quickly become irritating.

Though chairs and a large central table have great integrity and flexibility, built-in banquettes work equally well, particularly in cramped spaces. Bench seats squeeze a surprising number of people in for a meal and can be constructed as a fixture against a wall or as a lift-up seat on top of low units – the drawback is lack of comfort. Varying the style and material of furniture – a wooden table paired with plastic laminate cabinets – contributes warmth and humanity,

though sharp contrasts jar. Consistent colors and streamlined pieces effectively make close areas feel spacious.

Well-made, plain chairs that can be wiped down are the most practical. Since upholstered chairs and cushions acquire kitchen smells, sensibly dress them in loose, washable covers or covers that are removable. Use patterned fabrics with care, or the kitchen will feel cluttered.

Most new furniture designs are loose interpretations of old standards like the classic linen press and pie safe, farmhouse or refectory table, and are available in the raw honesty of wood, as well as in modern metals whose vigor and wit are self-evident. Originals are costly, but reproduction pieces can be crafted to adhere to the principles of tradition. Cheap, basic dining tables are numerous. Err on the side of casualness with kitchen tables, reserving furniture with more formal polish for the dining room (if you have one).

HARDWARE
There is something satisfying in the act of opening and shutting a door, releasing a clasp or grasping and turning a handle. Using distinctive hardware is the cheapest way to customize your kitchen. Classic hardware abounds, from antique knobs in porcelain to hooks hammered in steel.

They don't need to match; designers often mount complementary but not identical hardware on upper and lower cabinets.

Brass hardware needs to be thoroughly lacquered or left natural. Unlacquered brass, even if it is top quality, must be polished or it will tarnish from moisture in the air and from your hands, looking disfigured and soiled very rapidly.

Stainless steel and iron hardware are fairly trouble free. The most universal designs of knobs have generous oversize grips that are easy for rheumatoid, arthritic and young fingers to open.

COUNTER-HEIGHT SEATING
High stools continue to be popular thanks to the proliferation of kitchen islands and built-in bars. They have transcended the basic and come in a multitude of styles and dimensions. When sitting, the user should be able to rest elbows comfortably on the countertop. Some stools are more like chairs; others are virtual perches. Those that shine through the dross have footrests and back supports; stretchers between the legs are designed to prevent someone from kicking the stool out from under the user. Backless models are fine as long as a countertop or armrest is close by. A collapsible stool that is a combination step ladder and seat is a great, versatile kitchen tool.

Classic Lloyd Loom basket chairs and a black metal pedestal table define the eating side of an open-plan kitchen/diner. A change in flooring demarcates the two spaces (TOP).

Dining furniture is the focus of interest in a cool, tranquil space, screened from kitchen bustle by a high-level counter (ABOVE).

Padded barstools make a comfortable perch at a kitchen counter with a view out the window (TOP).

The unbeatable Windsor chair, a traditional country design, is tailormade for relaxing in the mellow setting of a sun-filled farmhouse kitchen (ABOVE).

Simple wooden upright chairs and a classic wooden country table make a pleasingly hospitable focus for an airy, spacious kitchen, a comfortable and compatible blend of styles (LEFT).

A dining alcove off a main kitchen area is equipped with built-in bench seating on cantilevered steel supports. With minimal furnishing and low-key decor, nothing distracts from the pleasures of eating (BELOW).

A marble-topped pine kitchen table doubles up as an additional preparation area in a seamlessly integrated white kitchen (CENTER LEFT).

Folding chairs and a simple modern table bring the warmth of wood to a room in a nicely judged combination of materials (LEFT).

Equipping

A capacious American refrigerator, an elegant icon of domestic design with its gentle streamlined curves, injects a note of retro style in a modern kitchen (LEFT).

The best kitchen hardware repays investment in performance and sheer esthetic pleasure (RIGHT).

Tailoring the size of appliances to the space at your disposal makes good design sense. This small oven is a perfect fit for a restricted layout (ABOVE).

*F*rom dishwasher to microwave, appliances have revolutionized the kitchen in less than a century. The days of monotonous, labor-intensive chores have gone for ever; drudgery is banished at the press of a button. But domestic machines make their own demands, as anyone who has recently ventured into a manufacturer's show-room is well aware. Abstruse jargon, complex specifications and the sheer pace of technological change can make a simple replacement purchase seem daunting.

Positioning equipment for efficient use is only half the equation. Fundamental decisions must also be made on the range of functions you require, the level of sophistication and the merits of different sources of power. There are questions of budget, maintenance, energy savings and performance to be considered. If you make the wrong choice, you'll have wasted time and money, and you'll be losing valuable kitchen space that could be put to better use.

This survey of kitchen equipment and appliances provides an invaluable summary of what's available, from the basic to the technological cutting edge. What's important is making sure that the machines you choose serve your purposes.

Modern appliances offer a range of functions to maximize kitchen convenience. This American refrigerator incorporates a cold-water and ice dispenser in one of the doors (BELOW).

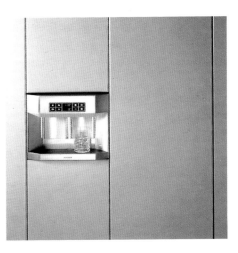

RANGES, OVENS AND COOKTOPS

Integrated into the architecture of the room, this generous cooktop is built in to a concrete partition. Adequate ventilation is ensured by the exhaust hood which is ducted up through the concrete block, out through the back of it and along the kitchen ceiling to an outside wall (RIGHT).

In response to city-scale apartments, several manufacturers have gone small scale. A pint-sized stove, with two burners and a broiler, is still the first-time stove for many people. It's easy to clean and consumes minimal fuel. If space and budget are tight, consider unitary one-piece kitchens which are cost and space effective.

TOP OF THE RANGE

The best manufacturers in the restaurant business have introduced their professional range, a model boasting the industrial look, quality and assets of catering equipment without the disadvantages. These ranges take their cue from the hearth. Whether cast iron or polished steel, pastel enamel or honed matte black, for some they are the ultimate cooking machine.

Garland, Wolf, Viking, and Brown Co.'s "Five Star" ranges are the most sought-after of the new commercially-styled ranges. These stainless steel and enamel behemoths feature surface burners with ratings of between 14,000 to 15,000 BTUs (compared to the normal 8,000 to 9,000 BTUs per burner for the average stove), a prized asset because it enables them to generate intense amounts of heat in a hurry. They also feature large, built-in griddle plates and extra-large ovens.

It is important to note that even though these ranges are designed for home use, they can require bigger gas lines and more extensive ventilation.

French ranges feature indoor barbecues, griddle plates, a hot roasting oven and one for baking, classic trims and from four to six gas burners. They are known for the delicacy of their ovens and flat cooking surfaces. Such quality does not come cheap.

Balance the total functionality and good looks of a range against how much you will use it and what you cook, the space these wider and deeper appliances lay claim to, and the weighty price. Unless they are placed as free standing appliances, they will also need custom-made cabinets.

Even if you plan to sell your house in a few years' time, when it comes to the kitchen's primary cooking instrument you want high-quality appliances. One way – though risky – to reduce cost is to buy brand-name merchandise from appliance specialists that is damaged, a floor model, display, or without its instructions.

STOVES

A stove with four hot plates or gas burners on the top and one or two ovens below is the most cost-effective cooking appliance, whether it is free standing or slots between base cabinets. For those with a limited space and budget, a 20in (500mm) wide stove with four burners, a broiler and one oven will do the job. While it may not be a thing of beauty, it is cheap. Installing a free standing stove costs two to four times less than installing a separate oven and cooktop which each require a cabinet box.

Broilers used to be a separate external, eye-level compartment. More and more, a broiler is set inside the oven or in its own cooking cavity. If a broiler is inside the oven and it is the only oven, simultaneous roasting and broiling will not be possible.

The Aga is a classic cooking fixture of the traditional English country kitchen. Part of the charm of these sturdy, dependable ranges is the way they mellow with use and age (ABOVE).

1 French range with double oven, four gas burners and wok ring

2 Side-by-side double oven with six gas burners and central hot plate

3 Single oven with four gas burners and griddle

1

2

3

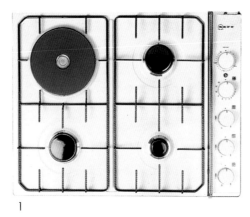

1

2

3

4

5

6

7

8

To make the most of counter space, these Italian gas burners fold back when not in use to clear extra room on the marble countertop. They are secured in an upright position by hooks over a metal rail from which other utensils hang (FAR RIGHT).

1 Combination gas and electric cooktop
2 Ceramic halogen combination cooktop
3 Electric cooktop
4 Gas cooktop
5 Electric halogen cooktop
6 Grill
7 Deep fryer
8 Hot plate
9 Combination gas and electric cooktop
10 Electric cooktop
11 Griddle plate, exhaust and gas cooktop
12 Large and small gas wok rings and deep fryer

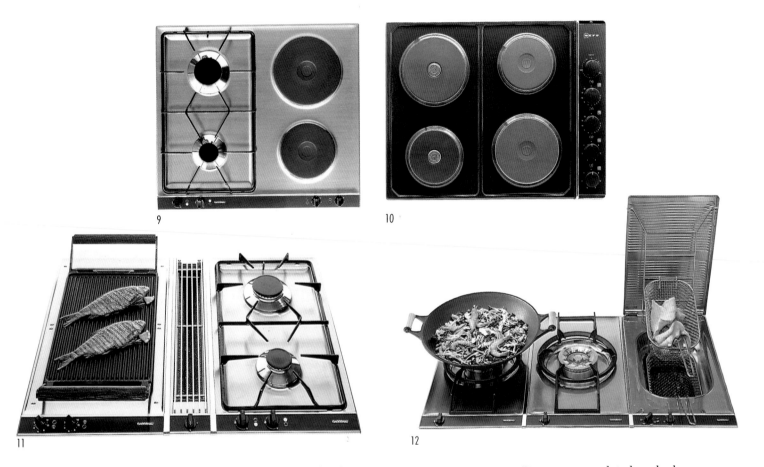

9

10

11

12

SEPARATE COMPONENTS

The stove has enjoyed a long monopoly. Locating cooktops in a countertop and an oven elsewhere increases the cost, but as two individual units they offer more visual and functional design flexibility than bulkier one-piece cookers. Ovens can be built in to wall cabinets at whatever height feels most comfortable for the user.

The biggest advantage of separation is having dual fuel. For cooktops, most gourmet cooks prefer natural gas because it heats more quickly and cheaply, and is more controllable. Gas burners also last indefinitely, whereas electric ones burn out. Whether gas or electric is better for the oven is a personal preference. Developed first, electric ovens are favored owing to their even temperature, accuracy and ability to self-clean more effectively.

COOKTOPS

Separating cooktops into four electric or four gas burners is a bit like food books without recipes: you are hungry for more variation. Since appliances are a supply-and-service industry, manufacturers have developed modular component systems valued for their looks and flexibility. A two-burner unit can be either gas or electric and can be combined with a griddle, grill, hot plate, surface-mounted extractor (page 150) or deep fryer; if you're a fan of Oriental food, it may be worth investing in a special wok ring. Ceramic electric cooktops are easy to clean, and those with halogen heating come close to providing the speed and versatility of gas. Components eliminate wasted space usually found in the middle of a four-burner cooktop – you can rest equipment on the countertop.

Pizza ovens and indoor barbecues are additional components. Barbecue modules are fueled like electric cooktops. Heat-conducting volcanic rock assures outdoor grilling flavor. When juices or grease spatter on to these lava rocks, food takes on a barbecued taste. Cleaning up is messy, despite the fact that the rocks can be tossed into the dishwasher. A countertop ventilating unit will also be necessary.

Countertops with a separate control box can be a nuisance. Ensure the connecting cable is long enough to reach from the cooktop to the control box. Cable often comes in short lengths and extensions are not easy to organize. Watch out, too, for gas burner grates without corner supports; inadequately supported small pots easily tilt and tip when pulled slightly off the heat on insubstantial grates.

OVENS

Not only are today's ovens more versatile and automated, their cooking capabilities have expanded. Finding the oven – or combination of ovens – that best suits your kitchen, cooking style, and budget requires research and a systematic approach. But the time you take to analyze your cooking needs and investigate the different options will be well rewarded.

There are four basic types of ovens on the market: conventional electric or gas, convection, microwave and multiple function. It is important to remember that there can be significant variations in the quality and time it takes to prepare food in different types of oven.

In a conventional gas or electric oven, 60 to 70 percent of the heat is radiant heat; the remainder is convection. In the conventional electric oven, the heating elements are located within the oven itself, at the top and bottom. As they become hot, they radiate heat into the food. In a gas oven, heat comes from a burner beneath the oven floor. Both gas and electric ovens are excellent for browning and making things crispy. But because air must constantly be introduced to fuel the flame in gas ovens, they have a reputation as being more drying to food. Temperatures in gas ovens also tend to be more uneven, due to the fact that the gas flame must continuously rise and fall as part of its normal operation. Unlike microwave, convection, and some of the new multi-function ovens which cook food faster, conventional ovens take their own, measured time.

The convection oven is forced-air cooking. Heating elements are combined with the motion of a fan to heat, then circulate, air. Heat penetrates food faster and more uniformly than in a conventional oven, generally reducing cooking time which keeps food moister. Cakes come out higher and lighter; meats brown beautifully and remain juicy and tender. A drawback is that you have to adjust your recipes to the oven.

Some multi-function ovens combine conventional operation and convection; others integrate conventional operation and microwave; and convection and microwave.

Self-cleaning ovens, which are almost standard nowadays, use intense heat to burn grime and grease off oven walls. The extra insulation in these ovens translates into cooler cooking. Continuous-cleaning ovens have an interior coating that, when activated by the oven's heat, oxidizes food splatters as they occur. But continuous-cleaning ovens are susceptible to nicks and the surface can never seem to get clean.

As a general rule, the bigger the cavity the better. Be aware that even though models may have similar exterior dimensions, their capacities can differ due to shelf supports. An oven window is a desirable feature because it allows you to see inside without opening the door. "Preheat" settings, which heat the oven quickly, and programmable controls that allow you to preset times and temperatures over a 24-hour period are also features worth considering. Before buying any model, be sure to check that it has a ventilation system that will work with your kitchen design.

MICROWAVE OVENS

Microwaves aren't really "ovens" at all. Radio-frequency waves penetrate deep into the food, vibrating water molecules so they generate heat. This heat is what cooks the food. Some people use their microwave simply as a handy reheating and defrosting machine, resuscitating leftovers, thawing frozen meats and making popcorn. Others use it as a true cooking appliance, and work from cookbooks on microwaving. The combination microwave and convection oven has resulted from a new appreciation of the microwave's directness and the realization that consumers want to be able to switch back and forth between the two cooking modes. These combination machines are useful if there is only one other oven in the kitchen – they provide a second.

Power, performance and capacity vary according to the manufacturer and model. Mid-sized ovens with 600–800 watts of power are considerably less bulky than large-sized models. Some have electronic sensing systems which determine how much and how long raw food needs to be cooked. Variable power levels, turntables, browning devices and interior lights are worthwhile options.

Though some microwaves come with simulated wood-grain cabinets, they are available in white, almond and charcoal gray cabinet colors with pinstripes and other design treatments. If the main function of a microwave is for heating snacks, a good spot is near the refrigerator. If it is a cooking utensil, it might be used to create a second oven area much the way a second sink creates an additional food preparation center. Microwaves can perch on countertops, be suspended under cabinets, be installed above conventional ovens or be built in to custom-built base or wall cabinets. In some instances, the ventilation hood and microwave can be combined.

Many microwaves cannot tolerate oven heat and should not be mounted above a regular oven. The majority of manufacturers have devised built-in wall model microwave/oven pairs. An existing microwave can be adapted with special vents and baffles to top off a new oven, but this kind of custom craftsmanship is costly.

STEAM OVENS

The built-in steam oven is a European reinvention of the pressure cooker, not yet widely available in America. It looks rather like a pressure cooker turned horizontal with a window. Steam ovens are plumbed into the water supply and programmed as you would a pressure cooker. The machine draws in water, heats it, forces it into the chamber as steam, pressure cooking foods. A steam oven complements a multi-function oven and a microwave, since it handles dry products with aplomb.

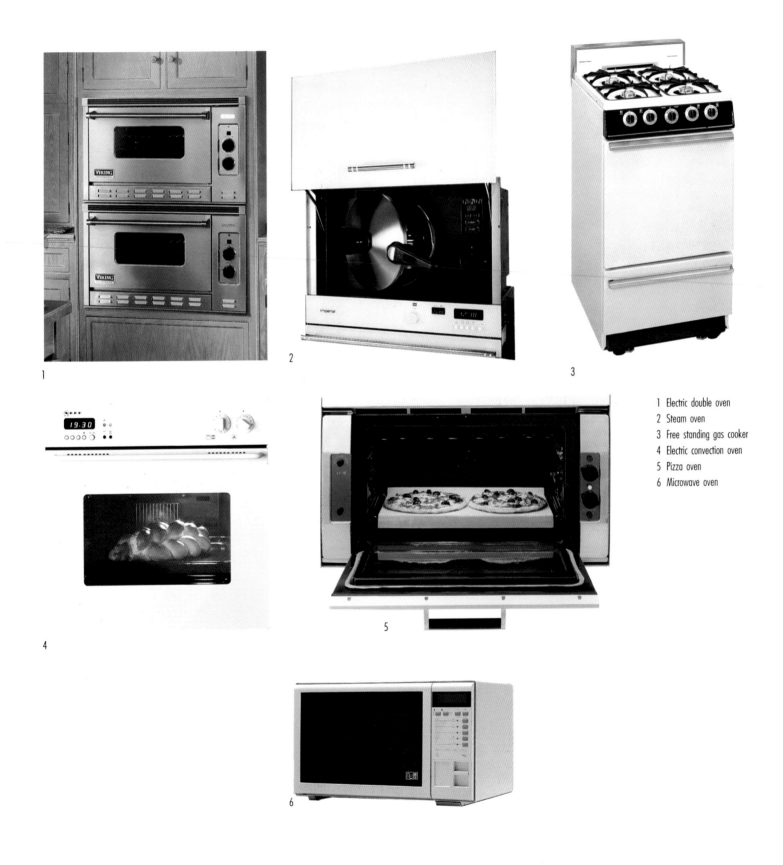

1

2

3

1 Electric double oven
2 Steam oven
3 Free standing gas cooker
4 Electric convection oven
5 Pizza oven
6 Microwave oven

5

4

6

REFRIGERATORS

The hunt has always been on for ways to prolong the life of perishable foods. Before 1000 BC, the Chinese used ice cellars. The Roman emperor Nero had pits lined with straw and filled with ice. Relics of eighteenth-century ice-houses, cellars likewise insulated with straw and filled with ice, still exist. A first attempt at a domestic apparatus was made about 150 years ago and was literally an ice box. Consumers, however, didn't immediately accept refrigeration. It was to be some time between then and now before the refrigerator became an absolutely essential kitchen ingredient.

Choose a model of refrigerator based on the size (and potential size) of your family; your work, shopping and cooking habits; the size and style of your kitchen; and, of course, your budget. Next on the list of priorities is quietness, esthetics and the flexibility of the refrigerator's interior storage facilities.

When evaluating a refrigerator's size, don't be misled by gross interior volume. How the space is organized is just as important as how much of it there is. There should be provisions for easy access to things you buy frequently, such as milk, butter and fresh fruits and vegetables, and preferably see-through bins so you can readily see what's in store and whether it needs replacing or throwing out.

If you stash away supermarket bargains or buy in bulk, you'll want a large, conveniently located freezer. If cooking with fresh fruits and vegetables is your forte, you'll probably want a refrigerator with separate compartments and humidity controls or vents for the individual meat, fruit and vegetables.

Refrigerators come in several configurations: side-by-side; with the freezer on top or the freezer below. Appliances may be free standing, built under, integrated or built in. Many large side-by-side models come equipped with ubiquitous iced-water and crushed-ice dispensers in the door.

1

WHICH ONE TO CHOOSE?

Refrigerators are prominent kitchen fixtures so it is worth choosing carefully.

- Do you want to sacrifice countertop space for a full-height refrigerator?
- Will you be moving on? A free standing model might be a better proposition than a built-in unit.
- Do you prefer the refrigerator to be unassuming? Undercounter styles and refrigerators designed to be installed flush in a built-in kitchen are less intrusive.

- Do you prefer them to be invisible? More expensive "integrated" models come with unfinished doors so you can disguise them with panels that match kitchen units. You can recess standard-size refrigerators or build the cabinets themselves deep enough to make the refrigerator less obtrusive.
- Is time precious? A frost-free unit, in which air is changed continuously, means there is no build up of ice. No-frost models automatically defrost the refrigerator and adjust humidity.

1 Full-size refrigerator with iced water and ice dispenser
2 Mini refrigerator with ice box
3 Stacking refrigerator and freezer
4 Undercounter, side-by-side refrigerator and freezer with doors to match kitchen units

2

3

4

ENERGY FACTORS

Refrigerators and freezers are basically insulated containers. A compressor, consisting of an electric motor which drives a pump, circulates gases which attract heat and dissipate warm air out of the refrigerator and freezer. The gases act as coolants.

Today's new refrigerators use much less energy compared to models built in the early 1970s. For example, a new 20.6cu. ft (0.5cu. m) refrigerator with top freezer uses about as much electricity as a 100-watt lightbulb, constantly burning. However, some refrigerators are more energy-efficient than others. Most new appliances are required to wear an "Energy guide" sticker, designed to help you compare models of similar size and with similar features. Bear in mind that while an energy-efficient appliance may cost you more, you will probably quickly recoup that extra money and more in energy savings over the life of the unit.

Avoid buying a larger refrigerator than you need, don't overchill food, and open doors as little as possible. Models with the compressor on top are more energy efficient (and quieter) than those with the compressor located at the back or bottom.

Unfortunately, domestic refrigerators contain ozone-destroying CFC coolants (chlorinated fluorocarbons) and CFC foam insulation which may be environmentally destructive. However, refrigerators with CFC-free refrigerant and CFC-free insulation are in developmental stages and expected to be available in the near future from major American and European appliance manufacturers.

SINKS AND FAUCETS

Selecting a sink based on function, space and style is the best way to ensure that using it never becomes a drudgery. Whether you want one, two or three bowls depends on your work habits, available space and budget. With sinks, simple and big are often best. Single-bowl sinks are streamlined and flexible, roomy enough for oversize pans and cutting boards. Identical twin basins simplify washing and rinsing dishes and food preparation. A sink with one large and one small bowl is sensible for the majority of households; it doesn't hog a huge amount of work space while still allowing secondary tasks to go on.

Avoid sinks with overly generous expanses of drainer which eat up work space. Good drainers are only slightly sloped and without grooves, which collect dirt and are useless on a shallow incline, so that the surface can double as a countertop.

A sink should cleanse and inspire. Place sinks as close to the countertop brim as possible. Under-mounted rimless sinks, flush with countertops, eliminate the metal strip that tends to hold water. Small single sinks maximize space and work well as second sinks, too.

MATERIALS
Stainless steel sinks come in a range of quality levels, depending on the gauge of metal, amount of detailing, and the finish. Better sinks contain more nickel, giving the sink a richer luster, warmer color, better cleanability, and resistance to water spotting and scratches. The thicker the gauge, the quieter and sturdier the sink. Stainless steel has more "give" than porcelain, so fewer breakages occur. Other metallic possibilities include white bronze (an alloy of copper, manganese and zinc), brass, sand-cast aluminum and copper. Each gives a sink a warmer nuance than the cold sheen of steel or iciness of porcelain.

Porcelain-enameled, cast-iron sinks retain their gloss for years, are heavy and sturdy and come in as many colors as paint.

Porcelain glazing cleans easily and takes hard use. Its finish, though, is less than resilient; a heavy frying pan can chip it, rusting the cast iron beneath. Serious stains must be bleached.

Belfast and farmhouse sinks of porcelain-coated fire clay have a predominantly boxy silhouette. They afford the depth of commercial sinks and a stain- and heat-resistant surface. Granite and marble sinks espouse the aesthetic of archetypal basins.

Synthetic sink materials are essentially a composite material containing quartz and plastic. Less polished than stone, they are more flexible and chip resistant.

1

Corian and other solid surfacing materials free the imagination. Sinks are handsome, soberly modern, and very expensive. They come customized, either as an integral bowl molded seamlessly into a counter of the same material or as a drop-in sink with the lip resting on the surrounding countertop and sealed in place.

FAUCETS
Faucets may be the single most used item in the kitchen. The best turn on at a touch or via infra-red technology, with water of a preset temperature flowing when heat sensors detect your hands underneath. A qua-

lity standard faucet requires only a gentle quarter turn for it to be fully on or off; water flow should be steady and smooth.

Which style faucet is best for you rests with your personal preference and the style of your kitchen. There are single-handle faucets and those that swivel with the swing of an elbow; mixer faucets integrate hot and cold water; separate pillar faucets keep temperatures segregated; a tall, goose-neck spigot facilitates filling tall pots; and a pull-out spray spout can be useful for rinsing pots and pans with very hot water.

A tap with a ceramic disc valve provides more years of drip- and leak-free service

2

than a tap that relies on a plastic valve to control the flow of water. Ask your designer, architect or a plumbing fixture and fittings supplier about the different ceramic disc valves available.

The best faucets are heavyweights, cast of solid brass (copper and zinc) for maximum corrosion resistance. Look for faucets with a hard, smooth finish and deep luster. Polished chrome finishes stay shiny for years and clean easily. Epoxy coatings are tough, smooth and come in many colors. At the high end of the price scale, gold and silver plate are fashionable but quality and durability vary greatly.

3

4

5

6

7

8

1 Belfast sink and cherry countertop with mixer faucet

2 Granolithic sink and countertop with wall-mounted mixer faucet

3 Stainless steel double sink and countertop with mixer faucet and additional "showerhead" mixer faucet

4 Polished metal double sink and surround with countertop mixer faucet

5 Copper sink and wood countertop with individual countertop faucets

6 Stainless steel sink and concrete island with countertop mixer faucet

7 Stainless steel sink and stained wood countertop with wall-mounted mixer faucet

8 Stainless steel sink and wood countertop with individual faucets

DISHWASHERS AND WASHING MACHINES

1

Tucking a dishwasher under the counter and close by to the sink is usually the best place in a kitchen for it. Particularly dirty dishes can be rinsed under the faucet and then placed in the dishwasher while you wait for a full load to accumulate. Storage for everyday dishes and pans is located in the immediate vicinity of the dishwasher so that clean items can be unloaded and returned to their proper places with a minimum of effort (ABOVE).

Meticulous engineering continues to improve the productivity and unobtrusiveness of these labor-saving devices. However, find out what the long-term value and expected life is of the model under consideration. Products that come and go waste money and squander environmental resources, although most dishwashers and washing machines have built-in water softeners and energy-saving features. Ascertain what you want and ignore the sales pitch. Even the largest domestic dishwasher will only take five full place settings, despite exaggerated claims.

Always match the appliance to the dimensions and design of the kitchen. They all come in standard sizes although there are narrower and smaller models available for the tiny kitchen. If you want to do first-hand research, call your local repair com-

panies and ask them which models and makes break down most and least often and why. Don't go for complicated machines with excess gadgets. There's more to go wrong.

DISHWASHERS

What you want are efficiently cleaned and dried dishes. Be conscious of energy, water and detergent consumption. Make sure the operating noise is a barely audible hum. Soundproofing materials vary even within models of the same brand. Quality dishwashers incorporate a number of silencers: layers of insulation as sound filters and separated, cushioned motors and pumps. Each layer of padding adds to the cost.

Machines with two revolving spray arms, fitted top and bottom, wash best. A filtration system keeps dirty water exiting and clean water circulating, and stops food from

1 A fully loaded dishwasher

2 A European-style clothes dryer stacked on top of a front-loading washing machine

3 A top-loading washing machine alongside a front-loading clothes dryer

2

3

splashing back on to china. Better models have a large strainer to catch bulky dirt, followed by a finer drainage system. Invest in a machine with an anti-flood design: hidden sensors detect water levels and automatically shut off the water inlet valve and start up the drainage pump in the event of an overflow or leak.

Dishwashers are highly complex pieces of machinery and are therefore produced by just a handful of manufacturers and rebranded by others. The branding involves the brand name putting on its own parts, upgrades and logo. So shop around: an expensive model may not be any better than a medium-priced one with fewer "refinements." Essentials in a top machine are a drop door, removable racks, baskets that glide out on rails and few limitations on plate size. Stainless steel interiors are more

durable and less likely to take on odors or stain than enamel. The one proviso is that copper, silver and aluminum items discolor when they're washed in steel due to a reaction between the metals.

THE LAUNDRY

Having a washing machine and clothes dryer in the kitchen or in close proximity to it can be very convenient. The heart of a washing machine is its motor which controls how well it washes, how thoroughly it rinses and how many revolutions it spins. Most machines are quite happy with cold fill only. A capacity of between 14–16lb (30–35kg) is adequate for the average family wash.

Buy a brand with a good repair history. Costlier machines offer elaborate electronics and custom-cycle programming.

But these frills don't necessarily improve performance, and they can make the machine more expensive to service.

The ultimate clothes dryer dries clothes without shrinkage, returning them soft, free of lint, and in wearable condition. Look for large, easy-to-clean, removable filters. Clothes dry more quickly, gently and with minimal creasing in drums of large volume. Dryers usually operate more efficiently and economically with gas rather than electricity. Some electronic models stop automatically when clothes are dry by reading the humidity level inside the machine.

Not much heed is paid to manufacturing quiet laundry machines. Assess noise before you buy. With a machine grinding and spinning away for up to 90 minutes you'll soon resort to shouting, and wish you had a soundproof door.

The Well-Stocked Kitchen

A metal strip fixed across the length of a kitchen wall is hung with meat hooks to provide an adaptable and practical method of storing colanders, ladles, strainers and other kitchen accoutrements (ABOVE).

Pickled vegetables, dried foods, beans and pulses form the basis of an open display. The gleaming metal shelves are softened and harmonized by the wicker baskets and the rich variety of ingredients jostling for space (RIGHT).

The sight of a row of gleaming saucepans or a rack of honed knives can be esthetically pleasing as well as essential for the preparation of good food. Once you've planned and decorated your kitchen, the real work begins as you learn to get the best from it.

Before supermarkets, television, mass tourism and color magazines it would have been possible to draw up a list of ingredients most people in any given area of the world regularly used. In a confident expectation of tastes and preferences, early kitchen cabinets from the 1920s and '30s often incorporated checklists and menus on the insides of the doors.

Cooking is no longer so predictable. Supermarkets selling fresh produce from far-flung corners of the globe and restaurants that offer every conceivable type of cuisine mean that the pantry at home is just as likely to contain lemongrass as lemons. The eclecticism of the modern cook goes along with an increasing willingness to experiment with new recipes, so if you won't find the same provisions from one household to the next, you won't necessarily find the same ingredients from one month to the next.

THE ESSENTIAL PANTRY

Even if no definitive list can be drawn up to suit everyone's taste and diet, certain fundamental considerations apply. Foodstuffs, wherever they hail from, fall into basic categories, each with their own storage requirements – length of keeping, correct levels of temperature and humidity, bulk and size – which dictate the type and amount of space they require. Some ingredients are used every day and need to be close by; others can be stored out of sight for that rare occasion when you need them. Those types of food that form a staple of your diet or mainstay of your cooking may be more economically bought in bulk.

STOCKING UP

Food storage should be intimately related to cooking habits and the space at your disposal. But many people overstock their kitchens. There is a primitive instinct to hoard when it comes to food. Many people overbuy, comforted by the feeling that a little extra might come in handy. There's nothing more satisfying than being able to fling together a meal for unexpected guests; nothing more dispiriting than finding the pantry bare. But whatever you buy that is surplus to requirements is more likely to end up wasted, or to languish forgotten in some dark corner.

Bulk buying can make good economic sense, particularly those items which are relatively stable in price and which you use a large amount. And it makes good ecological sense, too, since there will be less wastage in the form of packaging and fewer trips to the supermarket. But bulk buying can be a false economy and you need to think carefully before indulging in that tempting special offer. Does a bulk purchase genuinely represent a good investment for your money? Is storing great quantities of provisions the best use you can make of the space in your house? Will you consume more of the product than usual if there is more of it around? Will you get tired of it before you finish the packet?

A windowsill array of bottled preserves – lovely to look at, satisfying to make and great to have on hand. Reviving traditional methods of preserving food – either cheap seasonal produce bought in bulk or surplus from the back yard – extends the scope of the pantry and the cook's repertoire (LEFT).

Pull-out basket trays make a sensible storage arrangement for fresh fruit and vegetables that benefit from well-aerated conditions. Fruit and vegetables that will be used up quickly do not require refrigeration in temperate conditions; storing fresh ingredients just beneath the main preparation area makes good ergonomic sense (LEFT).

In Sir Terence Conran's Provençal kitchen, the eating area features a wall of display shelves, with a waist-high marble cantilevered shelf. An angled strip of mirror above the shelf reflects bowls piled high with local produce, an appetizing and colorful display. Shelves above hold dishes and glassware in daily use (LEFT).

Large canned goods may appear a good buy, but once the can is opened, the contents have a limited life and you may end up throwing a substantial portion away before you get around to using it up – unless you freeze in sensible quantities.

Even in the best run households, things do tend to accumulate. Special ingredients bought in a fit of enthusiasm tried once and never repeated, half-used jars of uncertain provenance or not-quite-empty packets of pasta can be found cluttering up cabinets and lurking behind the cereal boxes on the shelf. There is no real remedy for this accumulation of ingredients short of sticking to a dull routine and stifling all the impulses and creative experiments that make cooking so worthwhile. But it is a good idea periodically to have a really thorough spring-cleaning session. Study sell-buy dates and throw out anything you can't remember buying and about which you have the slightest doubts. You may find a hidden treasure or two or discover that your tastes have moved on and that some items can be crossed off the shopping list while others can be bought in larger sizes.

Restaurant management can provide some tips for home economies. Ordering stocks for a professional kitchen involves treading a tightrope between underbuying and running the risk of disappointing customers, and overstocking, which means wastage and money down the drain. In a good restaurant where food is bought in fresh on a daily basis and no meal has ever seen the inside of a freezer or microwave, ordering is a precision art that demands an application of supply and demand. The chef needs an intuitive sense of what customers are going to want to eat as well as good lines of communication with suppliers to take advantage of seasonal bargains. The pattern of previous orderings must be considered but there is also the need to respond to less predictable factors such as changes in the weather which can enormously influence what people want to eat.

Basics, especially dried goods, are always kept in stock and reviewed every day. The stocks of fresh meat, fish, vegetables and fruit are governed more by seasonal variation and cost. Good suppliers will offer special deals for certain foods which an imaginative chef can turn to creative advantage. Ingenuity has a real role to play if supplies of a certain ingredient suddenly run out, or there is too much left at the end of the day. Ensuring that the menu offers a near alternative if the worst happens and a dish runs out can help to alleviate customers' annoyance, while an overorder of fish, for example, can be creatively recycled the following day as the basis for a stock or paté. A surplus of less expensive ingredients may find their way into staff dinners.

Many of these principles can be put into practice on the domestic front. Stocking a pantry doesn't have the make-or-break urgency of restaurant ordering, but with a little planning and forethought, the savings can add up significantly. The essential discipline is to learn as you go along, noting the rate at which you consume certain items and how your eating habits change over time. It is also important to allow a little flexibility to take advantage of seasonal price changes.

A PLACE FOR EVERYTHING

Visibility plays an important part in maintaining a good turnover of supplies and minimizing food wastage. Deep shelves where cans and packages can get pushed to the back and forgotten are a bad idea in the kitchen. So are awkwardly shaped cabinets that you can't see into properly or those placed too high or too low to encourage regular inspection. Flavor is fugitive and anything out of sight or mind for any length of time will probably not be worth eating when you finally rediscover it, even if it is still in a condition to be consumed. This applies particularly to spices and dried herbs which lose their pungency and bite and must be regularly replaced.

The indispensible kitchen pantry, with perimeter shelving that keeps everything on view, is still one of the best ways of storing a range of foodstuffs and ingredients. With full visibility, little will be overlooked or wasted, and if the pantry is sited against external walls, natural cooling will provide optimum keeping conditions (OPPOSITE).

A sunny bay window is an ideal location for an indoor herb garden. Most herbs flourish in containers; in some cases, such as the invasive mint, pot-growing is the best way of preventing the plants from over-running the back yard (ABOVE).

Modern manufacturers have responded to the complexity of kitchen storage needs by tailoring units, cabinets and drawers to suit different requirements. Kitchens have to work harder now and yet be more pleasant than the days when a "cabinet" was likely to be a wooden tub filled with flour or an earthenware jar packed with cookies. Basket drawers to take vegetables that need aerating, pull-out trays to enable you to keep the contents of deep drawers well organized and insert racks for bottles and upright containers help to eliminate clutter and confusion behind the scenes by asigning items a specific space.

We have come to rely more and more on the refrigerator to store perishable items and the bulk of all fresh food purchases; but there are certain disadvantages in relying too heavily on it. There is a limit to the amount of space at your disposal and then there is the risk of flavors spreading and contaminating other food unless each item is well wrapped or sealed. Unquestionably many types of food, especially in warm climates or conditions, demand refrigeration. The refrigerator should not be too tightly packed or it won't function properly, so for foods which don't absolutely need this level of chilling, alternative means of storage should be adopted.

A wine rack placed on an alcove shelf keeps bottles in relative cool and darkness, but on hand when the time arises (ABOVE LEFT).

In many built-in kitchens, the space between the top of the wall cabinets and the ceiling is wasted. This ingenious design uses notches carved in the tops of the cabinets to hold the necks of wine bottles, storing the wine so that it's out of the way but still easily accessible (ABOVE).

Investing in wine on such a scale as this is little more than a dream for most of us, but the sight of reviewing dozens of bottles laid down to mature is undeniably rewarding. Building the wine cellar around the spiral staircase visually enhances the effect of splendor and plenty (RIGHT).

In a similar way freezers once seemed to promise the solution to all food storage problems. They have proved to share many of the drawbacks of other methods of keeping food for long periods and should not be used simply as a depot for all kitchen surplus. Large freezers situated out of the main kitchen area can easily become repositories for forgotten leftovers and bulk purchases where food is filed, frozen and forgotten. Freezers come into their own in large households where there is a great turn-over in food, or where there is an abundance of produce from the back yard. They also play an important role in reducing kitchen drudgery; sauces, stews and stocks, best made in large quantities, can be individually portioned for future use, saving much labor.

Natural refrigeration in the form of a pantry is a time-honored way of keeping a wide variety of foods fresh. Away from the heat of the kitchen but without the deep chill of the refrigerator, the pantry allows certain foods to mature and improve with age and keeps many others in perfectly acceptable condition for considerable periods of time. The traditional location for a pantry is on the side of the house that never sees the sun, with as many external walls as possible to benefit from natural chilling and good ventilation. Fitted out with tiled stone or slate surfaces, the ambient temperature can be low enough to preserve vegetables and fruit, game, ham, sausages and salamis, jars of preserves, racks of wine and the odd leftover for overnight storage. In warm climates, you may consider the option of a walk-in chilled room, where air conditioning keeps the temperature at a regulated level. The pantry also makes an ideal location for bulk stores which can be decanted for everyday use in the kitchen.

The kitchen itself, with heat-producing apparatus of refrigerator and stove, as well as fluctuating levels of humidity, is better for storing utensils than food. But there is a need to balance ideal keeping conditions with ease of working and there will inevitably be some indispensable items that you need to keep close at hand. Rather than run to the pantry every time you need a pinch of salt, it makes good sense to keep an array of basic condiments, oils and flavorings near the main work surface even if bulk supplies are better kept elsewhere.

Today we are educated about the risks of badly kept food. As health regulations multiply, food is irradiated on our behalf and labeled to rigorous standards. It is hard to imagine how previous generations managed to eat safely without such safeguards. But despite such restrictions, there is an increasing move towards reviving the old techniques of preserving, pickling and salting food that stood our ancestors in such good stead. A living pantry – kitchen yard or herb patch – is an excellent way of responding to seasonal fluctuations of supply and of keeping the kitchen well stocked with everyday provisions.

STORING WINE

All wine, wherever it's kept and in whatever quantities, will benefit from correct storage. Few people have either the space or the money to be able to lay down an extensive wine cellar. If you are lucky enough to have a cellar, it is best (though not essential) for it to be ventilated; and it's worth labeling bottles so that you can see what's what at a glance, without having to disturb the bottles unduly.

Wine should be kept at an even temperature, ideally around 60°F (15.5°C), in a dark place, and on its side to keep the cork moist, to prevent air entering the bottle and to allow sediment to settle. In the kitchen, beware of storing wine too close to the stove unless it's extremely well insulated, otherwise the variation in temperature will be too great. Simple wire or wooden racks can be adapted to fit most spaces and will carefully cradle your wine. Properly stored, it simply remains for you to enjoy the contents of your bottles.

BASIC KITCHEN ACCOUTREMENTS

A lot of kitchen equipment and gadgets are baffling and quickly end up buried at the back of cabinets, taking up valuable storage space. Some items that packed up working ages ago somehow remain, vying for special shelf space with more regularly used cooking equipment.

As a rule of thumb, any item in your kitchen should be able to answer the burning question "What does it do?" on sight and should be put to regular use. If it isn't, chances are it doesn't deserve house room. On the following pages you'll find a collection of the most essential pieces of kitchen equipment. Some of the items illustrated are the very best of the range available and, as such, quite costly. But whilst it's worth buying the best knives and saucepans you can afford, you don't have to break the bank to equip your kitchen so that it functions to its fullest potential.

Stock one of everything you would not be without: a lemon squeezer, strainer, funnel, colander, carving fork (unless all the members of your household are vegetarian), can opener, corkscrew, potato peeler, potato masher, apple corer, balloon whisk, ladle, basting spoon, spatula, rolling pin, pastry brush (avoid one with nylon bristles), cheese grater, salt bowl, pepper mill, stove-top kettle and a large chopping board (the best are made from end-grain maple). All of these perform very specific tasks that are difficult to improvise and that will certainly take you longer and require a greater expense of effort if you don't have the right tool to hand. A pair of sharp kitchen scissors will perform the tasks of gadgets such as poultry shears and herb snippers, as well as trimming fat or the stems of cut flowers, clipping recipes and coupons, and cutting through packaging.

Well-made chefs' knives make food preparation as effortless as possible. You'll need three in 3in (8cm), 5in (12cm) and 8in (20cm) sizes, plus some skewers, a carving knife, a narrow spatula and a bread knife with a serrated edge. The best knives are

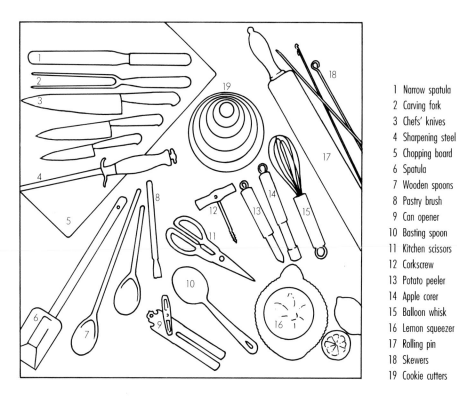

1 Narrow spatula
2 Carving fork
3 Chefs' knives
4 Sharpening steel
5 Chopping board
6 Spatula
7 Wooden spoons
8 Pastry brush
9 Can opener
10 Basting spoon
11 Kitchen scissors
12 Corkscrew
13 Potato peeler
14 Apple corer
15 Balloon whisk
16 Lemon squeezer
17 Rolling pin
18 Skewers
19 Cookie cutters

forged by hand and hammered into shape when hot. Carbon steel edges last longest but rust, whereas stainless steel blades won't corrode but are hard to sharpen. High-carbon stainless steel is best of all, forming a rust- and abrasion-resistant knife with a razor-sharp edge – and the sharpening steel will ensure that it stays that way. Wooden spoons are essential for a variety of tasks, and good enough to take to the table.

Three good-quality saucepans of different sizes should satisfy basic requirements. Plain, heavy-gauge anodized aluminum is a better conductor and retainer of heat than copper or enameled cast iron. The bases of the pans should be thick and heavy, and the sides quite high so that food can be stirred and liquid ingredients can be easily added at later stages. Make sure that lids are tight fitting for efficient simmering.

A roasting pan is a must; non-stick pans are coated to resist fat and ease cleaning, but, if you buy one, it's best to stick to brand-name varieties since the term "non-stick coating" has no legal definition. You'll also want a skillet and an omelette pan so that you can match the size to the type and quantity of food being cooked. Steel versions can be expensive but are multipurpose – beware of aluminum pans, which can affect the taste and color of ingredients such as wine and spinach. An enameled cast-iron casserole and gratin dish are both perfect for cooking and handsome enough to serve from at the table. Judge the size you'll need according to the number of people you regularly cook for, but if in doubt then err on the generous side. Casseroles, in particular, reduce in bulk as they stew, but the raw ingredients can take up a surprising amount of space.

Keen cooks will want adequate baking equipment, typically a couple of pudding bowls and cake pans, a loaf pan, a pie dish, a soufflé dish and accompanying cocottes, a loose-bottomed flan pan and cookie cutters.

ANTIQUES

Check out local flea markets, salvage yards and antique shops. The following specialize in kitchenware:

Hollywood Stove
5118 Santa Monica Blvd
Santa Monica
CA 90029

Judith Van Amringe
107 Greene Street
New York
NY 10012

APPLIANCES

AEG Appliances
65 Campus Plaza
Edison
NJ 08837

Admiral
740 King Edward Avenue
Cleveland
TN 37311

Amana Products
Amana
IA 52204

Asko, Inc.
903 North Bowser
Richardson
TX 75081

Bosch Corporation
2800 South 25th Avenue
Broadview
IL 60153

Broan
PO Box 140
Hartford
WI 53027

La Cornue French Ranges
from: Purcell-Murray Co.
113 Park Lane
Brisbane
CA 94005

Dacor
950 South Raymond Avenue
Pasadena
CA 91109

Euroflair
6000 Perimeter Drive
Dublin
OH 43017

Five Star Division
Brown Stove Works, Inc.
PO Box 2490
Cleveland
TN 37320

Frigidaire
6000 Perimeter Drive
Dublin
OH 43017

Gaggenau USA
425 University Avenue
Norwood
MA 02062

Garland Commercial Industries
185 East South Street
Freeland
PA 18224

General Electric Appliances
4700 Allmond Avenue
Louisville
KY 40225

Heartland Appliances, Inc.
5 Hoffman Street
Kitchener
Ontario
N2M 3M5

Jenn-Air Co.
3035 Shadeland Avenue
Indianapolis
IN 46266

Kenmore
Scans Tower Brand Central
25th Floor
Brand Central
Chicago
IL 60684

KitchenAid, Inc.
701 Main Street
St Joseph
MI 49085

Maytag Company
1 Dependability Square
Newton
IA 50208

Miele Appliances Inc.
22D World's Fair Drive
Somerset
NJ 08873

Modern Maid
403 North Main Street
Topton
PA 19562

Panasonic Company
1 Panasonic Way
Secaucus
NJ 07094

Sharp Electronics
Sharp Plaza
Mahwah
NJ 07430

Sub-Zero Freezer Co., Inc.
PO Box 4130
Madison
WI 53711

Thermador
5119 District Boulevard
Los Angeles
CA 90040

Viking Range Corporation
PO Box 8012
Greenwood
MS 28930

Whirlpool Home Appliances
PO Box 405
St Joseph
MI 49085

WolfRange Co.
19600 South Alameda Street
Compton
CA 90221

CABINET MANUFACTURERS

Allmilmo Corporation
70 Clinton Road
Fairfield
NJ 07004

Aristokraft
PO Box 420
Jasper
IN 47547-0420

Bulthaup USA
153 South Robertson Boulevard
Los Angeles
CA 90048

Downsview Kitchens
2635 Rena Road
Mississauga
Ontario L4T 1G6

European Country Kitchens
PO Box 125
Route 202
The Mall at Far Hills
NJ 07931

KraftMaid Cabinetry, Inc.
16052 Industrial Parkway
PO Box 1055
Middlesfield
OH 44062

Merillat Cabinetry
PO Box 1946
Adrian
MI 49221

Plain 'n' Fancy Kitchens, Inc.
PO Box 519
Schaefferstown
PA 17088

Schiffini
From: Charles Braham &
Associates
37 West 17th Street
5th Floor
New York
NY 10011

Schrock
217 South Oak Street
Arthur
IL 61911

SieMatic Corporation
PO Box F286
Langhorne
PA 19047-0934

Smallbone
from: SieMatic Corporation
PO Box 936
Langhorne
PA 19047

Snaidero International USA, Inc.
201 West 132nd Street
Los Angeles
CA 90061

Triangle Cabinets
475 Keap Street
Brooklyn
NY 11211

Wellborn Cabinet, Inc
PO Box 1210
Ashland
AL 36251

WM OHS
5095 Peoria Street
Denver
CO 80239

Woodworks, Inc
7710 West Shawnee Mission
Parkway
Shawnee Missions
KS

COUNTERTOPS

Abet Laminati
725 River Road
Suite 112
Edgewater
NJ 07020

Avonite
1945 Highway 304
Belen
NM 87002

Ceramic Stiles
51 West 19th Street
New York
NY 10011

Custom Tile
102 West Seward Avenue
Sand Springs
OK 74063

Du Pont Company (Corian)
Room G-50849
Wilmongton
DE 19801

Eco Timber International
PO Box 882461
San Francisco
CA 94188

Formica Corporation
1 Stamford Road
Piscataway
NJ 00854

Foro Marble
160 Third Street
Brooklyn
NY 11231

French Country Living
10130 Calvin Run Road
Great Falls
VA 22006

Marble Supply
901 West Division
Chicago
IL 60622

Monarch Flooring
PO Box 999
Florence
AL 35631

Nevamar Corporation
8339 Telegraph Road
Odenton
MD 21113

Petrafina
964 Third Avenue
New York
NY 10155

Ryerson Steel
PO Box 23070
Emeryville
CA 94523

Syndesis (Syndecrete)
2908 Colorado Avenue
Santa Monica
CA 90404-3616

Vermont Soapstone Company
PO Box 168
Perkinsville
VT 05151

Vermont Structural Slate
PO Box 98
3 Prospect Street
Fair Haven
VT 05743

Walker Zanger
8901 Bradley Avenue
Sun Valley
CA 91352

Ralph Wilson Plastics
600 General Bruce Drive
Temple
TX 76503

FLOORING

Armstrong Vinyl Flooring
PO Box 3001
Lancaster
PA 17604

Azrock Industries
PO Box 696060
San Antonio
TX 78269

Bruce Hardwood Floors
16803 Dallas Parkway
Dallas
TX 75248

Ceramic Stiles
51 West 19th Street
New York
NY 10011

Country Floors
1706 Locust Street
Philadelphia
PA 19103

Decorative Wood Floors
8687 Melrose Avenue
#B680
West Hollywood
CA 90069

Eco Timber International
PO Box 882461
San Francisco
CA 94188

Florida Tile Industries, Inc.
Lakeland
FL 33802

Hispanic Design
1275 Merchandise Mart
Chicago
IL 60654

Kentucky Wood Floors
PO Box 33276
Louisville
KY 40213

NAFCO
PO Box 354
Florence
AL 35631

Nairn Linoleum
PO Box 989
Lancaster
PA 17603

Ryerson Steel
PO Box 23070
Emeryville
CA

LM Scofield Company
13601 Preston Road
Suite 418
Dallas
TX 75240

Sheoga Hardwood Flooring and Paneling Inc.
13851 Station Road
Burton
OH 44201

Summitville Tile
PO Box 73
Summitville
OH 43962

Walker Zanger
8901 Bradley Avenue
Sun Valley
CA 91352

FURNITURE AND HARDWARE

Chris Collicott
1151 1/2 North LaBrea Avenue
Los Angeles
CA 90038

Colonial Bronze Company
PO Box 207
Torrington
PA 19020

Lexington Furniture
PO Box 1008
Lexington
NC 27293

McGuire
151 Vermont Street
San Francisco
CA 94103

Merit Metal Products Corporation
242 Valley Road
Warrington
PA 18976

Modern Objects
1 Muller Avenue
Norwalk
CT 06851

George Tylor Specialities
187 Lafayette Street
New York
NY 10013

Wendover's Ltd of England
6 West 20th Street
New York
NY

KITCHEN DESIGNERS AND ARCHITECTS

Aileron Design
16 Powers Street
Brooklyn
NY 11211

Pierce Allen Architects
118 West 22nd Street
New York
NY

Beech Associates
145 East 94th Street
New York
NY 10128

Al Boland
6016 Pratt
Alexandria
VA 22310

Chartier, Newton & Associates
1101 Capital of Texas Highway
South
Building G, Suite 256
Austin
TX 78746

Frederick Hlavacek
1257 North 55th Street
Milwaukee
WI 53208

LLG Contracting
295 East 8th Street
New York
NY 10009

William McDonough Architects
116 East 27th Street
New York
NY 10016

Walz Designs
143 West 20th Street
New York
NY 10011

Deborah Weintraub
1540 North Sierra Bonita
Los Angeles
CA 90046

SINKS AND FAUCETS

American Standard
1 Centennial Plaza
Piscataway
NY 08855-6820

Blanco America
1001 Lower Landing Road
Suite 607
Blackwood
NJ 08012

Blanco Canada
Mississauga
Ontario

Chicago Faucet Company
2100 Clearwater Drive
Des Plaines
IL 60018

Delta Faucet Company
55 East 111th Street
PO Box 40980
Indianapolis
IN 46280

Elkay Manufacturing Company
2222 Camden Court
Oak Brook
IL 60521

Franke Kitchen Systems
212 Church Road
North Wales
PA 15239

Grohe America, Inc.
241 Covington Drive
Bloomingdale
IL 60108

Kohler Company
444 Highland Drive
Kohler
WI 53044

KWC
2610 South Yale Street
Santa Ana
CA 92704

Vance Industries, Inc.
7401 West Wilson Avenue
Chicago
IL 60656

Vermont Soapstone Company
PO Box 168
Perkinsville
VT 05151

UNIVERSAL DESIGN

Advanced Living Systems
428 North Lamar Boulevard
Oxford
MI 38655

Barrier-free Design Centre
150 Eglinton Avenue East
Suite 400
Toronto
Ontario M4 1E8

Barrier-free Environments, Inc.
PO Box 30634
Raleigh
NC 27622

Center for Accessible Housing
North Carolina State University
School of Design
PO Box 8613
Raleigh
NC 27695-8613

Good Grips
230 Fifth Avenue
New York
NY

Lifespec Cabinet Systems, Inc.
428 North Lamar Boulevard
Oxford
MI 38655-3204

**National Rehabilitation
Information Center (NARIC)**
8455 Colesville Road
Silver Spring
MD 20910-3319

**Resource Center for Accessible
Living**
Architectural Modification
Consultation
602 Albany Avenue
Kingston
NY 12401

Elizabeth Ringwald
11818 South-East 78th Street
Renton
WA 98056

INDEX

Page numbers in *italic* refer to the illustrations

A

accoutrements, *73, 84, 119,* 202, *202,* 210–13, *211–12*
Agas, 71, *74,* 111, *112,* 190, *190*
Aicher, Otl, 36
air-conditioning, 143
air filters, 148
alcove kitchens, *116*
aluminum:
  cabinet doors, 171
  saucepans, 211
  sinks, 198
amboyna wood, 171
Antium countertops, 165
apothecary drawers, *179*
apple corers, 10, 211, *211*
appliances, 189–201, *189–201*
  building in, 64
  dishwashers, 200–1, *200*
  priorities, 118
  refrigerators and freezers,
    196–7, *196–7*
  sinks and faucets, 198–9, *198–9*
  storage, 175
  stoves, ovens and cooktops,
    190–3, *190–5*
  universal design, 140–1
  washing machines, 200–1, *201*
architectural features, *110*
Arts and Crafts movement, *61*
ash wood, 163, 171
Avonite countertops, 165
Avron countertops, 165

B

backsplashes, 158, 160
bains maries, 10–11
baking equipment, 211
balconies, *105*
Baleine, 26
balloon whisks, 211, *211*
banquettes, 184
bar stools, *184, 186*
barbecues, 104, 106–7, *107,* 193
Barton Court, *41*
basements, 116
basket drawers, *204,* 208

basting spoons, 211, *211*
Beauvilliers, 26
beech wood, *170,* 171
Beecher, Catherine, 21
Beeton, Isabella, 19
Belfast sinks, 58, 71, 198, *198*
bench seats, 184, *187*
bentwood furniture, 98, 100
birch wood, 171
blinds, 181, *182*
blue color schemes, 52, 55, 72
boilers, 143
Boulanger, 26
bowls, 211, 213, *213*
Braddell, Mrs Darcy, *23*
brass:
  cabinet doors, 171
  hardware, 184
  sinks, 198
  taps, 198
bread knives, 211
breakfast bars, 69, *83,* 99, 100,
  101
brick floors, 154, *155*
Brillat-Savarin, Anthelme, 26
bronze sinks, 198
Brueghel, Pieter, *14*
built-in kitchens, 56, *56,* 58–61,
  59, 64, 92, 168
bulk buying, food, 204
Bulthaup, Gerd, 38
Bulthaup kitchens, 36–8, *36–9,*
  126–7
Burke, David, 32
butcher blocks, *48,* 71, *74,* 162,
  163, *163*

C

cabinets, 22, 92, 168–71, *168–71*
  built-in kitchens, 59
  construction, 168
  doors, 168, 170
  ergonomics, 122, *122*
  glass-fronted, *93,* 171, *175, 176,*
    178
  lighting inside, 146
  materials, 170–1, *170–1*
  pantries, 177
  as screens, 181
  shelves, 175
  storage in plinths, 174

cabinets (continued):
  under-cabinet lighting, 146
  unfitted kitchens, 62
  universal design, 140
cake pans, 211, *213*
can openers, 211, *211*
cane:
  chairs, 100
  split cane shades, *107*
canisse, *107*
canned food, 207
Carême, Antoine, 26
carousels, corner cabinets, 175
carving forks, 211, *211*
carving knives, 211
casseroles, 211, *213*
cast iron:
  casseroles, *213*
  saucepans, 211
  sinks, 198
cedar wood, 171
ceilings, lighting, 145
central heating, 143
ceramic cooktops, *192,* 193
ceramic tiles, 54
  countertops, 162, 164, *164–5*
  floors, 154, *155*
  walls, *160–1*
ceramics, displays, *93, 94, 97*
CFCs, refrigerators, 197
chairs, *74,* 98, 100, 184, *186–7*
charcoal braziers, 106–7
Château Bagnol, *24*
cheese graters, 211, *213*
chefs, 31
children, 120
  family kitchens, 77
  safety, 118, 140
chopping boards, *151,* 162, 211,
  211
  see also butcher blocks
chrome taps, 198
coal-burning stoves, 92
coal fires, 17
cocottes, 211, *213*
colanders, 211, *213*
color, *44, 45,* 52, *53–5*
  country kitchens, 71
  lighting and, 52, 144
  multipurpose areas, 49
  walls, 158
combination ovens, 194

compressors, refrigerators, 119,
  197
concertina doors, 181
concrete:
  countertops, 166, *167*
  floors, 157, *157*
condensation, 148
Conran, Terence, 132
conservatory kitchens, 102, *102–3*
contemporary kitchens, 64–6,
  64–9
convection ovens, 194, *195*
conventional ovens, 194
cookie cutters, 211, *211*
cooktops, *190, 191–3,* 193
  ceramic, *192,* 193
  combined fuels, 142
  electric, 22, 142, 190–3, *190–5*
  exhaust hoods, 148
  gas, *191–3,* 193
  halogen, *192,* 193
  universal design, 141
copper:
  cabinet doors, 171
  saucepans, 211
  sinks, 198, *199*
Le Corbusier, 28
Corian:
  countertops, 162, 165, *165*
  sinks, 198
cork floors, 157, *157*
corkscrews, 211, *211*
corner cabinets, 175
corridor kitchens, 67, 82, 123–4,
  123
countertops:
  built-in kitchens, 59
  concrete, 166, *167*
  Corian, 162, 165, *165*
  ergonomics, 122–3, *122*
  granite, *87,* 162, 164, *164*
  laminate, 162, 166, *166–7*
  layouts, 123–4, *123–5*
  marble, 162, 163, *163*
  materials, 162–7, *162–7*
  as partitions, 99, *101*
  rubber, 167
  sinks, 163, 164, 198
  slate, 164, *164*
  stainless steel, 162, *162,* 167,
    167
  terrazzo, 162, 165

countertops (continued):
 tiles and mosaic, 164, *164–5*
 wood, 64, 162, 163, *163*
 zinc, 162, 167, *167*
country kitchens, 55, 56, *57*, 70–1,
 70–5
cushions, 184
cutting boards, *151*, 162, 211, *211*

D

David, Elizabeth, 7, 88
deep fryers, *192*, 193, *193*
design, 108–12
desks, 77
dichroic halogen lights, 145
dimmer switches, 100, 142, 144,
 146
dining areas, 49
dining furniture, 100
disabled people, 140–1
dishwashers, 22, 141, 142, 200–1,
 200–1
display, 92–5, *92–7*
distemper, 159
doors:
 cabinets, 168, 170
 glass-fronted, *93*, 171, *175*, *176*,
 178
 space dividers, 181, *181*, *183*
double boilers, 10
double glazing, 143
downlighters, 100, 145, *145*, 146,
 146
drainers, sinks, 198
drains, 142
drawers, 176, *176*, *179*
drawing plans, 120–1, *121*
dressers, 15, 22, 62, 71, *71*, 92,
 101
drinking-water taps, 142
Drölling, Martin von, *9*
dryers, 142, 201, *201*
Durcon countertops, 165, *167*

E

earth colors, 52
eating in the kitchen, *98–101*,
 99–100
Ecart, *28*
eggshell paint, 158–9

electrical appliances, 22
 dishwashers, 200–1, *200*
 heaters, 143, *143*
 refrigerators and freezers,
 196–7, *196–7*
 storage, 175
 stoves, ovens and hobs, 22, 142,
 190–3, *190–5*
 universal design, 140–1
 washing machines, 200–1, *201*
electrical supply, installation, 142
elevations, drawing, 121, *121*
emulsion paint, 158, 159
enamel paint, 158
equipment:
 accoutrements, 202, *202*,
 210–13, 211–12
 appliances, 189–201, *189–201*
ergonomics, 111, 122–5, *122–5*
essential services, 142–3
exhaust fans and hoods, *42*, 66,
 118–19, 143, 148, *148–9*, 190

F

family kitchens, 76–7, *76–7*,
 126–7, *126–7*
farmhouse kitchens, 70, 88, 132,
 132–3
farmhouse tables, 100
faucets, 198, *198–9*
filters:
 air, 148
 water, 142
fire safety, 118
flagstone floors, 155
flan pans, 211, *213*
floor plans, 120–1, *121*
floors:
 materials, 154–7, *155–7*
 multi-purpose rooms, 49, *68*,
 100
 universal design, 141
fluorescent lighting, 144, 146
food:
 displays, *202*
 refrigerators, 196–7, *196–7*
 storage, 176–7, *177*, 204–9,
 204–9
food processors, 213, *213*
framed cabinets, 168
frameless cabinets, 168

freezers, 196–7, *196–7*, 209
French doors, 181
French ranges, 190, *191*
fuels, choosing, 142
funnels, 211, *213*
furniture, 184, *184–7*
 outdoor eating, 107
 see also cabinets; chairs;
 dressers; tables

G

gadgets, 43, 66, 95
gardens, 102
gas, 142
 condensation from, 148
 cooktops, *191–3*, 193
 heaters, 143
 stoves, 22, 142, 194, *195*
George, Owain, 134–5
George, Prince Regent, 16, 26
glass:
 cabinet doors, *93*, 171, *175*,
 176, *178*
 displays, *94*, *96*
 shelves, *94*, *96*, 175
 tables, 100, *184–5*
gloss paint, 158–9
granite:
 countertops, 87, 162, 164, *164*
 floors, 156, *156*
 sinks, 198
 wall tiles, 159
graters, *213*
gratin dishes, 211, *213*
gray color schemes, 52
griddles, 193, *193*
grills and broilers, 190, *192*, 193
grout, 154, 160, 164
Guérard, Michel, *27*

H

halogen cooktops, *192*, 193
halogen lights, 145, 146
Hamlyn, Helen, *24*
Hammerite, *171*
handles, furniture, 141, 184
hanging racks, 146, *178*
hard water, 142
hardware, furniture, 184
hardwoods, cabinets, 171

hasteners, 17
Hazelins House, Stockholm, *17*
heating systems, 142–3
herbs, *207*
hibachi stoves, 107
history, 10–22
Hobbs, Keith, 32
Hoexter's Market, Boca Raton, 29
hot plates, *192*, 193
hot-water cylinders, 143
hygiene, 92

I

ice dispensers, *189*, 196, *196*
ice-houses, 196
"ice safes," 22
idiosyncratic kitchens, 86, *86–7*
incandescent lighting, 144
incinerators, 151
Indians, American, 106
insulation, 148
internal windows, 68, 181, *182*
iron:
 hardware, 184
 sinks, 198
 see also cast iron
island units, *41*, *47*, 49, 64, 66,
 112, *119*, 124, *124*, 181

J

Jacobsen, Arne, *185*
Jaffe, Walter, 136
Japanese food, *30*
Japanese style, 90, *90*

K

King, Paul, 136–8
kitcheners, 18
knives, 211, *211*
knobs, 184

L

L-shaped kitchens, 100, 124, *124*,
 140, *141*
ladles, 211, *213*,
laminates, 64
 countertops, 162, 166, *166–7*
laundry, 201

Lavau Franche, *13*
layouts, ergonomics, 123–4, *123*
lead piping, 142
lemon squeezers, 211, *211*
lighting, 144–6, *144–7*
    and color, 52, 144
    dimmer switches, 100, 142,
        144, 146
    electrical supply, 142
    fluorescent, 144
    halogen, 145
    incandescent, 144
    restaurant kitchens, 31, 32
    switches, 146
    tables, 100
lime wood, 171
linoleum, 22, 156, *156*
linseed oil, 155
Lloyd Loom chairs, *186*
loaf pans, 211, *213*
London plane wood, 171
louvered doors, *183*

M

maple wood, 163, *163*, 171, 211
marble, 54, *69*
    countertops, 162, 163, *163*
    floors, 155, *155*
    sinks, 198
    tables, 100
Maschler, Fay, *115*, 128–31
matchboarding, *96*
Matharu, Bennie, 126–7
Mather, Rick, *114*, 128–31
MDF (medium-density
    fiberboard), cabinets, 171, *171*
measuring jugs, 213, *213*
meat, spit-roasting, 17, *24*
meat hooks, *202*
Mediterranean kitchens, *88*, *91*
melamine shelves, 175
metals:
    cabinets, 171, *171*
    sinks, 198, *199*
    see also aluminum; brass;
        copper; stainless steel
Mexican style, *89*, *91*
microwave ovens, *115*, 125, 141,
    194, *194*
mixer faucets, 198, *198*
mixing bowls, *213*

mosaic, 156, *156*, *161*, 164, *165*
Mouli-legumes, 213, *213*
multi-generation design, 140–1
multi-purpose areas, 49, 68, 181
multifunction ovens, 194

N

narrow spatulas, 211, *211*
natural gas, 142
neon lights, *146*
neutral colors, 52
noise, 118–19, 200, 201
non-stick pans, 211
notice boards, 77

O

oak wood, 163, 171
omelette pans, 211, *213*
one-wall kitchens, 123, *123*
open-plan areas, 49, 68, 181
Oriental cooking, *90*
outdoor kitchens, 104–7, *104–7*
outlets, electric, 142, 175
ovens, *189*, 190, 193, 194
    convection, 194, *195*
    conventional, 194
    electric, 142, *195*
    gas, *191*
    microwave, *115*, 125, 141, 194,
        194
    pizza, 193, *195*
    ranges, 18, *191*
    steam, 194, *195*
    universal design, 140

P

paint, walls, 158–9, *158–9*
paneling, wood, 160
pantries, 176–7, 204–9
partitions, 49, 68, 99, 181
pastry brushes, 211, *211*
pattern, 54
Pawson, John, *30*
pendant lights, 146, *147*
peninsular kitchens, 124, *124*
pepper mills, 211, *213*
perimeter kitchens, 124, *125*
pestles and mortars, *10*, *91*
pie dishes, 211, *213*

pine wood, *170*, 171
pipes, lead, 142
pizza ovens, 193, *195*
planning, 115–51
    built-in or unfitted, 56–63
    color, pattern and texture, 52–5
    defining areas, 44–9
    design, 110–12, 120–1
    ergonomics, 122–5, *122–5*
    essential services, 142–3
    lighting, 144–6, *144–7*
    planning from scratch, 116
    priorities, 118–19
    waste disposal, 150–1
planning permission, 121
plans, drawing, 120–1, *121*
plants, 102
plaster, walls, 159
plate racks, 175
plate warmers, *114*
plumbing, 142
Pompeii, *11*
Le Pont de la Tour, London, *25*,
    28, *32*, *33–5*
porcelain sinks, 198
potato mashers, 211, *213*
potato peelers, 211, *211*
pots and pans, 174, *174*, 211, *213*
pottery, displays, *93*, *94*, *97*
poultry shears, 211
preserves, *204*
pressure cookers, 194
primary colors, 52
priorities, 118–19
professional kitchens, 24–39, 64
propane, refrigerators and
    freezers, 197
pudding bowls, 211, *213*
Putman, Andrée, *28*
PVC wallpaper, 159

Q

Quaglino's, London, 31
quarry tiles, 164

R

ranges, 18, *19*, 71, 111, 190,
    190–1
    restaurant kitchens, 31, *35*, 64
recessed lights, 145

recycling rubbish, 150, 151
refectory tables, *61*, 184
refrigerators, *189*, 196–7, *196–7*
    compressors, 119, 197
    food storage, 208
    glass-fronted, 95
    history, 22
    noise, 119
    universal design, 141
    work triangle, 122, 125
restaurant kitchens, 26–31, 207
reverberation, 119
roasting pans, 211, *213*
Rogers, Richard, *65*
roller blinds, 181
rolling pins, 211, *211*
Roman de Renaud de Montauben,
    13
Royal Pavilion, Brighton, *16*
rubber:
    countertops, 167
    floors, 157, *157*
rubbish disposal, 150–1, *150–1*

S

Sadeler, Justus, *15*
safety:
    family kitchens, 77
    oven doors, 194
    planning, 118
    universal design, 140
salt bowls, 211, *213*
saucepans, 174, *174*, 211, *213*
scales, 213, *213*
scissors, 211, *211*
screening, *180–3*, 181
sculleries, 19, 49
sealants, tile floors, 154–5
self-cleaning ovens, 194
shade, outdoor eating areas, 106,
    107
Shakers, *20*, *57*
sharpening steels, *211*
shelves, 50, *93*, *96*, 175, *175*,
    176–7, *176*, *182*
shutters, 181
sinks, 198, *198–9*
    Belfast, *58*, 71, 198, *198*
    countertops, 163, 164, 198
    drains, 142
    lighting, 146

sinks (continued):
  plumbing, 142
  universal design, 140
  waste-disposal units, 150, *150*
  work triangle, 122
skewers, 211, *211*
skillets, 211, *213*
slate, 54
  countertops, 164, *164*
  floors, 156, *156*
  walls, *160*
sliding doors, 181
small kitchens, 78–82, *78–85*, 116,
  134–5, *134–5*
soapstone, 162
softwoods, cabinets, 171
solar heating, 143
soufflé dishes, 211–13, *213*
sound insulation, 118, 200, 201
spatulas, 211, *211, 213*
spices, 11, 13, 174, 207
spit-roasting, 17, *24*
spoons:
  basting, 211, *211*
  wooden, 211, *211*
spotlights, 100, *147*
stained wood, 171
stainless steel, 54, *59*, 64
  cabinets, 171, *171*
  countertops, 162, *162*, 167,
    167
  hardware, 184
  knives, 211
  saucepans, 211
  shelves, 175
  sinks, 198, *199*
  walls, *159*
Starck, Philippe, *69*
steam ovens, 194, *195*
steel *see* stainless steel
stencils, *159*
stone, 54, 71
  floors, 154, *155*
  sinks, 198
stools, *98*, 184, *184, 186*
storage, 174–7, *174–9*
  displays, 92–5, *92–7*
  food, 204–9, *204–9*
  planning, 120
  storage jars, *213*
  wine, *114*, 208, 209
  see also cabinets

store cupboards, *see*
  pantries
stoves, 190–3, *190–5*
  combined stove/boilers, 143
  electric, 22, 142
  exhaust hoods, 148
  gas, 22, 142, 194, *195*
  work triangle, 122, 125
strainers, 211, 213, *213*
style, 40
switches, lighting, 146
sycamore wood, 163, 171
Syndecrete, *167*

T

tables, 100, 184, *186–7*
  country kitchens, 71
  family kitchens, *76*
  farmhouse, 100
  lighting, 100
  refectory, *61*, 184
  trestle, 100
  universal design, 141
taun wood, 171
teak countertops, 163
technology, 22
telephones, 77
terra cotta, 71, 154, *155*
terraces, *104*
terrazzo:
  countertops, *162*, 165
  tiles, *154*, 156, *156*
texture, 52–4
  plaster, 159
tiles, 64
  backsplashes, 158
  ceramic, 54
  cork, *157*
  countertops, 164, *164–5*
  floors, 154–7, *154–7*
  granite, *159*
  grout, 154, 160, 164
  vinyl, *156*, 157
  walls, 160, *160–1*
timber *see* wood
tin, cabinet doors, 171
tongue-and-groove wood, 160,
  160
track lights, 145
trash compactors, 150–1, *151*
trays, *204*

trestle tables, 100
tumble dryers, 142, 201, *201*
tungsten lighting, 144
turbo grilling, 194

U

U-shaped kitchens, 124, *125*, 140,
  140
ultraviolet light, 144
underfloor heating, 143
unfitted kitchens, 56, *57*, 62,
  62–3, 168
units, cabinets, 168–71, *168–71*
universal design, 140–1, *140–1*
uplighters, *146*
utility cabinets, 175
utility rooms, 181

V

Vefour, 26
veneers, cabinets, *170*, 171
venetian blinds, 181, *182*
ventilation, 31, 148, *148–9*
vernacular kitchens, 88–90, *88–91*
vibrations, 118
Villa Turque, *28*
vinyl:
  floorings, *156*, 157
  wallpaper, 159

W

Wagamama, London, *30*
wall lights, 145
wallpaper, 159
walls, 158–60
  multi-purpose rooms, 100
  paint, 158–9, *158–9*
  plaster, 159
  tiles, 160, *160–1*
  wallpaper, 159
  wood, 160, *160*
warm-air heating, 143
washer/dryers, 201
washing machines, 142, 201, *201*
waste disposal, 150–1, *150–1*
waste-disposal units, 142, 150, *150*
water filters, 142
water heaters, electrical supply,
  142

water-purification systems, 142
water-softening systems, 142
weighing scales, 211, *213*
Weintraub, Deborah, 136
wheelchair access, 141
whisks, 211, *211*
white color schemes, 52
windows:
  double glazing, 143
  internal, *68*, 181, *182*
Windsor chairs, *74, 98, 186*
wine, storage, *114*, 208, 209
woks, 193
wood, 50, 54, 64
  cabinets, 170–1, *170*
  chairs, 100
  countertops, 64, 162, 163, *163*
  country kitchens, 71
  floors, 154, *155*
  shelves, 175
  veneers, 171
  wall coverings, 160, *160*
wooden spoons, 211, *211*
work triangle, 122–5
Wright, Merlin, 134

Y

yellow color schemes, 52

Z

zinc, 54
  cabinet doors, 171
  countertops, 162, 167, *167*

ACKNOWLEDGMENTS

The publisher thanks the following photographers and organizations for their kind permission to reproduce the photographs in this book:

1 Alexander Bailhache; **4** left Pierre Hussenot/Agence Top; **4** right Marie Claire Maison/Bailhache/Comte; **5** left Dominique Vorillon (Architects/owners: Jeffrey Biben/Peggy Bosley, courtesy of Metropolitan Home); **5** center Clive Frost; **5** right Simon McBride; **6** Lars Hallen/Design Press; **7** above Jonathan Pilkington (Hardwood Flooring Company); **7** center Tom Leighton (Mark Landini, Designers: The Edge); **7** below David George/Cassell/Elizabeth Whiting and Associates; **8** left Ann Ronan at Image Select; **8–9** AKG, Berlin; **11** Ancient Art & Architecture Collection; **12** left Charmet/Explorer/Mary Evans Picture Library; **12–13** René Stoeltie; **13** right Mary Evans Picture Library; **14** AKG, Berlin; **15** left Hulton Deutsch Collection; **15** right Mary Evans Picture Library; **16–17** Angelo Hornak (Courtesy of the Royal Pavilion, Brighton); **17** right René Stoeltie; **18** Mary Evans Picture Library; **19** above left AKG, Berlin; **19** above right and below Paul Ryan/International Interiors; **20** left Michael Freeman; **20–1** Hulton Deutsch Collection; **21** right Explorer/Collection: Lausat; **22–23** Hulton Deutsch Collection; **24** Hugh Johnson; **26–7** Jacques Dirand/World of Interiors; **27** right Marie Claire Maison/Chabaneix/Postic; **28** Richard Bryant/Arcaid (Courtesy of EBEL Watchmakers, interior design by Andrée Putman); **29** © Kim Sargent; **36–9** Bulthaup; **40** right Simon McBride; **40–1** David Brittain; **42** Jean-Paul Bonhommet; **43** left Evelyn Hofer; **43** right Scoop/Elle Décoration © G. de Laubier (Courtesy of Anthony Collett Associates); **44** James Merrell; **44–5** Paul Ryan/International Interiors; **46** above Guy Bouchet; **46** below Henry Bourne (Paxton Locher Architects); **47** above Paul Warchol; **47** below left Paul Ryan/International Interiors; **47** below right George Mott (Designer: Clodagh, N.Y.); **48** Trevor Richards; **49** Yves Duronsoy; **50** above left David Phelps; **50** above right John Freeman (Designer: Patrick Daw); **50** below Tom Leighton (George Fenton); **51** above Derry Moore; **51** below George Mott; **52** David Phelps; **52–3** Rodney Hyett/Elizabeth Whiting and Associates (B.B.P. Architects, Melbourne, Australia); **54** above left Camera Press; **54–5** above Richard Ludbrook/Vogue Living (Designer: Tony Masters); **54** below Tim Street-Porter (Designer: Buzz Yudell); **55** above center Rodney Hyett/Elizabeth Whiting and Associates (Architect: Kevin Barland, Melbourne, Australia); **55** above right Peter Baistow; **55** below left Dan Lepard/Elle Decoration (Designed by Philip Hooper, courtesy of Claire McLean & Nick Welch); **56** above Tim Street-Porter (Architect: Scott Johnson); **56** below John Hollingshead; **57** above ESTO/Peter Aaron (Architects: Greene and Greene); **57** below left René Stoeltie; **57** below right Paul Ryan/International Interiors; **58** above left Alberto Piovano/Arcaid; **58** above right Trevor Richards; **58** below Jean-Paul Bonhommet; **59** above Deidi von Schaewen (Colette & Jim Rossant, N.Y.); **59** below Rodney Weidland/BELLE Magazine (Designer: Lissa Grey); **60** left Fritz von der Schulenburg (Lars Bolander); **60–1** Camera Press; **61** above right Fritz von der Schulenburg (Andrew Wadsworth); **61** below right Tim Street-Porter (Architect: Mark Mack); **62** above Tim Street-Porter (Designer: Brian Murphy); **62** below Paul Ryan/International Interiors; **63** above left Simon Brown; **63** above right Tim Beddow; **63** below Tom Leighton (Mark Landini, Designers: The Edge); **64** left Stylograph/Brackrock; **64** right Trevor Richards; **65** Richard Bryant/Arcaid (Courtesy of Sir Richard & Lady Rogers); **66** above Alberto Piovano/Arcaid (Architect: Giancarlo Gariboldi); **66** below Michael Crockett/Elizabeth Whiting and Associates (Designer: Alfred Munkenbeck); **67** left Deidi von Schaewen (Architect: Michel Seban/Babel); **67** right Jean-Paul Bonhommet; **68** Tim Beddow; **69** above left Dominique Vorillon (Architects: Miriam Mulder/Richard Katkov, courtesy of the L.A. Times); **69** above right Jean-Pierre Godeaut (Designer: Philippe Starck); **69** below left Jeremy Cockayne/Arcaid (Paxton Locher Architects); **69** below right Paul Warchol; **70** above Joshua Greene; **70** below Roland Beaufre/Agence Top (Chez: Kim & Odile Moltzer); **71** above Marianne Haas (Designer: Jacques Grange); **71** below IPC Magazines/Robert Harding Syndication; **72** above left Tim Beddow; **72** center left Jean-Paul Bonhommet; **72** below left Jean-Pierre Godeaut (Mayo); **72–3** Pascal Chevalier/Agence Top; **73** above right Marie-Louise Avery/IMP; **73** below right Roland Beaufre/Agence Top (Chez: Kim and Odile Moltzer); **74** above left Simon McBride; **74** above right Pascal Chevalier/Agence Top; **74** below Jean-Pierre Godeaut (Ashcan, Nairobi); **75** Tim Beddow/World of Interiors (Designed by Neil Ware); **76** below Ianthe Ruthven (Harvey Clark Design); **76–7** above Walter Smalling Jr.; **77** below Peter Woloszynski/Elizabeth Whiting and Associates; **78** Richard Bryant/Arcaid (Eva Jiricna Architects); **79** above left Alberto Piovano/Arcaid (Courtesy: David Mellor, Architect: Michael Hopkins); **79** above right Dia Press; **79** below Rodney Hyett/Elizabeth Whiting and Associates (Architect: Chris Jones, Melbourne, Australia); **81** Geoff Lung/Vogue Living (Designer: Brian Tetu, Sydney, Australia); **82** above left Tim Street-Porter (Designer: Russell Leland); **82** above right Francesco Radino/Abitare; **82** below Rodney Hyett/Elizabeth Whiting and Associates (Architect: Col Bandy, Melbourne, Australia); **83** Jonathan Pilkington (Designer: Dido Farrell, mural by David Marrian); **84** above Clive Frost; **85** above left Peter Woloszynski; **85** above right William Stites; **85** below Paul Ryan/International Interiors; **86** above Richard Bryant/Arcaid (Architect: John Young); **87** above Laura Jeannes; **87** below left Clive Frost; **87** below right Jean-Pierre Godeaut; **88** left Peter Woloszynski; **88** right Alexander Bailhache; **89** Peter Woloszynski; **90** above from "Oriental Style" by Stafford Cliff & Suzanne Slesin, photo: Gilles de Chabaneix; **90** below left Michael Freeman; **90** below right Pascal Chevalier; **91** above left Tim Street-Porter/Elizabeth Whiting and Associates; **91** above right Peter Woloszynski; **91** below Marie Claire Maison/Chabaneix/Postic; **92** Christian Sarramon; **93** above left Laura Jeannes; **93** above right William Sites; **93** below Paul Ryan/JB Visual Press; **94** above left Tim Beddow/World of Interiors (Designed by Neil Ware); **94** below left Simon McBride; **94–5** David Phelps (Courtesy of Decorating and Remodelling Magazine); **95** right Tom Leighton (George Fenton); **96** above left Dominique Vorillon (Architects/owners: Jeffrey Biben/Peggy Bosley, courtesy of Metropolitan Home); **96** above center Simon Butcher/Houses & Interiors; **96** above right Trevor Richards; **96** below Mick Hales; **97** left William Stites; **97** above right Trevor Richards; **97** below right William Stites; **98** Scoop/Elle Décoration © G. de Laubier (Courtesy of Anthony Collett Associates); **99** Paul Warchol; **100** Deidi von Schaewen (Courtesy of M. and Mme. Lecetre, Paris); **101** above Tom Leighton (Charles Rutherford); **101** below left William Stites; **101** below right Jean-Paul Bonhommet; **102** above left Deidi von Schaewen (Colette & Jim Rossant, N.Y.); **102** above right and below Jean-Paul Bonhommet; **103** Tim Street-Porter/Elizabeth Whiting and Associates (Architect: Frank Gehry); **104** Simon McBride; **105** above David Massey; **105** below left Simon McBride; **105** below right Annet Held; **106** left Karen Bussolini (Zeus Goldberg); **106–7** Lars Hallen/Design Press; **107** above left Bent Rej; **107** above right Jerome Darblay (Bantherotte); **107** below Jean-Paul Bonhommet; **108–9** Tim Street-Porter (Designer: Francisco Kripacz); **110–1** Paul Ryan/International Interiors; **111** right Richard Ludbrook/Vogue Living (Kitchen by Gieffe); **112** above John Gollings/Vogue Living (Architect: Andrew Metcalf); **112** below Trevor Richards; **113** Julie Phipps/Arcaid; **116** above Balthazar Korab; **116** below Camera Press; **117** Lars Hallen/Design Press; **119** above Tim Beddow; **119** below Christian Sarramon; **120** Walter Smalling Jr.; **122** Courtesy of Smallbone of Devizes; **132** Christian Sarramon; **143** Antoine Rozes; **144** Jean-Paul Bonhommet; **145** Simon Brown/Conran Octopus (Colorist: Don Kaufman); **146** Rodney Hyett/Elizabeth Whiting and Associates (Neo Metro Design, Melbourne, Australia); **146–7** above Peter Mauss/ESTO (Architects: Kurth and Kurth); **147** above right Karen Bussolini (Architect: Abraham Rothenberg); **147** below left Annet Held (Mitch Bell & Gerald Sabine); **147** below right Christian Sarramon; **149** Dominique Vorillon (Architects/owners: Jeffrey Biben/Peggy Bosley, courtesy of Metropolitan Home); **150** Earl Carter/BELLE Magazine (Architects: Ivan and Anne Rijavec); **151** left and center Bulthaup; **151** right KitchenAid; **152** John Hall (Studio Morsa); **153** above Tim Street-Porter (Architect: Mark Mack); **153** below Rodney Hyett/Elizabeth Whiting and Associates; **153** center Mick Hales; **154** Earl Carter/BELLE Magazine (Architect: Norman Day); **155** above left Rodney Hyett/Elizabeth Whiting and Associates (B.B.P. Architects, Melbourne, Australia); **155** above right Camera Press; **155** center left Tom Leighton (Liz & Paul Edmonds); **155** center Simon McBride; **155** center right Alexander Bailhache; **155** below left Marie Claire Maison/Chabaneix/Bayle; **155** below right Peter Woloszynski; **156** above left Paul Ryan/International Interiors; **156** above center Trevor Richards; **156** above right Areen Stonecraft; **156** below right Paul Warchol; **157** above left Michael Garland (Designer: Peter Shire); **157** center left Wicanders (UK) Ltd; **157** below left Tim Street-Porter/Elizabeth Whiting and Associates (Designer: Kent); **157** right Christian Sarramon (Architect: Claudio Silvestria); **158** Tim Street-Porter (Architect: Mark Mack); **159** above left Rodney Hyett/Elizabeth Whiting and Associates (Architect: Ken Charles, Melbourne, Australia); **159** above center Jean-Pierre Godeaut (Michel Klein); **159** above right René Stoeltie; **159** below left Bulthaup; **159** below right Paul Ryan/International Interiors; **160** above right Richard Bryant/Arcaid (Architect: Gianfranco Cavaglia); **160** below Eduard Hueber (Architects: Franke, Gottsgen, Cox); **160–1** Christian Sarramon; **161** above left Rodney Hyett/Elizabeth Whiting and Associates (Designer: Susan Hennessey, Melbourne, Australia); **161** above right Camera Preess; **161** center Michael Dunne/Elizabeth Whiting and Associates; **161** below Antoine Rozes; **162** Richard Bryant/Arcaid (Architect: David Chipperfield); **163** above left Christian Sarramon; **163** above right Rodney Hyett/Elizabeth Whiting and Associates (Designer: Kelly Hoppen); **163** center Rodney Hyett/Elizabeth Whiting & Associates (Architects: Bochsler & Partners, Melbourne, Australia); **163** below David Phelps; **164** above left Richard Bryant/Arcaid (Architect: David Wild); **164** below John Hall; **164–5** above Marianne Haas (Designer: Teddy Millington-Drake, Courtesy of Alexander & Diana Di Carcaci); **165** center Richard Waite/Elle Decoration; **165** below Courtesy of Corian; **166** above Rodney Hyett/Elizabeth Whiting and Associates; **166** below left Tim Street-Porter (Designer: Buzz Yudell); **166** below center Rodney Hyett/Elizabeth Whiting and Associates; **166** below right Neil Lorimer/Elizabeth Whiting and Associates; **167** above left Richard Bryant/Arcaid (Eva Jiricna Architects); **167** center Courtesy of Syndesis, Inc. 1990; **167** below Dan Lepard/Elle Decoration (Designed by Philip Hooper, courtesy of Claire McLean & Nick Welch); **167** above right Richard Bryant/Arcaid (Architect: John Young); **168–9** John Hall (Studio Morsa); **169** above center Rodney Hyett/Elizabeth Whiting and Associates (Architect: Barsbara Crowl, Hong Kong); **169** above right Agence Top/Pascal Chevalier; **169** center Rodney Hyett/Elizabeth Whiting and Associates (Architects: Guildford Bell & Graham Fisher, Melbourne, Australia); **170** above left Neil Lorimer/Elizabeth Whiting and Associates; **170** below Nicolas Millet/Abitare; **171** center Richard Bryant/Arcaid (Architect: John Young); **171** right Richard Bryant/Arcaid (Eva Jiricna Architects); **172** above left Tim Street-Porter (Designer: Peter Shire); **172** above right Fritz von der Schulenburg (John Stefanidis); **172** below ESTO/Peter Aaron (Architects: Moore/Rubel/Yudell); **172–3** center Marianne Haas (Designer: Jacques Grange); **173** above Dominique Vorillon (Architect/owner: Bernardo Uquieta, courtesy of Elle Decor); **173** below Fritz von der Schulenburg (Mimi O'Connell); **174** above left John Hall (Designer: Alison Spear); **174** above center Jean-Paul Bonhommet; **174–5** below Pia Tryde; **175** right Ianthe Ruthven (Harvey Clark Design); **176** above Camera Press; **176** below left Tim Wood

Furniture; **176** below center Michael Dunne/Elizabeth Whiting and Associates; **176** below right Michael Garland (Architect: Michael Lewis); **177** above Peter Woloszynski/Elizabeth Whiting and Associates; **177** below Dominique Vorillon (Architects/owners: René David/Christine Killory, courtesy of Home); **178** above left Tim Street-Porter (Architects: Koning/Eizenberg); **178** right Jean-Pierre Godeaut; **178** below left Bulthaup; **179** above William Stites; **179** below left Paul Ryan/J B Visual Press; **179** below right Annet Held; **180–1** Tom Leighton (Charles Rutherford); **181** right Rodney Hyett/Elizabeth Whiting and Associates (B.B.P. Architects, Melbourne, Australia); **182** above Jerome Darblay; **182** below Jean-Paul Bonhommet; **182–3** Christian Sarramon; **183** above William Stites; **183** below Ianthe Ruthven; **184** Tim Street-Porter (Designer: Brian Murphy); **185** Paul Warchol; **186** above left Bulthaup; **186** above right HPR White/Stylograph; **186** below left René Stoeltie; **186** below center © Image/Dennis Krukowski, "The Farmhouse," Bantam Books, USA; **186–7** below Jean-Paul Bonhommet; **187** above Warwick Kent/BELLE Magazine; **187** below center Walter Smalling Jr.; **187** below right Paul Ryan/International Interiors; **188** Tim Street-Porter (Architect: David Conner); **189** above Rodney Hyett/Elizabeth Whiting and Associates (Neo Metro Designs, Melbourne, Australia); **189** below Gaggenau (UK) Ltd; **190** Paul Ryan/International Interiors; **191** above left Clive Frost;

191 above and below right Viking Range Corporation; **191** below left Fourneaux de France, London W2; **192** above left Neff UK Ltd; **192** above right Miele Co. Ltd; **192** center (left to right) Miele Co. Ltd; Miele Co. Ltd; Gaggenau (UK) Ltd; Neff UK Ltd; Neff UK Ltd; Neff UK Ltd; **192** below Alberto Piovano/Arcaid (Architect: M. Romanelli); **193** above left and below Gaggenau (UK) Ltd; **193** above right Neff UK Ltd; **195** above left Viking Range Corporation; **195** above center Imperial UK; **195** above right General Electric Co.; **195** center left Neff UK Ltd; **195** center right Gaggenau (UK) Ltd; **195** below Moulinex Swan Holdings Ltd; **196** General Electric Co.; **197** left Zanussi; **197** center Hotpoint; **197** right Miele Co. Ltd; **198** right Christian Sarramon; **199** above left Geoff Lung/Vogue Living (Designer: Trevor Crump & Associates, Sydney, Australia); **199** above center Rodney Hyett/Elizabeth Whiting and Associates; **199** above right Nadia Mackenzie; **199** below left Paul Warchol; **199** center Simon Brown; **200** left Ianthe Ruthven (Harvey Clark Design); **200** right Gaggenau (UK) Ltd; **201** left Miele Co. Ltd; **201** right Whirlpool Corporation; **202** Fritz von der Schulenburg (Janet Fitch); **203** Trevor Richards; **204** above IPC Magazines/Robert Harding Syndication; **204** below Yves Duronsoy; **205** Christian Sarramon; **206–7** William Stites; **208** left Spike Powell/Elizabeth Whiting and Associates; **208–9** Rodney Hyett/Elizabeth Whiting and Associates (Architect: Gary Catt, Melbourne, Australia).

The following photographs were specially taken by Nadia Mackenzie for Conran Octopus:

Bulthaup UK Ltd: 126, 148.
Designers: Owain George and Merlin Wright: 115 above, 135, 198 left, 208 right.
Charles Hurst Workshop: 160 above left, 171 left, 199 below right.
Meryl & John Lakin: 169 below.
Rick Mather Architects: 114, 130–1
Johnson Naylor Design: 86 above, 115 below, 165 above right.
Architect: David Tooth (Jeremy Brock & Helen Greaves): 55 below right, 156 below left, 174–5 above.
Designers: Grahame Thomas & Bogdan Starzec: 2, 84 below, 115 centre.
Wagamama, London WC1: 4 centre, 30.
Nato Welton and Dawn Williamson: 80, 165 above centre, 170 above right, 189 centre.

by Hugh Johnson for Conran Octopus: 24–5.
by Robert Mort for Conran Octopus: 34–5.
by Richard Foster for Conran Octopus: 210–3.
by Steve Gross and Susan Daly for Conran Octopus: (Courtesy of Paul King and Walter Jaffe; Architect: Deborah Weintraub) 108 left, 136–9.

The kitchen plans reproduced on pages 126–139 are copyright © the architects and designers credited in the text. They can be contacted as follows:

Plan 1: Bennie Matharu for Bulthaup UK Ltd, 37 Wigmore Street, London W1H 9LD
Plan 2: Rick Mather Architects, 123 Camden High Street, London NW1 7JR
Plan 3: Sir Terence Conran, c/o Conran Octopus, 37 Shelton Street, London WC2H 9HN (mark envelope, "Kitchen Design")
Plan 4: Owain George and Merlin Wright, Boss House, 3rd Floor, Boss Street, London SE1
Plan 5: Deborah Weintraub A.I.A. 1540 N. Sierra Bonita, Los Angeles, Ca. 90046.

The kitchen plan of Le Pont de la Tour (page 33) is copyright © Keith Hobbs and Sir Terence Conran.